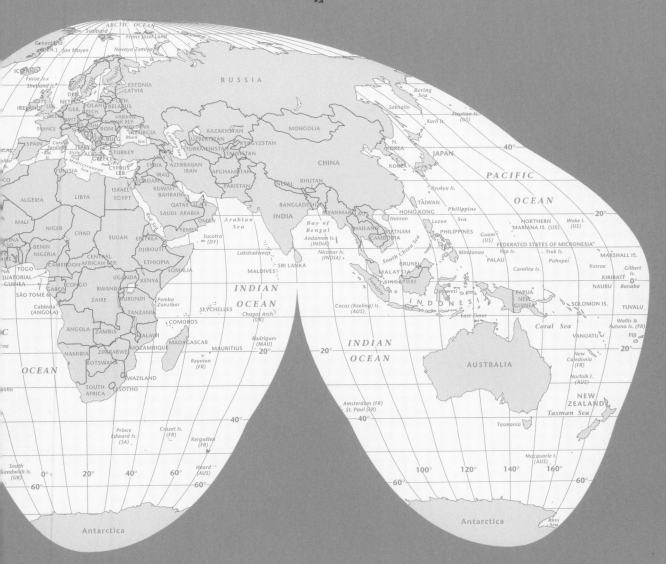

Junior Worldmark Encyclopedia of the Nations

VOLUME 9

Junior
Worldmark
Encyclopedia
of the

Nations

An imprint of Gale Research
An ITP Information/Reference Group Company

Changing the Way the World Learns

NEW YORK • LONDON • BONN • BOSTON • DETROIT
MADRID • MELBOURNE • MEXICO CITY • PARIS
SINGAPORE • TOKYO • TORONTO • WASHINGTON
ALBANY NY • BELMONT CA • CINCINNATI OH

VOLUME

Uganda to Zimbabwe

JUNIOR WORLDMARK ENCYCLOPEDIA OF THE NATIONS

Timothy L. Gall and Susan Bevan Gall, *Editors*
Rosalie Wieder, *Senior Editor*
Deborah Baron and Daniel M. Lucas, *Associate Editors*
Brian Rajewski and Deborah Rutti, *Graphics and Layout*
Cordelia R. Heaney, *Editorial Assistant*
Dianne K. Daeg de Mott, Janet Fenn, Matthew Markovich,
    Ariana Ranson, and Craig Strasshofer, *Copy Editors*
Janet Fenn and Matthew Markovich, *Proofreaders*
Maryland Cartographics, Inc., *Cartographers*

U·X·L Staff

Jane Hoehner, *U·X·L Developmental Editor*
Sonia Benson and Rob Nagel, *Contributors*
Thomas L. Romig, *U·X·L Publisher*
Mary Beth Trimper, *Production Director*
Evi Seoud, *Assistant Production Manager*
Shanna Heilveil, *Production Associate*
Cynthia Baldwin, *Product Design Manager*
Barbara J. Yarrow, *Graphic Services Supervisor*
Mary Krzewinski, *Cover Designer*
Margaret McAvoy-Amoto, *Permissions Associate (Pictures)*

∞™ This book is printed on acid-free paper that meets the minimum requirements of American National Standard for Information Sciences——Permanence Paper for Printed Library Materials, ANSI Z39.48-1984.

Library of Congress Cataloging-in-Publication Data
Junior Worldmark encyclopedia of the nations / edited by Timothy Gall
   and Susan Gall.
       p.   cm.
   Includes bibliographical references and index.
   ISBN 0-7876-0741-X (set)
   1. Geography--Encyclopedias, Juvenile. 2. History--Encyclopedias,
Juvenile. 3. Economics--Juvenile literature. 4. Political science--
Encyclopedia, Juvenile. 5. United Nations--Encyclopedias,
Juvenile. I. Gall, Timothy L. II. Gall, Susan B.
G63.J86   1995
910'.3--dc20
                                                    95-36739
                                                    CIP

ISBN 0-7876-0741-X (set)
ISBN 0-7876-0742-8 (vol. 1)   ISBN 0-7876-0743-6 (vol. 2)   ISBN 0-7876-0744-4 (vol. 3)
ISBN 0-7876-0745-2 (vol. 4)   ISBN 0-7876-0746-0 (vol. 5)   ISBN 0-7876-0747-9 (vol. 6)
ISBN 0-7876-0748-7 (vol. 7)   ISBN 0-7876-0749-5 (vol. 8)   ISBN 0-7876-0750-9 (vol. 9)

U·X·L is an imprint of Gale Research Inc.,
an International Thomson Publishing Company.
ITP logo is a trademark under license.

CONTENTS

Guide to Country Articles

Every country profile in this encyclopedia includes the same 35 headings. Also included in every profile is a map (showing the country and its location in the world), the country's flag and seal, and a table of data on the country. The country articles are organized alphabetically in nine volumes. A glossary of terms is included in each of the nine volumes. This glossary defines many of the specialized terms used throughout the encyclopedia. A keyword index to all nine volumes appears at the end of Volume 9.

Flag color symbols

Yellow Red Green Blue Orange Brown White Black

Alphabetical listing of sections

Agriculture	21	Income	18
Armed Forces	16	Industry	19
Bibliography	35	Judicial System	15
Climate	3	Labor	20
Domesticated Animals	22	Languages	9
Economy	17	Location and Size	1
Education	31	Media	32
Energy and Power	27	Migration	7
Environment	5	Mining	25
Ethnic Groups	8	Plants and Animals	4
Famous People	34	Political Parties	14
Fishing	23	Population	6
Foreign Trade	26	Religions	10
Forestry	24	Social Development	28
Government	13	Topography	2
Health	29	Tourism/Recreation	33
History	12	Transportation	11
Housing	30		

Sections listed numerically

1	Location and Size	19	Industry
2	Topography	20	Labor
3	Climate	21	Agriculture
4	Plants and Animals	22	Domesticated Animals
5	Environment	23	Fishing
6	Population	24	Forestry
7	Migration	25	Mining
8	Ethnic Groups	26	Foreign Trade
9	Languages	27	Energy and Power
10	Religions	28	Social Development
11	Transportation	29	Health
12	History	30	Housing
13	Government	31	Education
14	Political Parties	32	Media
15	Judicial System	33	Tourism/Recreation
16	Armed Forces	34	Famous People
17	Economy	35	Bibliography
18	Income		

Abbreviations and acronyms to know

GMT= Greenwich mean time. The prime, or Greenwich, meridian passes through Greenwich, England (near London), and marks the center of the initial time zone for the world. The standard time of all 24 time zones relate to Greenwich mean time. Every profile contains a map showing the country and its location in the world.

These abbreviations are used in references to famous people:
b.=born
d.=died
fl.=flourished (lived and worked)
r.=reigned (for kings, queens, and similar monarchs)

A dollar sign ($) stands for US$ unless otherwise indicated.

UGANDA

Republic of Uganda

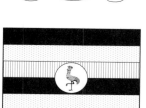

CAPITAL: Kampala.

FLAG: The national flag consists of six equal horizontal stripes of black, yellow, red, black, yellow, and red (from top to bottom); at the center, within a white circle, is a crested crane, the national bird of Uganda.

ANTHEM: Begins "O Uganda! May God uphold thee."

MONETARY UNIT: The new Uganda shilling (NUSh) was introduced in May 1987 with a value equal to 100 old Uganda shillings. NUSh1 = $0.01612 (or $1 = NUSh62.03). There are coins of 1, 2, and 5 shillings, and notes of 10, 20, 50, 100, 200, 500, and 1,000 shillings.

WEIGHTS AND MEASURES: The metric system is now in use.

HOLIDAYS: New Year's Day, 1 January; Labor Day, 1 May; Martyrs' Day, 3 June; Independence Day, 9 October; Christmas Day, 25 December; Boxing Day, 26 December. Movable holidays include Good Friday, Easter Monday, 'Id al-Fitr, and 'Id al-'Adha'.

TIME: 3 PM = noon GMT.

1 LOCATION AND SIZE

A landlocked country in east-central Africa, situated north and northwest of Lake Victoria, Uganda has a total area of 236,040 square kilometers (91,136 square miles), slightly smaller than the state of Oregon. It has a total boundary length of 2,698 kilometers (1,676 miles).

2 TOPOGRAPHY

The greater part of Uganda consists of a plateau. Margherita Peak on the western border reaches a height of 5,109 meters (16,762 feet), while on the eastern frontier Mount Elgon rises to 4,321 meters (14,178 feet). By contrast, a valley runs through the western half of the country, known as the Western Rift Valley. Its elevation is only 621 meters (2,036 feet)

around Lake Albert. The Victoria Nile has its source in Lake Victoria.

3 CLIMATE

Although Uganda is on the equator, its climate is warm rather than hot, and temperatures vary little throughout the year. Most of the territory receives an annual rainfall of at least 100 centimeters (40 inches). On Lake Albert, the mean annual maximum is 29°C (84°F) and the mean annual minimum 22°C (72°F). At Kabale in the southwest, 1,250 meters (4,100 feet) higher, the mean annual maximum is 23°C (73°F), and the mean annual minimum 10°C (50°F).

4 PLANTS AND ANIMALS

Plant life in Uganda varies from region to region, and includes cultivated plots of plantain, long grass, forest, short grass, and open woodland. At least 15 mammal species are found only in Uganda. Elephant, hippopotamus, buffalo, and many kinds of monkeys are plentiful. There are many species of birds but relatively few varieties of fish. Crocodiles are found in many areas.

5 ENVIRONMENT

Erosion is a major environmental problem due to overgrazing, primitive agricultural methods, and expansion of the desert. Attempts to control the reproduction of tsetse flies (flies that spread the disease called sleeping sickness) have resulted in the use of hazardous chemicals. The nation's water supply is threatened by toxic industrial pollutants; mercury from mining activity is also found in the water supply. Roughly 40% of the nation's city dwellers and 70% of the people living in rural areas do not have pure water. Uganda's three national parks total over 6,300 square kilometers (2,400 square miles). In 1994, 16 of the nation's mammal species and 12 of the nation's bird species were endangered, as well as 11 species of plants.

6 POPULATION

The most recent census in Uganda, in January 1991, registered a population of 16,671,705. A population of 23,401,000 was projected for the year 2000. Estimated population density is 75 persons per square kilometer (194 per square mile) of land. At the time of the 1991 census, Kampala, the capital and largest city, had a population of 773,463.

7 MIGRATION

At the end of 1992 there were 196,300 registered African refugees in Uganda, of which 92,100 were Sudanese, 85,800 Rwandese, and 15,600 Zairians. At the end of 1986 there were an estimated 170,000 Ugandan refugees in the Sudan and 23,000 in Zaire. The refugee population in Zaire remained steady, but the number in the Sudan dropped to 3,800 by the end of 1992.

8 ETHNIC GROUPS

The Baganda, who populate the northern shore of Lake Victoria, constitute the largest single ethnic group in Uganda (about 17% of the total population). Other important tribal groups include the Iteso, Banyoro, Banyankole, Batoro, and Basoga. Perhaps 6% of the population (not counting refugees) is of Rwandan descent, either Tutsi or Hutu. In 1989 the Asian population was estimated at about 10,000.

9 LANGUAGES

English is the official language. Bantu and Nilotic languages, particularly Luganda (the language of the Baganda), are widespread, and Central Sudanic clusters exist in the northwest. Kiswahili and Arabic are also widely spoken.

10 RELIGIONS

About 63% of the population is Christian: 41% Roman Catholic, and 22% Protestant (mostly Anglican). About 5% is Muslim. The rest practice traditional African religions.

11 TRANSPORTATION

A landlocked country, Uganda depends on links with Tanzania and Kenya for access to the sea. There is a total of 1,286 kilometers (799 miles) of railroad track in Uganda. In 1991 there were 26,200 kilometers (16,280 miles) of roads. In 1991 there were 12,865 passenger cars and 12,933 trucks and buses in Uganda. As of 1987, three Ugandan ferries were operating on Lake Victoria. Uganda's international airport, which serviced about 122,000 passengers in 1990, is at Entebbe.

12 HISTORY

Cushitic speakers from eastern Africa probably penetrated the area that is now Uganda around 1000 BC. In the first millennium (thousand years) AD, they were followed by Bantu-speaking peoples of central and southern Africa and later by people of central and western Africa. Europeans began to arrive in the nineteenth century, beginning with the British explorers John Hanning Speke and J. A. Grant in 1862. Members of the Church Missionary Society of Great Britain, came to Buganda (present-day southeast Uganda) in 1877.

The missionaries were welcomed by the kabaka (ruler) of Buganda, Mutesa I. He hoped to gain their support in his effort to fight off the Egyptian attempts to expand. Later Mutesa became less cooperative, and his son, Mwanga, who succeeded to the throne in 1884, was even more hostile, fearing the influence of both missionaries and Arab traders. When Mwanga began to persecute the ethnic Bagandan adherents of both Christianity and Islam, the

LOCATION: 4°7′N to 1°30′S; 29°33′ to 35°20′E.
BOUNDARY LENGTHS: Sudan, 435 kilometers (271 miles); Kenya, 933 kilometers (578 miles); Tanzania, 396 kilometers (247 miles); Rwanda, 169 kilometers (105 miles); Zaire, 765 kilometers (475 miles).

two groups joined forces to drive him from the country in 1888. He was restored to power early in 1890.

In 1894, the kingdom of Buganda became a British protectorate, which was extended in 1896 to cover most of what is now Uganda. In 1897, Mwanga led a revolt against the British, but he was quickly defeated and dethroned. Under the Uganda Agreement of 1900, Buganda was ruled indirectly by the British. Buganda's rejection of British policies following World War II marked the beginning of a conflict over independence for the territory. Kabaka Mutesa II was ousted in 1953 when he refused to force his chiefs to cooperate with the British, but was restored to power in 1955 under a compromise agreement.

At a 1961 constitutional conference in London, independence for a new state of Uganda, composed of Buganda and the kingdoms of Ankole, Bunyoro, and Toro, was agreed to, effective 9 October 1962. In 1963, Sir Edward Mutesa (Kabaka Mutesa II of Buganda) became Uganda's first president. In February 1966, the 1962 constitution was suspended and the prime minister, Milton Obote, assumed all powers of government. Parliament formally repealed the 1962 constitution on 15 April 1966, and adopted a new one which created the post of president and commander-in-chief; Obote was elected to fill this position on the same day.

Amin Seizes Power

On 25 January 1971, while Obote was out of the country, Major General Idi Amin led a successful military coup, and the Second Republic of Uganda was proclaimed on 17 March 1971, with Amin as president. In September 1972, Ugandans who had followed Obote into exile in Tanzania staged an unsuccessful invasion. They were immediately overpowered, but tensions between Uganda and Tanzania remained high.

Under Amin, Uganda suffered a reign of terror that had claimed 50,000 to 300,000 lives by 1977. The expulsion of Asian noncitizens from Uganda in August 1972 took a heavy toll on the economy, especially on trade. Agricultural and industrial production also fell, and educational and health facilities suffered from the loss of skilled personnel. An Israeli commando raid on Entebbe Airport on 3–4 July 1976 freed 91 Israeli passengers and 12 crew members held captive by pro-Palestinian radicals in a hijacked aircraft. This raid was a severe blow to Amin's prestige. By January 1979, Tanzanian forces, supported by anti-Amin rebels, entered Ugandan territory. Kampala was taken on 11 April 1979, and all of Uganda was cleared of Amin's forces by the end of May. A provisional (temporary) government was formed, and parliamentary elections were held on 10 December 1980. The elections were administered by Paulo Muwanga and other supporters of Obote, who returned from exile in Tanzania. The election results gave Obote's Ugandan People's Congress (UPC) a clear majority, and he was sworn in as president on 15 December 1980. Obote's second term in office was marked by continued fighting between the army and guerrilla factions, especially the National Resistance Army (NRA). On 27 July 1985, Obote was overthrown in a military coup and Lieutenant General Tito Okello, commander of the armed forces, was installed as president.

The NRA continued fighting, and on 26 January 1986 it occupied Kampala; by

Photo credit: AP/Wide World Photos.

Children play jump-rope in the deserted village of Rakai, Uganda, where it is thought the Uganda AIDS epidemic started.

April it formed the National Resistance Movement (NRM) government, with Yoweri Museveni as president, and took control of most of the country. Armed rebels remained active in northern and northeastern Uganda, but by 1990 most were defeated. By 1992, work on a draft constitution had progressed. Parliament declared a ban on party politics, but opposition parties became more active. General elections were held at the end of 1994. The government has introduced constitutional changes allowing the Baganda to restore their monarchy (purely for ceremonial purposes). Ronald Mutebi, son of the former king, was installed as kabaka (ruler) on 31 July 1993.

13 GOVERNMENT

A 270-person National Resistance Council was established in 1986. An appointed cabinet advises the president. The government introduced legislation providing for the election of a constituent assembly with 180 nonpartisan members.

14 POLITICAL PARTIES

After the overthrow of Idi Amin, remaining parties included the Ugandan People's Congress (UPC); the Democratic Party (DP); the Uganda Patriotic Movement; and the Conservative Party. These parties, as well as Yoweri Museveni's National Resistance Movement and the Uganda Freedom Movement, were represented in the cabinet appointed in 1986. By 1991, party activity, although banned, began to increase. The Ugandan People's Democratic Movement (UPDM) operates from exile.

15 JUDICIAL SYSTEM

At the lowest level are three classes of courts presided over by magistrates. Above these is the chief magistrate's court, which hears appeals from magistrates. The High Court hears appeals and has full criminal and civil jurisdiction. The three-member Court of Appeal hears appeals from the High Court.

16 ARMED FORCES

In 1987, the National Resistance Army (NRA) was established as the national army in the wake of civil war. Thousands of defeated guerillas were given amnesty and integrated into the NRA, swelling its ranks to between 70,000–100,000.

17 ECONOMY

Uganda's economy is based on agriculture, with rural poverty a continuing problem. An economic reform process begun in 1986 has resulted in progress; the economic growth rate averaged about 7% in 1993.

18 INCOME

In 1992 Uganda's gross national product (GNP) was $2,949 million at current prices, or about $180 per person. For the period 1985–92 the average inflation rate was 91.1%, resulting in a real growth rate in per person GNP of 1.8%.

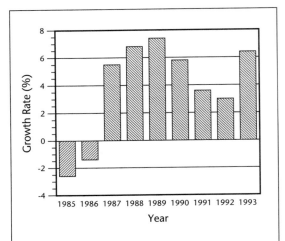

Yearly growth rate of the economy. This economic indicator tells by what percent the economy has increased or decreased when compared with the previous year.

19 INDUSTRY

Industrial output in 1985 was little more than a third of the post-independence peak levels of 1970–72. Industries include cotton, coffee, tea, sugar, tobacco, edible oils, dairy products, grain milling, brewing, vehicle assembly, textiles, and steel.

20 LABOR

Agriculture engaged over 90% of the total population of 16.7 million in 1991. Working conditions, hours of work, and paid holidays are negotiated with the unions.

21 AGRICULTURE

Uganda's economy is predominantly agricultural, employing 80% of the active labor force. In 1992, food production estimates included plantains, 8 million tons; cassava, 3.7 million tons; sweet potatoes,

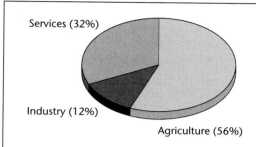

Components of the economy. This pie chart shows how much of the country's economy is devoted to agriculture (includes forestry, hunting, and fishing), industry, or services.

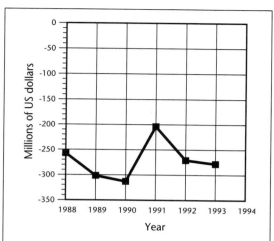

Yearly balance of trade measured in millions of US dollars. The balance of trade is the difference between what a country sells to other countries (its exports) and what it buys (its imports). If a country imports more than it exports, it has a negative balance of trade (a trade deficit). If exports exceed imports there is a positive balance of trade (a trade surplus).

1.7 million tons; bananas, 570,000 tons; finger millet, 593,000 tons; corn, 595,000 tons; sorghum, 375,000 tons; beans, 402,000 tons; and potatoes, 257,000 tons. Estimated production of major export crops in 1992 included coffee, 180,000 tons; cotton (lint), 11,000 tons; tea, 9,000 tons; and raw sugar, 49,000 tons.

22 DOMESTICATED ANIMALS

Uganda had an estimated 5,100,000 head of cattle, 3,350,000 goats, 1,980,000 sheep, and 880,000 hogs, and about 20 million chickens in 1992. An estimated 536,000 cattle, 1,173,000 goats, and 792,000 sheep were slaughtered in 1992; meat production was an estimated 193,000 tons.

23 FISHING

Lake Victoria and Lake Kyogo are the major commercial fishing areas. In 1991, the total catch was estimated at 254,900 tons.

24 FORESTRY

Forests covered 5,510,000 hectares (13,615,000 acres) in 1991. In 1991, production of roundwood was estimated at 15.7 million cubic meters. About 87% is used for fuel.

25 MINING

Small quantities of tin, tungsten, and phosphates are mined. Limestone is quarried for use in cement, and salt is obtained by evaporation of lakes and brine wells.

26 FOREIGN TRADE

In recent years, coffee has been by far the most important export (91.2% of total exports in 1990) and the principal earner

Selected Social Indicators

These statistics are estimates for the period 1988 to 1993. For comparison purposes, data for the United States and averages for low-income countries and high-income countries are also given.

Indicator	Uganda	Low-income countries	High-income countries	United States
Per capita gross national product†	$180	$380	$23,680	$24,740
Population growth rate	2.4%	1.9%	0.6%	1.0%
Population growth rate in urban areas	4.6%	3.9%	0.8%	1.3%
Population per square kilometer of land	75	78	25	26
Life expectancy in years	45	62	77	76
Number of people per physician	21,681	>3,300	453	419
Number of pupils per teacher (primary school)	35	39	<18	20
Illiteracy rate (15 years and older)	52%	41%	<5%	<3%
Energy consumed per capita (kg of oil equivalent)	23	364	5,203	7,918

† The gross national product (GNP) is the total dollar value of all goods and services produced by a country in a year. The per capita GNP is calculated by dividing a country's GNP by its population. The World Bank defines low-income countries as those with a per capita GNP of $695 or less. High-income countries have a per capita GNP of $8,626 or more. Less than 14% of the world's 5.5 billion people live in high-income countries, while almost 60% live in low-income countries.

> = greater than   < = less than

Sources: World Bank, *Social Indicators of Development 1995,* Baltimore: Johns Hopkins University Press, 1995. Central Intelligence Agency, *World Fact Book,* Washington, D.C.: Government Printing Office, 1994.

of income from abroad. The main exports include coffee, cotton, and corn. In 1989, Uganda's leading export partner was the Netherlands (16.2%), followed closely by the United States (15.8%), France (13.2%), and the United Kingdom. Imports came primarily from Kenya (31.4%), the United Kingdom (20.1%), and Germany (15.1%).

27 ENERGY AND POWER

In the early 1990s, hydroelectric potential was estimated at nearly 200,000 kilowatts. A total of 783 million kilowatt-hours was generated in 1991. Fuel wood and charcoal supply 95% of required energy.

28 SOCIAL DEVELOPMENT

Responsibility for social welfare rests primarily with the Ministry of Culture and Community Development, but voluntary agencies play a supplementary role.

29 HEALTH

AIDS (acquired immune deficiency syndrome) became a severe problem in the 1980s, with an estimated 800,000 Ugandans testing positive for human immunodeficiency virus (HIV) in 1989.

Containment of other serious diseases, such as cholera, dysentery, tuberculosis, and malaria, is made difficult by poor sanitation and unclean water. In 1992, there were 8 hospital beds per 100,000 inhabitants; there is 1 physician per 21,681 people. In 1990, the total health care expenditures were $95 million, with an estimated 61% of the population having access to health care services in 1992.

30 HOUSING

Most of the inhabitants live in thatched huts with mud and wattle (interwoven branches and reeds) walls. Even in rural areas, however, corrugated iron is used extensively as a roofing material.

31 EDUCATION

In 1988 there were 7,905 primary schools. At the primary level there were 2,632,764 pupils and 75,561 teachers in 1988, and at the secondary level, 260,069 pupils and 15,437 teachers. Makerere College became Makerere University in 1970. It offers degrees in the arts, sciences, and agriculture. In 1990 there were 15,578 pupils and 1,555 teachers in all higher level institutions. In 1990, the adult literacy rate was 48%.

32 MEDIA

Radio Uganda broadcasts daily in 22 languages, including English, French, and Swahili; television programs are in English, Swahili, and Luganda. In 1991 there were 1,975,000 radios, 187,000 television sets, and 61,046 telephones. The government-operated *New Vision,* had a 1991 circulation of 30,000. Other dailies

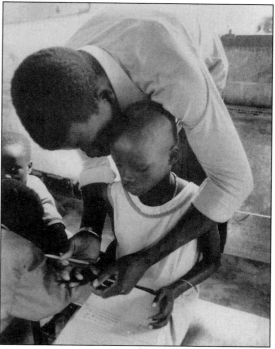

Photo credit: AP/Wide World Photos.

A young pupil under instruction in a third grade class at a Moroto primary school. Education is available, but many families do not make use of the system as their children are needed for agricultural work.

(with 1991 circulation figures), are *The Star* (13,000*), Munno* (14,000), *Ngabo* (15,000), and *Taifa Empya* (4,000). Weekly newspapers in Kampala include the *Equator, The Economy,* and *Mulengera.*

33 TOURISM AND RECREATION

Tourism facilities are adequate in Kampala but limited in other areas. There were 4,567 hotel beds in 1991, with a 32% occupancy rate. In 1991, 69,000 tourists visited Uganda. Wildlife is the major tourist attraction.

34 FAMOUS UGANDANS

Sir Apollo Kagwa (1890–1926), chief minister to Kabaka Mwanga, was one of the dominant figures in Uganda's history. Mukama Kabarega of Bunyoro (r.1896–99) led his people against British and Buganda forces until captured and exiled in 1899. Major General Idi Amin Dada (b.1925) overthrew Milton Obote in 1971 and led a military government until ousted in 1979. Yoweri Museveni (b.1944), leader of the National Resistance Movement, became president in 1986.

35 BIBLIOGRAPHY

Byrnes, Rita M., ed. *Uganda: A Country Study.* 2d ed. Washington, D.C.: Library of Congress, 1992.

Caputo, Robert. "Uganda—Land Beyond Sorrow." *National Geographic,* April 1988, 468–492.

Mutibwa, Phares Mukasa. *Uganda Since Independence: A Story of Unfulfilled Hopes.* London: Hurst & Co., 1992.

UKRAINE

Ukraina

CAPITAL: Kiev (Kyyiv).

FLAG: Equal horizontal bands of azure blue (top) and yellow.

ANTHEM: *The National Anthem of Ukraine.*

MONETARY UNIT: The official currency, introduced in early 1993, is the hryvnia. One hundred shahy equal one hryvnia.

WEIGHTS AND MEASURES: The metric system is used.

HOLIDAYS: New Year's Day, 1–2 January; Christmas, 7 January; Women's Day, 8 March; Spring and Labor Day, 1–2 May; Victory Day, 9 May; Ukrainian Independence Day, 24 August.

TIME: 2 PM = noon GMT.

1 LOCATION AND SIZE

Ukraine, the second largest country in Europe, is located in eastern Europe, bordering the Black Sea, between Poland and Russia. Comparatively, Ukraine is slightly smaller than the state of Texas with a total area of 603,700 square kilometers (233,090 square miles). Its boundary length totals 4,558 kilometers (2,834 miles). Ukraine's capital city, Kiev, is located in the north central part of the country.

2 TOPOGRAPHY

The topography of Ukraine consists mainly of fertile plains (steppes) and plateaus. Mountains (the Carpathians) are found only in the west and in the Crimean Peninsula in the extreme south. The most important river in Ukraine is the Dnipro (Dnieper), the third longest river in Europe.

3 CLIMATE

Precipitation is highest in the west and north, least in the east and southeast. Winters vary from cool along the Black Sea to cold farther inland. Summers are warm across the greater part of the country, but hot in the south. The mean temperature is 10°C (66°F) in July and -6°C (21°F) in January. Northern and western Ukraine average 69 centimeters (27 inches) of rainfall a year.

4 PLANTS AND ANIMALS

Ukraine is famed for its rich agricultural land. European bison, fox, and rabbits can be found living on the vast steppes of the country.

5 ENVIRONMENT

Three and one-half million hectares (8.6 million acres) of agricultural land and 1.5 million hectares (3.7 million acres) of forest were contaminated by radiation from the Chernobyl nuclear accident in 1986. Pollution from other sources also poses a threat to the environment. The water supply in some areas of the country contains toxic industrial chemicals up to 10 times the concentration considered to be within safety limits. Air pollution is also a significant environmental problem. The nation's industries produce 469,000 tons of carbon monoxide and 3,072,000 tons of anhydride sulphide.

6 POPULATION

The population of Ukraine was 51,706,742 in 1989. A population of 53,754,000 is projected for 2000. The estimated population density in 1993 was 85 persons per square kilometer (224 per square mile). Kiev, the capital, had a population estimated at the beginning of 1990 as 2,616,000.

7 MIGRATION

Ukraine had net immigration within the former Soviet Union of 79,300 in 1990 (more people moved into the Ukraine than left). Emigration (people leaving the country) in 1991 came to 59,436. There are about 12 million ethnic Ukrainians living outside of the Ukraine but within the former Soviet Union, and an additional 4 million Ukrainians are living in the United States, Canada, Australia, Western and Central Europe, and South America.

8 ETHNIC GROUPS

The population was 73% Ukrainian in 1989. Russians totaled 22%, mainly in eastern Ukraine. The population of the

Photo credit: Susan D. Rock.

Girls posing for a photo in a park in Yalta.

Crimean Peninsula is about 70% Russian. Crimean Tatars formed about 10% of the population of the Crimean Peninsula in 1992.

9 LANGUAGES

Like Russian and Belorussian, Ukrainian is an eastern Slavic language. Ukrainian began to emerge as a separate language from Russian in the late twelfth century.

10 RELIGIONS

The population is 76% Orthodox, but church life has been marked by disputes

LOCATION: 49°0′N; 32°0′E. **BOUNDARY LENGTHS:** Total boundary lengths, 4,558 kilometers (2,834 miles); Belarus, 891 kilometers (554 miles); Hungary, 103 kilometers (64 miles); Moldova, 939 kilometers (584 miles); Poland, 428 kilometers (266 miles); Romania (southeast), 169 kilometers (105 miles); Romania (west), 362 kilometers (225 miles); Russia 1,576 kilometers (980 miles); Slovakia, 90 kilometers (56 miles).

between the Ukrainian Orthodox Church and the Autocephalous (independent) Ukrainian Orthodox Church. In 1992 the two were united as the Kievan Patriarchy. Byzantine-rite Catholics account for some 15% of the population, and in 1990 there were 375,000 Jews.

11 TRANSPORTATION

As of 1991, there were 23,000 kilometers (14,295 miles) of railway. Highways in 1990 totaled 273,700 kilometers (170,100 miles). There were some 63 passenger cars per 1,000 population in 1990.

The main marine ports are Berdyans'k, Illichivs'k, Kerch, Mariupol', Odesa, and Sevastopol'. The merchant marine fleet includes 338 ships (1,000 gross registered tons or over) for a total capacity of 4,117,595 gross registered tons. The Dnipro (Dnieper) River is the primary inland waterway. The largest airports are in Kiev, Kharkiv, Donetsk, Odesa, and Simferopol.

12 HISTORY

Ukrainians, Russians, and Belarussians are eastern Slavs who trace their origins to the medieval Russian kingdom founded in Kiev in the ninth century AD. Internal strife in the twelfth century and the Mongol invasion in the thirteenth led to the destruction of this kingdom as a major power.

Ukrainian Cossacks (frontier people) were able to establish an independent state in the sixteenth and seventeenth centuries, but war between Russia and Poland resulted in the partition of Ukraine. Most of Ukraine's territory was absorbed by the Russian Empire.

A Ukrainian national movement arose in the nineteenth century. The fall of the Tsar in 1917 amid the chaos of the Russian revolution allowed Ukraine to assert its independence. In 1917, the National Ukrainian Assembly proclaimed the creation of the Ukrainian People's Republic. An independent Republic of Western Ukraine was declared on 1 November 1918 after the disintegration of the Austro-Hungarian Empire. On 22 January 1919, the two republics united and established an independent Ukrainian state, recognized by over 40 other nations.

By 1920, however, eastern Ukraine fell to the Bolsheviks (Communists) and became the Ukrainian Soviet Socialist Republic while Poland occupied most of western Ukraine. Small areas of the west went to Romania, Hungary, and Czechoslovakia. Early policy in the Soviet Union allowed for cultural autonomy and local administration by Ukrainian Communists. But Joseph Stalin changed this liberal policy in the 1930s and began the persecution of Ukrainian nationalists.

The 1939 Nazi-Soviet pact assigned Poland's Ukrainian territory to the Soviet sphere of influence. After Germany invaded the Soviet Union in 1941, a resistance movement led by nationalists fought both the Soviet and German armies. During World War II (1939–45), Ukraine lost six million people through death or deportation and a total of 18,000 villages were destroyed.

The Ukrainian resistance movement continued to fight in Soviet Ukraine, and it was not until the 1950s that they were completely defeated by the better-equipped Soviet Red (communist) Army.

On 24 August 1991, following the failed coup in Moscow, the parliament proclaimed the independence of Ukraine and declared that only the constitution and laws of Ukraine were valid on its territory. On 1 December 1991, 90.3% of Ukraine's citizens voted in favor of independence and elected Leonid Kravchuk as their first president.

Ukraine joined Russia, Belarus, and other nations of the former Soviet Union in creating the Commonwealth of Independent States (CIS) in December 1991. However, Ukrainian-Russian differences have arisen in several areas, including the command and control of nuclear weapons, the formation of a unified military command, and the character and pace of economic reform.

Since its independence, Ukraine has experienced unrest in some of its mostly Russian areas, notably the Crimean Peninsula (Crimea), which declared independence on 6 May 1992. Demands for secession in Crimea have continued to complicate Ukrainian-Russian relations.

13 GOVERNMENT

The Ukrainian parliament consists of a single chamber with 450 seats called the Rada. The prime minister and cabinet are nominated by the president and confirmed by the parliament. In Ukraine's first post-independence presidential elections, held in 1994, the incumbent Leonid Kravchuk was defeated by his former prime minister, Leonid Kuchma.

Ukraine is divided into 24 administrative regions (*oblasts*) plus the autonomous Republic of Crimea.

Photo credit: Susan D. Rock

Streetside produce vendor in Yalta.

14 POLITICAL PARTIES

There are some 30 political parties active in Ukraine. They fall roughly into four different categories: radical nationalist; democratic nationalist (including the influential Rukh Party, which gained 20 parliamentary seats in the 1994); liberal-centrist; and Communist-socialist. The most important party in the last group is the Communist Party of Ukraine, which won 75 seats in the 1994 elections.

Aside from the Communists and Rukh, all other parties won 12 seats or less. Independents hold most of the seats in the Rada.

15 JUDICIAL SYSTEM

The court system has not significantly changed since the former Soviet regime. The three levels of courts are *rayon* (also known as regional or people's courts), provincial or regional (*oblast*) courts, and the Supreme Court. All three levels provide first hearings for cases, the choice of court depending on the severity of the crime. They also hear appeals.

16 ARMED FORCES

Ukraine was able to quickly organize an impressive national army, in part because it had always been an important contribu-

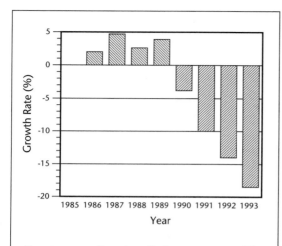

Yearly growth rate of the economy. This economic indicator tells by what percent the economy has increased or decreased when compared with the previous year.

tor to the Soviet armed forces. The armed forces numbered 230,000 in 1993. The army of 150,000 is organized into 19 divisions and more than 50 specialized brigades and regiments. The air force numbers 50,000 and the navy 30,000.

Of great international concern is the fate of the 176 ICBMs (intercontinental ballistic missiles) and 41 strategic bombers on Ukrainian soil, which are supposed to be sent to Russia for dismantling.

17 ECONOMY

The rich agricultural land of Ukraine (commonly called the "breadbasket" of the former Soviet Union) provided 46% of Soviet agricultural output in the 1980s. Ukraine's economic base is currently dominated by industry, but agriculture continues to play a major role in the economy.

The 1991 dissolution of the Soviet Union has led to shortages of supplies for business and industry, and of consumer goods as well. Inflation in 1992 averaged nearly 1,500%.

18 INCOME

In 1992, the gross national product (GNP) was $87,025 million at current prices, or about $2,210 per person. For the period 1985–92 the average inflation rate was 11.5%.

19 INDUSTRY

Ukraine is a major producer of heavy machinery and industrial equipment for industries including mining, steelmaking, and chemicals. Ukraine is also an important supplier of products—including automobiles, clothing, foodstuffs, timber, and paper—to other former Soviet republics.

20 LABOR

As of 1991, there were some 19,119,000 employees, including 6,913,000 in manufacturing, mining, and utilities, 1,639,000 in construction, and 1,699,000 in transportation, storage, and communications. In 1992, a minimum wage was established, but was well below the cost of living by the end of the year.

21 AGRICULTURE

Ukraine's steppe (plains) region in the south is possibly the most fertile region in the world. However, it is estimated that nearly 60,000 hectares (148,250 acres) of fertile land in the Chernobyl vicinity are now unavailable for cultivation. The production of grain in 1991 compared to

1989 fell by 12.5 million tons, sugar beets by 15.6 million tons, potatoes by 4.7 million tons, and vegetables by 1.5 million tons.

Production amounts in 1992 included (in 1,000 tons): sugar beets, 28,546; potatoes, 20,427; wheat, 19,473; dry peas, 2,776; fruit, 2,351; sunflower seeds, 2,100; cabbage, 1,140; grapes, 655; wine, 290; soybeans, 140; and tobacco, 19.

22 DOMESTICATED ANIMALS

Just over 10% of Ukraine's total land area is composed of permanent pastureland. As of 1992, there were 23.7 million head of cattle, 17.8 million pigs, 7.3 million sheep, 233 million chickens, and 10 million turkeys. Horses, goats, ducks, and rabbits are also bred and raised. In 1992, meat production included: beef, 1,676,000 tons; pork, 1,209,000 tons; and poultry, 605,000 tons. Milk and egg production in 1992 amounted to 19 million tons and 830,000 tons, respectively.

23 FISHING

In 1991, the total catch came to 816,000 tons. Fishing occurs mainly on the Black Sea.

24 FORESTRY

About 13% of the total area is forest and woodland. Forestry production in 1990 included: roundwood, 8 million cubic meters; sawn timber, 6 million cubic meters; wood pulp, 90,000 tons; paper, 353,000 tons; and cardboard, 463,000 tons.

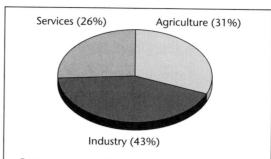

Components of the economy. This pie chart shows how much of the country's economy is devoted to agriculture (includes forestry, hunting, and fishing), industry, or services.

Services (26%)   *Agriculture (31%)*   *Industry (43%)*

25 MINING

Mineral production in Ukraine includes alumina, aluminum, antimony, coal, ferroalloys, graphite, iron ore, magnesium, manganese, mercury, nickel, potash, salt, soda ash, sulfur, talc, titanium, and uranium.

26 FOREIGN TRADE

Raw materials and consumer goods are the main items of export. Inter-republic trade (with other former Soviet Republics) accounted for 73% of its total imports in 1988, and 85% of its total exports. In 1992, inter-republic trade declined severely, and trade with other countries dropped as well.

27 ENERGY AND POWER

Most electricity is generated by coal, natural gas, or oil, but nuclear power plants generated over 25% of Ukraine's electricity in 1991. Power generation in 1992 fell from its 1990 level of 298,000 million kilowatt hours due to fuel shortages from

Selected Social Indicators

These statistics are estimates for the period 1988 to 1993. For comparison purposes, data for the United States and averages for low-income countries and high-income countries are also given.

Indicator	Ukraine	Low-income countries	High-income countries	United States
Per capita gross national product†	$2,210	$380	$23,680	$24,740
Population growth rate	0.0%	1.9%	0.6%	1.0%
Population growth rate in urban areas	0.9%	3.9%	0.8%	1.3%
Population per square kilometer of land	85	78	25	26
Life expectancy in years	69	62	77	76
Number of people per physician	224	>3,300	453	419
Number of pupils per teacher (primary school)	n.a.	39	<18	20
Illiteracy rate (15 years and older)	2%	41%	<5%	<3%
Energy consumed per capita (kg of oil equivalent)	3,960	364	5,203	7,918

† The gross national product (GNP) is the total dollar value of all goods and services produced by a country in a year. The per capita GNP is calculated by dividing a country's GNP by its population. The World Bank defines low-income countries as those with a per capita GNP of $695 or less. High-income countries have a per capita GNP of $8,626 or more. Less than 14% of the world's 5.5 billion people live in high-income countries, while almost 60% live in low-income countries.

n.a. = data not available   > = greater than   < = less than

Sources: World Bank, Social Indicators of Development 1995, Baltimore: Johns Hopkins University Press, 1995. Central Intelligence Agency, World Fact Book, Washington, D.C.: Government Printing Office, 1994.

declining Russian imports. In October 1991, the Ukrainian Parliament decided to shut down the Chernobyl nuclear power plant, site of a major accident in 1986, by the end of 1993.

Oil production totaled less than 100,000 barrels per day. Natural gas production was 0.8 trillion cubic feet (2 billion cubic meters) in 1991.

28 SOCIAL DEVELOPMENT

The average family size was 3.2 in 1989, and the divorce rate was 8.7 per 1,000 women. Estimates suggest that women may account for as many as 90% of Ukraine's unemployed.

29 HEALTH

According to United Nations reports, approximately one million people were exposed to unsafe radiation levels following the Chernobyl nuclear accident by eating contaminated food. The government created special dispensaries and commissions to assess the amount of disease caused by the accident. As of 1994, 15,000 people listed were listed as affected.

Photo credit: Susan D. Rock.

The Opera House in Odessa.

In 1993 there were 220,000 physicians and a total of 700,000 hospital beds in Ukraine. Total health care expenditures for 1990 (prior to independence) were $6,803 million. Average life expectancy in 1992 was 69 years. The leading causes of death were cardiovascular and respiratory diseases, cancer, traumas, and accidents.

30 HOUSING

In 1991, average housing space per person totaled 18 square meters.

31 EDUCATION

Ukraine has a 98% literacy rate, with nearly 15% of the adult population having completed higher education. There were 7.1 million students enrolled in the 21,900 general education schools in 1992. The 156 institutions of higher learning had 876,200 students.

32 MEDIA

Ukrainian TV and four radio networks broadcast from Kiev. In 1991 there were 41,300,000 radios and 17,100,000 television sets. Ukraine has about 7 million telephone lines, or 13.5 telephones for each 100 persons.

Among the leading daily newspapers (with 1991 circulation) are: *Silski Visti* (2,300,000); *Nezavisimost* (1,300,000); *Molod Ukrainy* (700,000); *Golos Ukrainy*

(330,000); *Robitnycha Gazeta* (300,000); and *Demokratychna Ukraine* (150,000).

33 TOURISM AND RECREATION

Kiev, Ukraine's major cultural center, is known for its beautiful churches and golden-domed cathedrals, although much of its classic architecture was destroyed or obscured by Communist planners in the 1930s. L'vin (formerly Lvov) offers architectural sights ranging from late-thirteenth-century Russian to sixteenth-century Gothic structures. Ukraine's tourism was affected by the after-effects of the 1986 Chernobyl nuclear accident.

34 FAMOUS UKRAINIANS

Leonid M. Kravchuk and Vitold P. Fokin were respectively the first president and prime minister of Ukraine. Leonid Brezhnev (1906–82) led the Soviet Union from 1966–82. Outstanding representatives of the culture and literature of Ukraine include poet Taras Sshechenko (1814–61) and the Jewish writer Sholom Aleichem (Solomon Rabinowitz, 1859–1916).

35 BIBLIOGRAPHY

Chirovsky, Nicholas L. *An Introduction to Ukrainian History.* New York: Philosophical Library, 1981.

Edwards, Mike. "Ukraine." *National Geographic,* May 1987, 595–631.

Shcherbitskii, V. V. *Soviet Ukraine.* Moscow: Progress Publishers, 1985.

UNITED ARAB EMIRATES

United Arab Emirates
Al-Imarat al-ʿArabiyah al-Muttahidah

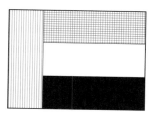

CAPITAL: Abu Dhabi (Abu Zaby).

FLAG: The flag consists of a red vertical stripe at the hoist and three equal horizontal stripes of green, white, and black.

ANTHEM: The National Anthem is an instrumental piece without words.

MONETARY UNIT: The United Arab Emirates dirham (UD), introduced as the currency in May 1973, is divided into 100 fils. There are coins of 1, 5, 10, 25, and 50 fils and 1 and 5 dirham and notes of 5, 10, 50, 100, 200, 500, and 1,000 dirhams. UD1 = $0.2724 (or $1 = UD3.6710).

WEIGHTS AND MEASURES: The metric system and imperial and local measures are used.

HOLIDAYS: New Year's Day, 1 January; Accession of the Ruler of Abu Dhabi (Abu Dhabi only), 6 August; National Day, 2 December; Christmas, 25 December. Muslim religious holidays include Lailat al-Miraj, ʿId al-Fitr, ʿId al-ʿAdha', Hijra New Year, and Milad an-Nabi.

TIME: 4 PM = noon GMT.

1 LOCATION AND SIZE

Comprising a total area of approximately 75,581 square kilometers (29,182 square miles), the United Arab Emirates (UAE), is in the eastern Arabian Peninsula. It consists of seven states, or emirates: Abu Dhabi, Dubayy, Ash Shariqah, Ra's al-Khaymah, Al Fujayrah, Umm al-Qaywayn, and ʿAjman. Comparatively, the area occupied by UAE is slightly smaller than the state of Maine. UAE has a total boundary length of 2,185 kilometers (1,358 miles). The UAE's capital city, Abu Dhabi, is located on the Persian Gulf.

2 TOPOGRAPHY

The UAE consists mainly of sandy desert. It is bounded on the west by an immense sebkha, or salt flat; the eastern boundary runs northward over gravel plains and high dunes. The flat coastal strip that makes up most of the UAE has an extensive area of sebkha subject to flooding.

3 CLIMATE

The months between May and October are extremely hot, with shade temperatures of between 38° and 49°C (100–120°F) and high humidity near the coast. Winter temperatures can fall as low as 2°C (36°F) but average between 17° and 20°C (63–68°F). Normal annual rainfall is from 5 to 10 centimeters (2–4 inches).

4 PLANTS AND ANIMALS

Vegetation of the marshes and swamps includes the dwarf mangrove, and there is a wide range of desert plants.

Animal life includes jerboa (desert rat), gazelle, mongoose, hare, fox, wolf, jackal, wildcat, and lynx. There are 14 species of reptile, and 4 types of land snake. More than 250 species of small birds have been reported in the UAE, along with many of the larger birds—kites, buzzards, eagles, falcons, owls, and harriers. Sea birds include a variety of gulls, terns, ospreys, waders, and flamingos. Popular game birds include the houbara (ruffed bustard), as well as species of ducks and geese.

5 ENVIRONMENT

The clearing of natural vegetation, livestock overgrazing on rangelands, and loss of forest land have led to desertification, or expansion of the desert. The oil industry has contributed to air pollution. Ninety-five percent of the city dwellers and 100% of the people living in rural areas have pure water.

The nation's cities produce 0.5 million tons of solid waste per year. The Al-'Ayn zoological gardens contain some 280 species of wildlife, including the gazelle, which had been on the verge of extinction in the region. In 1994, four of the country's mammal species were endangered. Seven bird species were threatened with extinction.

6 POPULATION

The population was estimated at 1,909,000 in 1991. The United Nations projected population for the year 2000 is 1,970,000.

The city of Abu Dhabi had 670,125 people in 1985.

7 MIGRATION

About 80% of the UAE's population originates from outside its borders. In the early 1980s, the government tried to reduce the immigration rate by limiting the number of visas issued to foreign workers.

8 ETHNIC GROUPS

South Asians (Asian Indians, Pakistanis, Bangladeshis, and Sri Lankans) account for about 45% of the population, followed by Arabs (about 33%, 13% of whom are from outside the UAE), and Iranians (17%). Westerners (Americans and Western Europeans) account for about 5%. Jordanians, Palestinians, Egyptians, Iraqis, and Bahrainis are employed throughout the government bureaucracy.

9 LANGUAGES

Arabic is the universal language. Farsi is spoken in Dubayy, and English is widely used in business.

10 RELIGIONS

Almost all UAE citizens and many immigrants are Muslims. Most are Sunni Muslims, with the exception of a comparatively large Shi'ite Muslim community in Dubayy. The non-Muslims are principally Christians and Hindus.

11 TRANSPORTATION

In 1991 there were 1,800 kilometers (1,118 miles) of bituminized highways. In 1992 there were 5.4 million registered vehicles.

Dubayy's Port Rashid is one of the largest artificial harbors in the Middle East. Other ports are the Jabal 'Ali complex and Abu Dhabi's Port Zayid. In 1991, the merchant fleet consisted of 51 ships with a capacity totaling 766,000 gross registered tons.

A new international airport in Abu Dhabi opened in 1982 and serviced 1,075,000 embarking and disembarking passengers in 1991. The other international airports in the UAE are in Dubayy, Ash Shāriqah, and Ra's al-Khaymah.

[12] HISTORY

Abu Dhabi island was settled by its present ruling family, Al-Nahyan, toward the end of the eighteenth century, and Dubayy was founded by an offshoot of the same family in 1833. The late eighteenth and nineteenth centuries brought the division of the area between the Nahyan and the Qawasim, who ruled Ra's al-Khaymah and neighboring territories.

Treaties signed in 1820 and 1835 established a formal relationship between the states of the southern Persian Gulf and Britain that was to last until 1971. In 1892, the United Kingdom promised to protect the coast from aggression by sea and land. In 1955, it intervened on the side of Abu Dhabi in its dispute with Sa'udi Arabia over the Al Buraymi oasis, near Al 'Ayn, control of which is now shared by Abu Dhabi and Oman.

When, in 1968, the United Kingdom announced the withdrawal of its forces from the area, an agreement was reached to establish a federation of Arab emir-

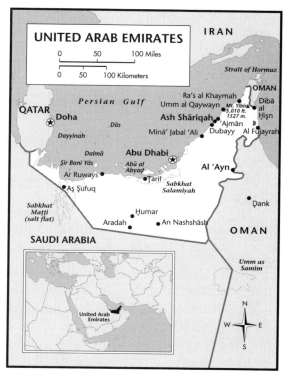

LOCATION: 51°3′ to 56°23′E; 22°30′ to 26°17′N.
BOUNDARY LENGTHS: Persian Gulf coastline, 1,318 kilometers (817 miles); Oman, 410 kilometers (256 miles); Sa'udi Arabia, 457 kilometers (285 miles). **TERRITORIAL SEA LIMIT:** 3 miles, except Ash Shariqah (12 miles).

ates—embracing the seven states of the present-day UAE, Bahrain, and Qatar. In 1971, six of the seven present-day UAE states agreed on the establishment of the United Arab Emirates. The UAE was officially proclaimed a sovereign, independent nation on 2 December 1971, with the seventh state, Ra's al-Khaymah, joining in early 1972.

UAE's independence created problems between the new state and its two powerful neighbors, Sa'udi Arabia and Iran.

Sa'udi Arabia claimed a group of oases (fertile areas in deserts) in the south of the UAE, and Iran laid claim to its offshore islands. In 1974, a border agreement on the oases was signed with Sa'udi Arabia, but has not been fully recognized by the rulers of either country.

The dispute with Iran over the islands became tense when Iranian forces tried to claim the UAE section of Abu Musa (a tiny island west of Ra's al Khaymah) in 1992. The Iranian government in Tehran backed down and relations between the two countries returned to a cautious normality.

The UAE became a founding member in 1981 of the Gulf Cooperation Council (GCC), a political and economic alliance that includes all the Persian Gulf countries (Bahrain, Kuwait, Oman, Qatar, Sa'udi Arabia, and the UAE) except Iran. During the Iran-Iraq War (1980–88), the UAE gave aid to Iraq but also maintained diplomatic relations with Iran and sought to mediate the conflict.

In the Persian Gulf War of 1990, forces from the UAE participated with allied troops against Iraq and the government gave some $4.5 billion to the coalition war effort. The UAE's generosity with foreign aid to Arab states (over $15 billion through 1991) makes it a significant player in the affairs of the region.

In 1991, the international Bank of Commerce and Credit International (BCCI), which was based in the UAE and largely owned by the ruling family of Abu Dhabi, was accused of fraud and closed down, causing repercussions all around the world.

13 GOVERNMENT

The executive branch of government consists of the Supreme Council of Rulers, headed by the president, and the Council of Ministers. The Council of Rulers, composed of the hereditary rulers of the seven emirates, has responsibility for formulation and supervision of all UAE policies, ratification of federal laws, and oversight of the union's budget.

Sheikh Zayed bin Sultan al-Nahayyan, emir of Abu Dhabi, was elected president upon independence and reelected to five-year terms from 1976 to 1991. The president is assisted by the Council of Ministers, or cabinet, headed by the prime minister. The Federal National Council can question cabinet ministers and make recommendations to the Supreme National Council.

Most of the individual emirates (states) are governed according to tribal traditions, including open meetings in which citizens express themselves directly to their rulers.

14 POLITICAL PARTIES

No political parties exist in the UAE.

15 JUDICIAL SYSTEM

Abu Dhabi, Dubayy, and Ash Shariqah have developed relatively sophisticated judicial systems based, as in other Persian Gulf states, on a combination of Shari'ah (Islamic) law and modern legal codes. The 1971 constitution established a Supreme

Court and an unspecified number of lower courts.

16 ARMED FORCES

In 1993, the combined UAE forces totaled 54,000 men, all volunteers. One-third are Asian contract (hired) soldiers. The army had 50,000 men, organized into 6 brigades. The navy comprised 2,000 men and 19 patrol and coastal combatants. The air force had 2,500 men, 105 combat aircraft, and 19 armed helicopters.

17 ECONOMY

Traditionally, the economy of the UAE centered primarily on oil and oil-based industries. However, with its strategic location, modern communications and transportation facilities, and strong banking system, the UAE has also become the major trade center in the Gulf region. The UAE has one of the highest per person national incomes in the world—$21,430.

In Abu Dhabi, by far the wealthiest of the seven emirates (states), oil revenues are supplemented by income from a huge investment fund. Dubayy's role as a center for trade plays a major role in its economy.

Although there are small industries in 'Ajman and Umm al-Qaywayn, these poorer areas depend on federal aid. Oil production in Ash Shariqah began in July 1974, and manufacturing and tourism there have been expanded. Ra's al-Khaymah has cement plants, a pharmaceutical factory, a lime kiln, and the gulf's first explosives plant. Al Fujayrah remains predominantly agricultural.

18 INCOME

In 1992, United Arab Emirates' gross national product (GNP) was $37,068 million at current prices, or about $21,430 per person. For the period 1985–92 the average inflation rate was 2.4%.

19 INDUSTRY

The industrial complex in Abu Dhabi includes an oil refinery with a processing capacity of 120,000 barrels per day; a fertilizer factory, with a production capacity of 1,000 tons of ammonia and 1,500 tons of urea per day; and a gas liquefaction installation.

In Dubayy, the industrial port complex includes an aluminum smelter, which produced over 150,000 tons in 1985. The other developed industries produce construction-related materials such as cement, asphalt, and concrete blocks. The UAE has been introducing a wide spectrum of new industries: aluminum, cement, pharmaceuticals, fabricated metals, processed foods, fertilizer, and explosives.

20 LABOR

In 1992, the total work force was estimated at 700,000. The UAE leans heavily on foreigners for skilled labor and management ability. Non-UAE Arabs are employed at all economic levels, including the government bureaucracy and civil service. However, with declining oil revenues in the mid-1980s, well-paying, skilled jobs were becoming harder to find. A 1984 decree guarantees UAE nationals priority in hiring, in order to reduce dependence on foreign labor.

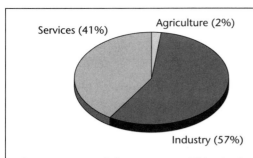

Services (41%)   Agriculture (2%)

Industry (57%)

Components of the economy. This pie chart shows how much of the country's economy is devoted to agriculture (includes forestry, hunting, and fishing), industry, or services.

21 AGRICULTURE

About 24% of cultivated land is used to grow vegetables, 30% fruit, 10% feed crops, and 36% for other uses. The main crops are tomatoes, melons, and dates. In 1992, UAE agriculture produced 361,000 tons of vegetables and 235,000 tons of fruit.

22 DOMESTICATED ANIMALS

In 1992, the UAE had 720,000 goats, 275,000 sheep, 132,000 camels, and 55,000 head of cattle. Local poultry and egg production satisfy 65% and 80% of domestic demand, respectively.

23 FISHING

Fishing is an important source of domestic food and animal feed. From 1988 to 1990, per person annual consumption of fish and shellfish in the UAE was 26.3 kilograms (58 pounds), more than any other country in the Middle East. Many varieties of fish are caught, including rock cod, tuna, mackerel, sardines, anchovies, jack, marlin, red mullet, bream, and snapper. The fish catch in 1991 was 92,300 tons, which supplied about 97% of local demand.

24 FORESTRY

Wooded areas covered only 3,000 hectares (7,400 acres), or about 0.04% of the total land area in 1991.

25 MINING

Apart from oil and natural gas, mining is limited to the production of construction materials, marble, and stone quarried in the northeast. In 1992, an estimated 20,000 tons of chromite ore were exported.

26 FOREIGN TRADE

Almost all export earnings derive from oil. In 1992, petroleum products accounted for around 75% of total exports, which amounted to $23.4 billion. The value of imports in 1992 was $17.4 billion. Consumer goods, especially food, accounted for about half of all imports, followed by business-related goods such as transportation equipment, oil-field equipment, and building materials.

Japan, Singapore, India, South Korea, the European Community countries, and the United States are the leading purchasers of petroleum from the UAE. Of the UAE's total 1992 imports, Japan supplied 15.3%, China 8.0%, the United States 7.9%, and Germany 7.4%.

27 ENERGY AND POWER

The UAE, with crude oil production of 2.3 million barrels per day in 1992, ranked as the third-largest Organization of Arab Petroleum Exporting Countries (OPEC) producer; total reserves of crude oil were estimated at 98.1 billion barrels. The UAE's proven natural gas reserves totaled about 5.8 trillion cubic meters (205 trillion cubic feet) in 1992, and net production amounted to 23.6 billion cubic meters. All electricity is thermally generated from oil or natural gas. Electric power production was 13,790 million kilowatt hours in 1991.

28 SOCIAL DEVELOPMENT

There is no social security law in the UAE, but many welfare benefits are available to citizens, relief for any domestic catastrophe, provided from a disaster fund. If the father of a family is unable to work because of illness, disability, or old age, he receives help under the National Assistance Law; should he die or divorce his wife, the woman's future is secured.

Female employment is growing in government service and in occupations such as education and health.

29 HEALTH

Modern hospitals have been built in Abu Dhabi, Dubayy, and other towns. The number of hospital beds totaled 6,025 in 1985. In 1991, there were 1,526 doctors. Typhoid fever and tuberculosis are rare; malaria remains a problem, however. Average life expectancy is 74 years. In 1992, 99% of the population had access to health care services.

30 HOUSING

The federal government is attempting to make modern low-cost homes available to poorer families and supplying them with piped water, sewage systems, and electricity.

31 EDUCATION

Education is compulsory for six years at the primary level. At the secondary level, children go through six years of education in two stages. In 1991, there were 231,674 pupils and 13,139 teachers at the primary level and 118,011 pupils and 9,430 teachers in secondary schools. United Arab Emirates University is at Al-'Ayn. In 1991, all higher level institutions had 10,405 students and 1,082 instructors.

32 MEDIA

In 1991, the UAE had 463,398 telephones. A color television network connects Abu Dhabi with Dubayy and Ash Shariqah. UAE Radio has broadcasting stations in four emirates (states); the first commercial station was opened in Abu Dhabi in 1980. There were an estimated 530,000 radios and 175,000 television sets in 1991.

Five Arabic-language dailies were published in 1991 in the UAE: *Al-Ittihad (Federation,* 1991 circulation 75,000), *Al-Fajr (The Dawn,* 20,000), and *Al-Wahdah (Unity,* 30,000), in Abu Dhabi; *Al-Bayan* (45,000) in Dubayy; and *Al-Khalij* (57,000) in Ash Shariqah. There were three English-language dailies: the *Gulf News* (54,100) and *Khaleej Times* (56,000), published in Dubai; and the *Emirates News* (15,000), published in Abu Dhabi.

Selected Social Indicators

These statistics are estimates for the period 1988 to 1993. For comparison purposes, data for the United States and averages for low-income countries and high-income countries are also given.

Indicator	United Arab Emirates	Low-income countries	High-income countries	United States
Per capita gross national product†	$21,430	$380	$23,680	$24,740
Population growth rate	2.6%	1.9%	0.6%	1.0%
Population growth rate in urban areas	3.3%	3.9%	0.8%	1.3%
Population per square kilometer of land	84	78	25	26
Life expectancy in years	74	62	77	76
Number of people per physician	1,095	>3,300	453	419
Number of pupils per teacher (primary school)	17	39	<18	20
Illiteracy rate (15 years and older)	32%	41%	<5%	<3%
Energy consumed per capita (kg of oil equivalent)	16,878	364	5,203	7,918

† The gross national product (GNP) is the total dollar value of all goods and services produced by a country in a year. The per capita GNP is calculated by dividing a country's GNP by its population. The World Bank defines low-income countries as those with a per capita GNP of $695 or less. High-income countries have a per capita GNP of $8,626 or more. Less than 14% of the world's 5.5 billion people live in high-income countries, while almost 60% live in low-income countries.

> = greater than   < = less than

Sources: World Bank, *Social Indicators of Development 1995,* Baltimore: Johns Hopkins University Press, 1995. Central Intelligence Agency, *World Fact Book,* Washington, D.C.: Government Printing Office, 1994.

33 TOURISM AND RECREATION

Tourism is encouraged in all areas. The UAE's varied scenery includes mountains, beaches, deserts, and oases. Tourist activities include visits to Bedouin markets, museums, zoos, and aquariums. Many large world-class hotels opened in the period 1985–95.

34 FAMOUS EMIRIANS

Sheikh Zayed bin Sultan an-Nahyan (b.1918) has been ruler of Abu Dhabi since 1966 and president of the UAE since 1971.

35 BIBLIOGRAPHY

Vine, Peter. *United Arab Emirates: Profile of a Country's Heritage and Modern Development.* London: Immel, 1992.

UNITED KINGDOM

United Kingdom of Great Britain and Northern Ireland

CAPITAL: London.

FLAG: The Union Jack, adopted in 1800, is a combination of the banners of England (St. George's flag: a red cross with extended horizontals on a white field), Scotland (St. Andrew's flag: a white saltire cross on a blue field), and Ireland (St. Patrick's flag: a red saltire cross on a white field). The arms of the saltire crosses do not meet at the center.

ANTHEM: *God Save the Queen.*

MONETARY UNIT: The pound sterling (£) is a paper currency of 100 pence. Before decimal coinage was introduced on 15 February 1971, the pound had been divided into 20 shillings, each shilling representing 12 pennies (p) or pence; some old-style coins are still in circulation. Under the new system, there are coins of 1, 2, 5, 10, 20, and 50 pence and 1 and 2 pounds, and notes of 5, 10, 20, and 50 pounds. £1 = $1.4822 (or $1 = £0.6747).

WEIGHTS AND MEASURES: Although the traditional imperial system of weights and measures is still in use (sample units: of weight, the stone of 14 pounds equivalent to 6.35 kilograms; of length, the yard equivalent to 0.914 meter; of capacity, a bushel equivalent to 36.37 liters), a changeover to the metric system is in progress.

HOLIDAYS: New Year's Day, 1 January; Good Friday; Easter Monday (except Scotland); Late Summer Holiday, last Monday in August or 1st in September (except Scotland); Christmas, 25 December; and Boxing Day, 1st weekday after Christmas. Also observed in Scotland are bank holidays on 2 January and on the 1st Monday in August. Northern Ireland observes St. Patrick's Day, 17 March; and Orangeman's Day, 12 July, commemorating the Battle of the Boyne in 1690.

TIME: GMT.

1 LOCATION AND SIZE

The United Kingdom (UK) is situated off the northwest coast of Europe between the Atlantic Ocean and the North Sea. It is separated from the Continent by the Strait of Dover and the English Channel, and from the Irish Republic by the Irish Sea and St. George's Channel. Its total area of 244,820 square kilometers (94,526 square miles) consists of the island of Great Brit-ain—formed by England, Wales, and Scotland—and Northern Ireland, on the island of Ireland. Comparatively, the area occupied by the United Kingdom is slightly smaller than the state of Oregon.

The United Kingdom also comprises several island groups and hundreds of small single islands. Its total boundary length is 12,789 kilometers (7,947 miles). The 0° meridian of longitude passes through the old Royal Observatory, located at Greenwich. The United Kingdom's capital city, London, is located in the southeast part of Great Britain, in England.

2 TOPOGRAPHY

England is divided into the hill regions of the north, west, and southwest, and the rolling downs and low plains of the east and southeast. The Cheviot Hills run from east to west at the Scottish border. The Pennines mountain range runs from the Scottish border to central England. South of the Pennines lies a plains region. The highest point in England is in the northwest. The longest river is the Thames in the southeast.

Scotland has three distinct topographical regions: the Northwest Highlands, occupying almost the entire northern half of the country and containing the highest point in the British Isles, as well as Loch Ness, site of the fabled "monster;" the area known as the Central Lowlands, containing Loch Lomond, Scotland's largest lake; and the Southern Uplands.

Wales is largely mountainous. The Cambrian Mountains occupy almost the entire area. There are narrow coastal plains in the south and west and small lowland areas in the north.

Northern Ireland consists mainly of low-lying plateaus and hills. At its center lies Lough Neagh, the largest lake in the United Kingdom.

3 CLIMATE

Despite its northern latitude, the United Kingdom generally has a temperate climate. Mean monthly temperatures range (north to south) from 3°C to 5°C (37°–41°F) in winter and from 12°C to 16°C (54°–61°F) in summer. Temperatures in summer rarely go over 32°C (90°F) or drop in winter below –10°C (14°F). Rainfall, averaging more than 100 centimeters (40 inches) throughout the United Kingdom, is heaviest on the western and northern heights (over 380 centimeters/150 inches), and lowest along the eastern and southeastern coasts. Known for its mists and fogs, the United Kingdom has little sunshine—averaging from half an hour to two hours a day in winter and from five to eight hours in summer.

4 PLANTS AND ANIMALS

With its mild climate and varied soils, the United Kingdom has many types of plant life. Fairly large forests remain in east and north Scotland and in southeast England. Oak, elm, ash, and beech are the most common trees in England, and pine and birch in Scotland. Almost all the lowland outside the industrial centers is farmland, with a variety of cultivated grasses and flowering plants. Wild plants of the United Kingdom's woods, fens and marshes, cliffs, and mountain slopes include heather, grasses, gorse, and the bracken of the moorlands.

The animals are similar to that of northwestern continental Europe, although there are fewer species. Some of the larger mammals—wolf, bear, boar, and reindeer—are extinct, but red and roe deer are protected

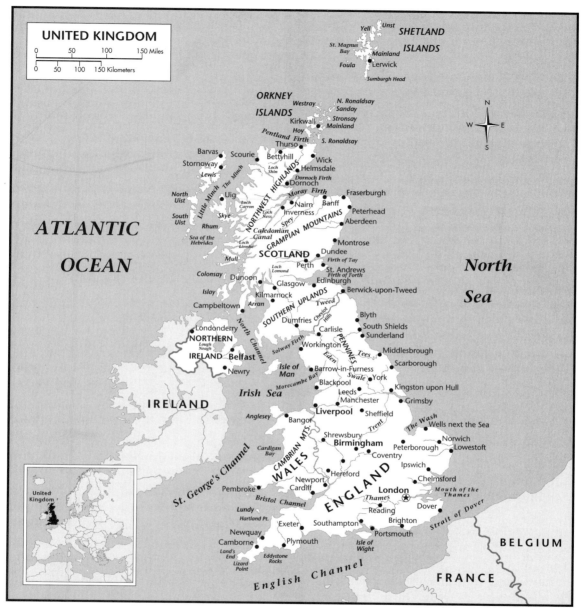

UNITED KINGDOM

0 50 100 150 Miles
0 50 100 150 Kilometers

SHETLAND ISLANDS
Yell · Unst
St. Magnus Bay · Mainland
Foula · Lerwick
Sumburgh Head

ORKNEY ISLANDS
N. Ronaldsay
Westray · Sanday
Kirkwall · Stronsay
Hoy · Mainland
Pentland Firth · S. Ronaldsay
Thurso

Barvas · Scourie · Bettyhill · Wick
Stornoway · Helmsdale
Lewis · Loch Shin
North Uist · Dornoch Firth · Dornoch
Moray Firth · Fraserburgh
Uig · Nairn · Banff
South Uist · Inverness · Peterhead
Skye · Loch Ness · Spey · Aberdeen
Rhum · Caledonian Canal · GRAMPIAN MOUNTAINS
Sea of the Hebrides · Loch Linnhe · Montrose
Mull · SCOTLAND · Dundee
Firth of Tay
Loch Lomond · Perth
Colonsay · Dunoon · St. Andrews
Firth of Forth
Glasgow · Edinburgh
Islay · Kilmarnock · Berwick-upon-Tweed
Campbeltown · Arran · SOUTHERN UPLANDS
Tweed · Cheviot Hills
Dumfries · Blyth
Londonderry · Carlisle · South Shields · Sunderland
NORTHERN · Lough Neagh · Workington
Solway Firth · PENNINES · Tees · Middlesbrough
IRELAND · Belfast · Eden · Scarborough
Newry · Isle of Man · Barrow-in-Furness
Swale · York
Morecambe Bay · Blackpool · Kingston upon Hull
Irish Sea · Leeds · Grimsby
Manchester
Anglesey · Liverpool · Sheffield
IRELAND · Bangor · Trent
The Wash · Wells next the Sea
Shrewsbury · Norwich
Cardigan Bay · CAMBRIAN MTS. · Birmingham · Peterborough · Lowestoft
WALES · Coventry · Ipswich
Newport · Hereford
Pembroke · Cardiff · ENGLAND · Chelmsford
Bristol Channel · London · Mouth of the Thames
Lundy · Thames · Dover
Hartland Pt. · Reading
Newquay · Exeter · Southampton · Brighton · Strait of Dover
Camborne · Plymouth · Portsmouth
Land's End · Isle of Wight
Lizard Point · Eddystone Rocks
English Channel

ATLANTIC OCEAN
North Sea
North Channel
St. George's Channel
The Minch
Little Minch
Loch Carron

BELGIUM
FRANCE

United Kingdom

N
W · E
S

LOCATION: 49°56′ to 60°50′N; 1°45′E to 8°10′W. **BOUNDARY LENGTHS:** Total coastline, 12,429 kilometers (7,722 miles), of which Northern Ireland's comprises 375 kilometers (233 miles); Irish Republic, 360 kilometers (225 miles). **TERRITORIAL SEA LIMIT:** 3 miles.

for sport. Common smaller mammals are foxes, hares, hedgehogs, rabbits, weasels, stoats, shrews, rats, and mice. Otters are found in many rivers, and seals frequently appear along the coast. Roughly 230 species of birds reside in the United Kingdom, and another 200 are migratory. Most numerous are the chaffinch, blackbird, sparrow, and starling. The rivers and lakes are full of salmon, trout, perch, pike, roach, dace, and grayling.

5 ENVIRONMENT

Air pollution is a serious problem for the United Kingdom. The country produces 564.2 million tons of particulate emissions and 2,276.7 tons of hydrocarbon emissions per year and contributes 2.4% of the world's total gas emissions. In addition, its sulfur adds to the acid rain problem in the surrounding countries of Western Europe. However, air quality has improved greatly in the United Kingdom as a result of the Control of Pollution Act of 1974 and other legislation. London is no longer densely smog-ridden, and winter sunlight has been increasing in various industrial cities.

Water pollution from farming is also a problem. The nation has 28.8 cubic miles of water of which 3% is used for farming activity and 77% for industrial purposes. The United Kingdom's cities produce 22 million tons of solid waste and 2,424.4 thousand tons of toxic waste per year. A major recent environmental problem is the regulation of oil and gas development and of large-scale dumping at sea.

The National Trust (for Places of Historic Interest or Natural Beauty), an orga-

nization of more than 1.3 million members, has acquired some 750 kilometers (466 miles) of coastline in England, Northern Ireland, and Wales. By 1982, the United Kingdom had designated 10 national parks, covering 13,600 square kilometers (5,250 square miles), or 9% of the area of England and Wales. Scotland has 40 national scenic areas. Northern Ireland has 8 designated areas of outstanding natural beauty, 7 country parks, and 1 regional park. There are also 7 forest parks in Great Britain and 9 in Northern Ireland. In 1994, 3 of the nation's mammal species and 22 bird species were endangered, as were 24 types of birds.

6 POPULATION

The mid-1994 population estimate for the United Kingdom was 57,965,456. A population of 58,810,000 is projected for the year 2000. The population of England was estimated at 48,378,000 in 1992, Wales 2,899,000, Scotland 5,111,000, and Northern Ireland 1,610,000.

Average population density was 236 persons per square kilometer (611 per square mile) for the period 1988–93. Major cities in England (with 1991 populations) include Greater London, 6,679,699; Birmingham, 938,000; and Leeds, 677,000. The major cities in Scotland, with their 1991 populations, are Glasgow, 654,000; and Edinburgh, 422,000. Belfast, the major city in Northern Ireland, had a 1991 population of 279,000; and Cardiff, in Wales, 277,000.

7 MIGRATION

Immigration is now on a quota basis. Between 1986 and 1991, 1,334,000 persons left the United Kingdom to live abroad, and 1,461,000 came from overseas to live in the United Kingdom, resulting in a net gain in population of 127,000. In 1991 there was a net gain of about 28,000. The total number of foreign residents in the United Kingdom was about 1,875,000 in 1990. Of these, more than a third were Irish (638,000). Indians were second (155,000) and Americans third (102,000). At the end of 1992 the United Kingdom had some 100,000 refugees.

8 ETHNIC GROUPS

The present-day English, Welsh, Scots, and Irish are descended from a long succession of early peoples: Iberians, Celts, Romans, Anglo-Saxons, Danes, and Normans, the last of whom invaded and conquered England in 1066–70. In 1991, about 93% of United Kingdom residents were native-born. The principal ethnic minorities are of West Indian or Guyanese descent (499,000) or of Indian (840,000), Pakistani (475,000), or Bengali (160,000) descent. There are also sizable numbers of Africans, Americans, Australians, Chinese, Greek and Turkish Cypriots, Italians, Spaniards, and Southeast Asians.

9 LANGUAGES

English is spoken throughout the UK. In northwestern Wales, Welsh (a form of Brythonic Celtic) is the first language of most inhabitants. According to the 1991 census, 19% of those living in Wales spoke Welsh (down from 26% in 1961).

Photo credit: Susan D. Rock

Punk rocker bagpipe player in Edinburgh, Scotland.

Some 80,000 or so persons in western Scotland speak the Scottish form of Gaelic. On the Isle of Man, the Manx variety of Celtic is used in official pronouncements.

10 RELIGIONS

The queen or king of England must be a member of the Church of England and, on taking the throne, promise to uphold the faith. In 1990, some 1.8 million people worldwide were members of the Church of England, whose membership also includes about 60% of the English population. In 1993, adult membership in the Church of Scotland was estimated at

839,000. The Roman Catholic Church in the United Kingdom had some 5 million members in 1991.

Other Protestant churches, with 1991 figures, include the Methodist Church (483,000 members); the Baptist Church (241,000); and the United Reformed Church (115,000). In 1991, the Presbyterian Church of Wales had some 58,000 members. The Salvation Army, founded in London in 1865, had 57,000 active members in the United Kingdom in 1991.

Many immigrants have established religious communities in the United Kingdom. Christian groups include Greek, Russian, Polish, Serbian Orthodox, Estonian and Latvian Orthodox, and the Armenian Church. Lutheran churches from various parts of Europe are also represented.

The Anglo-Jewish community, with an estimated 315,000 members in 1990, is the second-largest group of Jews in Western Europe. There are also sizable communities of Muslims (990,000 in 1991), Sikhs, Hindus, and Buddhists.

11 TRANSPORTATION

Under the 1968 Transport Act, national transport operations were reorganized, creating the National Freight Corporation, the Freight Integration Council, and the National Bus Company. In 1991, Great Britain had 339,483 kilometers (210,955 miles) of public highways; Northern Ireland had 23,499 kilometers (14,602 miles) of public roads. Licensed motor vehicles in Great Britain at the end of 1991 numbered 26.4 million, including 22.7 million passenger cars.

Eurotunnel, a British-French company, recently built two high-speed 50-kilometer (31-mile) rail tunnels beneath the seabed of the English Channel. The Channel Tunnel, referred to as the "Chunnel," links points near Dover, England, and Calais, France. The Channel Tunnel has the longest tunnel system (38 kilometers/24 miles) ever built under water.

There were 16,629 route kilometers (10,333 miles) of standard-gauge (1.435 meters) railway in Great Britain in 1991. Northern Ireland has about 332 kilometers (206 miles) of 1.6-meters-gauge track with 190 kilometers (118 miles) of double track. In 1985, British Rail carried 708 million passengers and 140 million tons of freight. Underground railway systems operate in London, Glasgow, and Liverpool.

Great Britain has about 2,291 kilometers (1,424 miles) of navigable inland waterways. Great Britain has some 300 ports, including the Port of London, one of the largest in the world. Other major ports include Liverpool, Southampton, Kingston upon Hull, and the inland port of Manchester. The British merchant fleet totaled 2.8 million gross registered tons in 1991.

London's Heathrow Airport handled 40.2 million passengers in 1991; Gatwick, London's second airport, handled 18.6 million. The Concorde, a supersonic jetliner, was developed jointly in the 1960s by the United Kingdom and France. British Airways (BA) carried 25.1 million passengers in 1992.

Photo credit: Susan D. Rock.

The mysterious stone monument at Stonehenge.

12 HISTORY

Beginnings

The stone circles of Stonehenge in Wiltshire are the remains of Britain's earliest inhabitants, whose origin is unknown. Celtic tribes from the Continent invaded before the sixth century BC. In the first century AD, the Romans occupied most of the present-day area of England, staying until the fifth century. With the fall of the Roman Empire, the Celtic tribes fought among themselves. Early raids by Germanic tribes from the Continent—Angles, Saxons, and Jutes—soon turned into full-scale invasions. The leaders of the invasions established kingdoms in the conquered territory, while the native Celts retreated into the mountains of Wales and the southwest of England.

Among the new kingdoms of the invaders, that of the West Saxons (Wessex) became the overall ruling kingdom, chiefly through the leadership of Alfred the Great. However, the West Saxons were overthrown, first by the Danes in 1017, then by William, Duke of Normandy, in 1066. William invaded England and defeated Harold the Saxon in the Battle of Hastings, beginning the Norman Conquest which lasted until 1070. He instituted a strong government, which continued through the reigns of his sons William II and Henry I. Henry II, who ascended the throne in 1154, and succeeding English kings expanded their holdings in France, beginning a long series of struggles between the two countries.

1215–1328

Long-standing conflict between the nobles and the kings reached a climax at Runnymede (on the bank of the Thames River, southwest of London) in 1215 when King John was forced to sign the Magna Carta—a document guaranteeing fundamental rights and privileges to the average citizen. Just half a century later, in 1265, Simon de Montfort, earl of Leicester, summoned the first Parliament, with representatives not only of the nobility but also of the boroughs and towns. In 1282, the last Welsh king, Llewellyn ap Gruffydd, was killed in battle, and Edward I completed the conquest of Wales.

By the end of the sixth century, four separate kingdoms had been established in Scotland. Most of the country was unified under Duncan I (r.1034–40). The Scottish king William the Lion (r.1165–1214) was captured by Henry II of England in 1174 and forced to accept the Treaty of Falaise, by which Scotland came under English control. Scotland later purchased its freedom from Richard I. In 1305, Edward I reestablished English rule, but after the decisive defeat of the English at Bannockburn (a town in central Scotland), Edward III signed a treaty once again giving Scotland its freedom in 1328.

1337–1588

Under Edward III, the Hundred Years War (1337–1453) with France was begun, which would eventually end with the English being driven out of France. The fourteenth and fifteenth centuries were a time of confusion and change for England. The plague, known as the Black Death, broke out in England in 1348, wiping out a third of the population. John Wycliffe led a religious reform movement and criticized many established doctrines and practices. Richard II ruled from 1377–99, then was overthrown and succeeded by Henry IV, the first king of the house of Lancaster. The Wars of the Roses (1455–85), in which the houses of Lancaster and York fought for the throne, ended with the accession of Henry VII, a member of the Tudor family, marking the beginning of the modern history of England.

Under the Tudors, business and trade were expanded, English sailors ranged far and wide, and conflicts with Spain grew worse. In 1531, Henry VIII separated the Anglican Church from Rome and proclaimed himself its head in order to divorce the first of his six wives. After his death (1547), the succession to the throne became a major issue during the reigns of Edward VI (1547–53), Mary I (1553–58), and Elizabeth I (1558–1603).

French influence in Scotland grew under James V (r.1513–42). His daughter, Mary, Queen of Scots, married the dauphin (prince) of France, where she lived and later ruled as queen. By the time Mary returned to Scotland (1561), a pro-English faction had the support of Queen Elizabeth I against the pro-French faction. Mary, who claimed the throne of England, was imprisoned and executed in 1587 by Elizabeth. Under Elizabeth, England acquired its first colony, Newfoundland, in 1583 and in 1588 defeated the Spanish Armada. It also experienced the beginning of a golden age of drama, literature, and music, which produced many great artists, including William Shakespeare.

1603–1707

Elizabeth was succeeded by Mary's son, James VI of Scotland, who became James I of England (r.1603–25), establishing the Stuart line. Under James and his son, Charles I (r.1625–49), the rising middle classes (mainly Puritan in religion) wanted to make Parliament superior to the king. The English Civil War broke out in 1642, and Charles I was tried and executed in 1649. Oliver Cromwell, as Protector, ruled the new Commonwealth until his death in 1658. In 1660, Charles II, eldest son of the executed king, regained the throne.

The following period, known as the Restoration, was marked by a reaction against Puritanism and by greater wealth. Charles II's younger brother, James II (r.1685–88), who tried unsuccessfully to restore Roman Catholicism, was overthrown in 1688. He was succeeded by his daughter, Mary II, and her Dutch husband, William III, who were invited to rule by Parliament. This transfer of power is known as the Glorious Revolution.

English colonial expansion developed further in the seventeenth and eighteenth centuries, and the English merchant marine became more successful than the Dutch. At home, the Act of Union of Scotland and England was approved by the two parliaments in 1707, thereby formally creating the kingdom of Great Britain under one crown and with a single Parliament composed of representatives of both countries.

1714–1922

George I of the House of Hanover took the throne in 1714 and established the modern cabinet system, with the king leaving much of the governing to his ministers. The eighteenth century was a time of rapid colonial expansion, internal stability, and literary and artistic achievement. Britain expanded its control of North America and India in the Seven Years' War (ended in 1763 by the Treaty of Paris). However, the American Revolution (1775–83) cost Britain its most important group of colonies. A few years later, Britain colonized Australia and New Zealand.

In 1800, with the Act of Union of Great Britain and Ireland, the United Kingdom formally came into being. Although the act established Irish representation in Parliament, the Irish question continued to cause trouble. There was a growing division between the 26 counties of southern Ireland and the 6 counties of the north, popularly called Ulster. While the north gradually became Protestant and industrial, the rest of Ireland remained Catholic and rural. Eventually, the northern Irish began a campaign that ended in the 1920 Government of Ireland Act, which established separate governments for the north and south, as well as continued representation in the United Kingdom Parliament. The 6 northern counties accepted the act and became Northern Ireland. The 26 southern counties, however, did not. In 1921, the Anglo-Irish Treaty was signed, by which these counties left the United Kingdom to become the Irish Free State (now the Irish Republic, or Éire), which was officially established in 1922.

The Industrial Revolution, beginning in the second half of the eighteenth century, provided the money needed for British colonial and military expansion throughout the 1800s. However, the growth of the factory system and cities also brought new social problems. The Reform Acts of 1832, 1867, and 1884 increased the rights and power of the new middle class and the working class. Factory acts, poor laws, and other humanitarian legislation did away with some of the worst abuses. The long reign of Queen Victoria (1837–1901) saw commercial and industrial growth like never before. This was a period of great colonial expansion, especially in Africa, where at the end of the century Britain fought settlers of mostly Dutch origin in the South African (or Boer) War.

1930s–1990s

The terrible economic and human losses of World War I, in which nearly 800,000 Britons were killed, brought on serious disturbances in the United Kingdom as elsewhere. The economic depression of the 1930s resulted in the unemployment of millions of workers. During the late 1930s, the government of Prime Minister Neville Chamberlain hoped to avoid war by appeasing (making compromises with) Nazi Germany. But after Hitler invaded Poland, the United Kingdom declared war on Germany on 3 September 1939, mark- ing the beginning of World War II. Although it won the war, the United Kingdom suffered much destruction from German bombing, and the military and civilian death toll exceeded 900,000.

The United Kingdom has remained firmly within the Atlantic alliance since World War II. A founding member of the North Atlantic Treaty Organization (NATO) and the European Free Trade Association (EFTA), the United Kingdom joined the European Community (EC) on 1 January 1973. The principal domestic problems in the 1970s were rapid inflation, labor disputes, and the continuing conflict in Northern Ireland. Civil rights protests in 1969 by Catholics drew a violent Protestant reaction. The Irish Republican Army (IRA), seeking the union of Ulster with the Irish Republic, began committing terrorist acts in both Northern Ireland and England. British troops were sent to Belfast and Londonderry in August 1969. In November 1985, the United Kingdom and the Irish Republic signed an agreement committing both governments to recognize Northern Ireland as part of the United Kingdom and to cooperate with each other.

In 1979, a Conservative government headed by Margaret Thatcher came to power with a program of income tax cuts and reduced government spending. Thatcher, who won reelection in 1983 and 1987, began a policy of "privatizing"— selling to private business—many of the United Kingdom's government-run businesses. The United Kingdom fought a brief but intense war (2 April–14 June 1982) after Argentina occupied the Falkland

Islands off the south Atlantic coast of South America. British government was restored to the islands at the end of the war. In November 1990, Thatcher withdrew from power and was replaced by John Major. Major's government sought to redefine Conservative values with a renewed emphasis on law and order.

13 GOVERNMENT

The United Kingdom is a monarchy in form but a parliamentary democracy in substance. In British terms, the sovereign—Elizabeth II since 1952—reigns but does not rule. Although head of state, the sovereign is considered under the law rather than above it, ruling only by approval of Parliament and acting only on the advice of her ministers.

The United Kingdom is governed, in the name of the sovereign, by Her Majesty's Government—a body of ministers responsible to Parliament. Parliament itself, the supreme legislative authority in the realm, consists of the sovereign, the House of Lords, and the House of Commons. All four countries of the kingdom—England, Scotland, Wales, and Northern Ireland—are represented in the Parliament at Westminster, London. Northern Ireland had its own parliament (Stormont) as well; however, because of civil conflict in Ulster, the Stormont was suspended on 30 March 1972, and direct rule was imposed from Westminster.

The sovereign formally calls and dismisses Parliament. The House of Lords is comprised of about 1,200 peers, including hereditary peers, spiritual peers (archbishops and bishops of the Church of

Photo credit: Susan D. Rock.

Big Ben and Houses of Parliament, London.

England), and life peers. Over the centuries, its powers have gradually been reduced. Today, its main function is to bring the wide experience of its members into the process of lawmaking. In early 1994, the House of Commons, which is elected, had 651 members: 524 for England, 38 for Wales, 72 for Scotland, and 17 for Northern Ireland. All British subjects 18 years old and over may vote in national elections.

Executive power rests with the prime minister, who, though formally appointed by the sovereign, is traditionally the leader of the majority party in Parliament. The prime minister is assisted by ministers chosen from the majority party—mostly from the House of Commons, which must approve general government policy and important specific measures. The ministers with the most seniority, about 20, compose the cabinet, which meets regularly to decide policy on major issues.

As of 1985, the United Kingdom was divided into 53 counties and 369 districts. Below the district level are some 10,000 parishes in England and about 1,000 communities in Wales. Scotland is divided into 9 regions and 3 island areas: Orkney, Shetland, and the Hebrides. Northern Ireland has a system of 26 districts.

14 POLITICAL PARTIES

The main political parties represented in Parliament today are the Conservative Party, the Labour Party, and the Liberal Democrats (a coalition of the Liberal and Social Democratic parties, which voted in favor of a formal merger in 1988).

The Liberal Party was a major force during the late nineteenth century. Since World War I, the Labour Party has replaced the Liberal Party as the official opposition to a Conservative government. The Labour Party favors public ownership of manufacturing, improvement of the social and economic conditions of the people, defense of human rights, cooperation with labor and socialist organizations of other countries, and peaceful solutions to international disputes. In foreign affairs, there has been little difference between the Labour and Conservative Parties since World War II. They differ mainly on the degree of state control to be applied to industry and commerce. The Conservative supports free enterprise, individual initiative, and restraining the power of the unions.

After World War II, Labour was in power during 1945–51, 1964–70, and 1974–79; the Conservatives have held office during 1951–64, 1970–74, and since 1979. The general election of 9 April 1992 resulted in a continuation of Conservative government under prime minister John Major with 42% of the vote and 336 seats. Labour followed with 34% of the vote and 271 seats. The Liberal Democrats took almost 18% of the vote and 20 seats. Minor parties received 3% of the vote and 17 seats.

15 JUDICIAL SYSTEM

The main civil courts in England and Wales are some 300 county courts for small cases and the High Court, which is divided into the chancery division, the family division, and the Queen's Bench division for the more important cases. Appeals from the county courts may also be heard in the High Court, though the more important ones come before the Court of Appeal. A few appeals are heard before the House of Lords.

In Scotland, civil cases are heard at the sheriff courts (corresponding roughly to the English county courts) and in the Outer House of the Court of Session, which is the supreme civil court in Scotland. Appeals are heard by the Inner House of the Court of Session.

Criminal courts in England and Wales include magistrates' courts, which try less serious offenses (some 98% of all criminal cases). These consist most often of three unpaid magistrates known as justices of the peace. There are about 90 centers of the Crown Court, presided over by a bench of justices or, in the most serious cases, by a High Court judge sitting alone.

In Scotland, minor criminal cases are tried without a jury in the sheriff courts and district courts, and more serious cases with a jury in the sheriff courts. The supreme criminal court is the High Court of Justiciary.

All criminal trials are held in open court. In England, Wales, and Northern Ireland, 12-citizen juries must unanimously decide the verdict unless (with no more than two jurors dissenting) the judge directs them to return a majority verdict.

16 ARMED FORCES

Total active army strength in 1993 was 145,400 (including 7,800 women), with 8,700 enlisted outside the United Kingdom. The regular reserves number 188,600. As of 1993, 12,000 British troops were on active duty in Ulster, along with the 6,000 soldiers of the Royal Irish regiment. Naval forces totaled 62,100 (4,000 women), with units stationed on Malta and the Falkland Islands. Naval reserves number almost 30,000. The Royal Air Force has a strength of 86,000 (7,000 women), with units deployed in Germany, Gibraltar, Cyprus, Hong Kong, Belize, and the Falkland Islands. Combat aircraft number 466.

The defense budget for 1992 was an estimated $42 billion. British troops are based in six different peacekeeping missions.

17 ECONOMY

The United Kingdom lives by manufacture and trade. It has few natural resources apart from coal and low-grade iron ore, some timber, building materials, hides and skins, natural gas and North Sea oil. Farming provides nearly two-thirds of the food needed. The rest of the United Kingdom's food and most raw materials for its industries have to be imported and paid for largely through exports of manufactured goods.

By the early 1990s the United Kingdom had far lower dependence on oil imports than in the past. Inflation averaged 6.3% a year during 1988–92 before falling to 1.6% in 1993. After falling to 5.8% in 1990, the unemployment rate crept up to 10.4% in 1993.

18 INCOME

In 1992 the United Kingdom's gross national product (GNP) was $1,024,769 million at current prices, or $18,060 per person. For the period 1985–92 the average inflation rate was 6.0%, resulting in a real growth rate in per person GNP of 1.5%.

19 INDUSTRY

The United Kingdom is one of the most highly industrialized countries in the world. Since World War II, some traditional industries have become far less important— such as cotton textiles, steel, shipbuilding, locomotives—and their place has been taken by newer industries, such as electronics, offshore oil and gas products, and synthetic fibers.

Metals, engineering, and allied industries—including steel, nonferrous metals, vehicles, and machinery—employ nearly half of all workers in manufacturing. Steel production was 16.2 million ingot tons in 1992. The United Kingdom is one of the world's largest exporters of commercial motor vehicles, with an output of 248,453 in 1992. Production of passenger cars was 1,291,880. Britain's aerospace industry is among the world's greatest.

The United Kingdom continues to produce high-quality woolen textiles. Certain smaller industries are noted for the quality of their products—for example, pottery, jewelry, goldware, and silverware. Other sectors are the cement industry (which focuses on the manufacture of Portland cement, a British invention); the rubber industry, the world's oldest; paper industries; and leather and footwear.

20 LABOR

The total working population of the United Kingdom in June 1991 was 28,230,000, including 12,060,000 (43%) women. Unemployment was 2,910,000 (10.4%) in September 1993. It is believed that recovery from the recession of the early 1990s will be gradual, with some 2.5 million unemployed by 1997.

Public administration, business services, trade, and commerce together accounted for 69% of all employment, with some 17,608,000 workers in 1992.

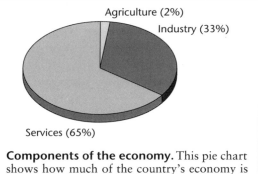

Components of the economy. This pie chart shows how much of the country's economy is devoted to agriculture (includes forestry, hunting, and fishing), industry, or services.

In 1990, distribution, hotels, catering, and repairs accounted for 20%; transportation and communications, 6%; construction, 6%; banking, finance, and insurance, 12%; public administration, 20%; manufacturing, 21%; and other services, 12%. Agriculture, forestry, and fisheries employed 2% of all workers. Energy and water supply, together with mining and quarrying, accounted for 1% of employment.

About 10.2 million persons were members of trade unions in 1992. Equal pay for men and women doing the same work has been required by law since the end of 1975.

21 AGRICULTURE

Just over 73% of Great Britain's land area was devoted to agriculture in 1992, some 6,600,000 hectares (16,309,000 acres) used for crops and 11,180,000 hectares (27,626,000 acres) for pastures. Most British farms produce a variety of products. Chief crops (with estimated 1992 production in tons) were barley, 7,386,000; wheat, 14,185,000; potatoes, 7,882,000; sugar beets, 8,500,000; oats, 523,000; and rapeseed oil, 1,166,000.

22 DOMESTICATED ANIMALS

Livestock continues to be the largest segment of the farming industry. The United Kingdom raises some of the world's finest pedigreed livestock and is the leading exporter of pedigreed breeding animals. Most of the internationally famous breeds of cattle, sheep, hogs, and farm horses originated in the United Kingdom.

In 1992 there were about 28.9 million sheep, 11.6 million head of cattle, 7.5 million hogs, and 124 million chickens and turkeys. Estimated output of livestock products for 1992 included 14,692,000 tons of milk, 1,069,000 tons of poultry, 970,000 tons of pork, 962,000 tons of beef and veal, 650,900 tons of eggs, and 355,000 tons of mutton and lamb.

23 FISHING

The waters surrounding the British Isles are excellent fishing grounds and breeding grounds for fish. The fishing industry has been declining, but it remains important to Scotland, which catches 69% by weight and 60% by value of all fish caught in the United Kingdom. The total catch of fish in the United Kingdom was 823,225 tons in 1991.

24 FORESTRY

The estimated total area of woodland in 1991 was 2.4 million hectares (5.9 million acres), or nearly 11% of Great Britain's land area. Roughly 40% of the area is in England, 49% in Scotland, and 11% in Wales. The lumber industry supplies the United Kingdom with 13% of its timber demand. Almost 90% of the national requirements in wood and wood products are met by imports.

25 MINING

Except for North Sea oil deposits, the United Kingdom has comparatively few mineral resources. Traditionally, coal has been by far the most important. In 1991, an estimated 97.7 million tons of coal were mined.

Other minerals mined in quantity are sand and gravel, 120 million tons in 1991; limestone and dolomite, 130 million tons; crushed igneous rock, 52 million tons; clays, 22 million tons; dimensional sandstone, 200,000 tons; gypsum and anhydrite, 4 million tons; fluorspar, 75,000 tons; and chalk, 12 million tons. Lead, zinc, and tungsten are worked on a small scale. The output of iron ore dropped from 916,000 tons in 1980 to 25,000 tons in 1991. The United Kingdom is the leading world producer and exporter of ball clay, and is the largest exporter and second largest producer after the United States of kaolin, fine white clay.

26 FOREIGN TRADE

The United Kingdom, the world's fifth largest trading nation, is highly dependent on foreign trade. It must import almost all its copper, ferrous metals, lead, zinc, rubber, and raw cotton; most of its tin, raw wool, hides and skins, and many other raw materials; and about one-third of its food. Principal exports in 1992 were

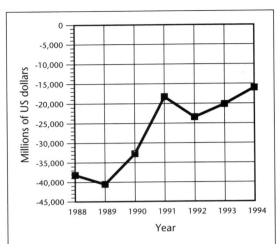

Yearly balance of trade measured in millions of US dollars. The balance of trade is the difference between what a country sells to other countries (its exports) and what it buys (its imports). If a country imports more than it exports, it has a negative balance of trade (a trade deficit). If exports exceed imports there is a positive balance of trade (a trade surplus).

machinery (excluding transport equipment); chemicals and related products; road vehicles; and food, beverages, and tobacco.

Entry into the European Community has resulted in some adjustment of United Kingdom trade patterns. The United States was the United Kingdom's leading market through 1989. It was then replaced by Germany, which has been the largest supplier since 1982. In 1992, Germany accounted for 14.6% of total United Kingdom trade, and the United States accounted for 11.1%. Trade with the European Community increased from 43% to 54% between 1980 and 1992. Other principal trade partners in 1992 were France, the Netherlands, Italy, Belgium-Luxembourg, Ireland, and Japan.

27 ENERGY AND POWER

Coal supplied 28% of the United Kingdom's primary energy consumption in 1992; oil, 40%; natural gas, 25%; nuclear energy and hydroelectricity, 7%.

The United Kingdom's proven oil reserves from the North Sea totaled 3.8 billion barrels at the end of 1992. Production reached 94.2 million tons in 1992, when the United Kingdom was the tenth largest oil producer in the world. In 1992, natural gas reserves were estimated at over 500 billion cubic meters. Production in 1992 was 53.6 billion cubic meters.

Most of the United Kingdom's electricity is produced by coal-fired steam generating stations. About 22% of the public electricity supply was generated by nuclear power stations in 1991. Total electricity generated by power stations in the United Kingdom in 1991 amounted to 322,133 kilowatt hours.

28 SOCIAL DEVELOPMENT

A system of social security, placed in full operation in 1948, provides national insurance, industrial injuries insurance, family allowances, and national assistance throughout the United Kingdom, although the system is administered separately in Northern Ireland. The National Insurance scheme provides benefits for sickness, unemployment, maternity, and widowhood, as well as guardian's allowances, retirement pensions, and death grants.

Selected Social Indicators

These statistics are estimates for the period 1988 to 1993. For comparison purposes, data for the United States and averages for low-income countries and high-income countries are also given.

Indicator	United Kingdom	Low-income countries	High-income countries	United States
Per capita gross national product†	$18,060	$380	$23,680	$24,740
Population growth rate	0.3%	1.9%	0.6%	1.0%
Population growth rate in urban areas	0.4%	3.9%	0.8%	1.3%
Population per square kilometer of land	236	78	25	26
Life expectancy in years	76	62	77	76
Number of people per physician	613	>3,300	453	419
Number of pupils per teacher (primary school)	n.a.	39	<18	20
Illiteracy rate (15 years and older)	<1%	41%	<5%	<3%
Energy consumed per capita (kg of oil equivalent)	3,718	364	5,203	7,918

† The gross national product (GNP) is the total dollar value of all goods and services produced by a country in a year. The per capita GNP is calculated by dividing a country's GNP by its population. The World Bank defines low-income countries as those with a per capita GNP of $695 or less. High-income countries have a per capita GNP of $8,626 or more. Less than 14% of the world's 5.5 billion people live in high-income countries, while almost 60% live in low-income countries.

n.a. = data not available   > = greater than   < = less than

Sources: World Bank, *Social Indicators of Development 1995,* Baltimore: Johns Hopkins University Press, 1995. Central Intelligence Agency, *World Fact Book,* Washington, D.C.: Government Printing Office, 1994.

Financial assistance for the needy is provided through supplementary benefits, in the form of a either a pension or an allowance. For needy families in which the head of the household has full-time employment, a family income supplement is paid.

Women's career progress in most sectors of the economy continues, although employed women earned about 25% less in 1993 than their male counterparts (despite the 1975 law requiring equal pay). Sexual harassment is a continuing problem in the workplace.

29 HEALTH

A comprehensive National Health Service (NHS), established in 1948, provides full medical care to all residents of the United Kingdom. Included are general medical, dental, pharmaceutical, and optical services; hospital and specialist services (in patients' homes when necessary) for physical and mental illnesses; and local health authority services (maternity and child welfare, vaccination, prevention of illness, health visiting, home nursing, and other services).

Life expectancy has increased from about 50 years in 1900–10 to about 76 years. Deaths from infectious diseases have been greatly reduced, although the proportion of deaths from circulatory diseases—including heart attacks and strokes—and cancer has risen. Since 1982, to help control the spread of AIDS, the government has begun measures for blood testing, research, public education, and other social services relating to the disease. In 1990, the United Kingdom had 6.3 hospital beds per 1,000 people, 80,200 physicians, and 37,832 pharmacists. The United Kingdom has about 1 physician per 613 people.

30 HOUSING

The United Kingdom is more crowded than most European countries. In 1991 there were 22,972,000 dwellings in the United Kingdom. About 50% of families now live in a dwelling built after 1945, usually a two-story house with a garden.

Most homeowners finance their purchase through a home mortgage loan from a building society, bank, insurance company, or other financial institution. The main providers of new subsidized housing are housing associations, which own, manage, and maintain over 600,000 homes in England alone and completed over 27,000 new homes for rent or shared ownership in 1991–92.

31 EDUCATION

Although responsibility for education in the United Kingdom rests with the central government, schools are mainly administered by local education authorities.

Nearly the entire adult population is literate. Education is compulsory for all children between the ages of 5 and 16. In 1990/91, about 9 million children attended Britain's 30,500 state schools while around 600,000 attended the 2,500 private schools. Of the 2,500 registered independent schools, the largest and most important (Winchester, Eton, Harrow, and others) are known in England as "public schools." Many have centuries of tradition behind them and are world famous.

In 1991, Britain had 47 universities with 334,000 full-time students and 30,000 lecturers. The Universities of Oxford and Cambridge date from the twelfth and thirteenth centuries, respectively. Nearly 1.5 million students are taking full-time, postsecondary courses. National policy states that no person should be excluded from higher education by lack of money. More than 90% of students in higher education hold awards from public or private funds.

32 MEDIA

The Post Office, founded in 1635, was the first in the world to use adhesive stamps as proof of payment for mail. British Telecommunications (Telecom) encompasses a system of some 29.5 million telephone exchange lines.

The British Broadcasting Corporation (BBC) broadcasts on two television channels: the Independent Television Commission on ITV; and Channel Four, which began operating in 1982. The BBC has 39 local radio stations, and there are 140 independent local radio stations. In September 1992, the first national commercial radio station, Classic FM, began broadcasting. There were an estimated 65,800,000 radios in use in 1991, and 25,000,000 television sets.

Although circulation totals have been decreasing, United Kingdom newspaper readership per person was the second highest in the world in 1992. As of that year there were about 130 daily and Sunday newspapers, some 2,000 weekly papers, numerous specialized papers, and about 7,000 periodicals. Nine Sunday papers and 12 daily morning papers are "national" in the sense of circulating throughout Britain.

Leading national dailies, with their average daily circulations in 1992, include *The Sun* (3,588,077); *The Daily Mirror* (2,868,263); *The Daily Mail* (1,688,808); *The Daily Express* (1,537,726); *The Daily Telegraph* (1,043,703); *The Daily Star* (808,486); *The Guardian* (418,026); *The Times* (390,323); and *The Financial Times* (291,915).

Wales has 1 morning daily, the *Western Mail,* with a 1992 circulation of 76,200, and 4 evening dailies with a circulation range between 32,500 and 80,900. Scotland has 6 morning, 6 evening, and 4 Sunday papers, plus the Scottish editions of the *Daily Mail* and the *Sunday Express.* Northern Ireland has 2 morning papers, 1 evening paper, and 3 Sunday papers with circulations ranging from 20,000 to 134,000, plus 45 weeklies.

Britain's ethnic minorities publish over 60 newspapers and magazines, most of them weekly, fortnightly (once every two

Photo credit: Susan D. Rock.

Beefeater at the Tower of London.

weeks), or monthly. These include the Chinese *Sing Tao* and *Wen Wei Po,* the Urdu *Daily Jang,* and the Arabic *Al-Arab* (all dailies), as well as newspapers in Gujarati, Bengali, Hindi, and Punjabi. The *Weekly Journal,* aimed at Britain's black community, was begun in 1992.

The 7,000 periodicals published weekly, monthly, or quarterly cover a huge range of special interests. *The Times Literary Supplement* is highly influential in cultural affairs. The chief news agency is Reuters.

33 TOURISM AND RECREATION

The world's seventh most popular tourist destination in 1991, the United Kingdom is rich in historic and cultural attractions. Among the many historic dwellings open to the public are medieval castles in Wales; 10-century-old Traquair House, the oldest continuously inhabited house in Scotland; the Palace of Holyroodhouse in Edinburgh; and Warwick Castle, near Stratford-upon-Avon, the birthplace of William Shakespeare.

Distinguished cathedrals include St. Paul's in London and those in Canterbury, Exeter, Norwich, Winchester, and York. At Bushmills, in Northern Ireland, is the oldest distillery in the world. Some of Scotland's 100 malt whiskey distilleries also offer tours.

Among London's attractions are Buckingham Palace, the Tower of London, and Westminster Abbey. London is particularly noted for its theater, including the Royal Shakespeare Company. Traditional community gatherings for music and dancing, called *ceilidhs*, are held in Scotland, and Edinburgh is the site of many music festivals.

Scotland, where golf developed in the fifteenth century, has many superb golf courses, as does the rest of the United Kingdom. Other popular sports include fishing, riding, sailing, rugby, cricket, and football (soccer). Wimbledon is the site of perhaps the world's best-known tennis competition.

Tourism brings in a great deal of money from overseas. In 1991, some 16.6 million foreign visitors spent $12.6 billion in the United Kingdom. The opening of the Channel Tunnel (under the English Channel) in 1994 has boosted travel to and from the Continent.

34 FAMOUS BRITONS

Well-known English rulers include William I (the Conqueror, 1027–87), duke of Normandy, who conquered England (1066–70); Henry VIII (1491–1547), who separated the Anglican Church from the Roman Catholic Church; and Victoria (1819–1901), who greatly expanded the British Empire.

Sir Winston Leonard Spencer Churchill (1874–1965) was prime minister during World War II, and won the Nobel Prize for literature in 1953. In 1979, Margaret (Hilda Roberts) Thatcher (b.1925) became the nation's first woman prime minister. The reigning monarch since 1952 has been Queen Elizabeth II (b.1926). The heir to the throne is Charles, prince of Wales (b.1948).

Noted anthropologists include husband and wife Louis Seymour Bazett Leakey (1903–72) and Mary Leakey (b.1913), who discovered important fossil remains of early hominids in Tanzania.

Important British scientists and inventors include Sir Isaac Newton (1642–1727), who discovered gravity; German-born physicist Gabriel Daniel Fahrenheit (1686–1736), who introduced the temperature scale named after him; and Charles

Darwin (1809–82), who advanced the theory of evolution.

Geoffrey Chaucer (1340?–1400), author of the *Canterbury Tales* and other works, is the best-known medieval English poet. William Shakespeare (1564–1616), is one of many fine poets and playwrights.

The mathematician Lewis Carroll (Charles Lutwidge Dodgson, 1832–98) became world-famous for two children's books, *Alice in Wonderland* and *Through the Looking Glass*. Rudyard Kipling (1865–1936), author of novels, stories, and poems, received the Nobel Prize for literature in 1907. Sir Arthur Conan Doyle (1859–1930) is known throughout the world as the creator of Sherlock Holmes. Novelist Charles Dickens (1812–70) is known for such works as *David Copperfield* and *Great Expectations*.

Important twentieth-century fiction writers include George Bernard Shaw (1856–1950), Dublin-born playwright, essayist, critic, and humorist.

Major contributors to the cinema have included the comic actor and director Charlie (Sir Charles Spencer) Chaplin (1889–1977); the director Sir Alfred Hitchcock (1899–1980); and actors Cary Grant (Archibald Alexander Leach, 1904–86), Sir Alec Guinness (b.1914), Welsh-born Richard Burton (1925–84), Irish-born Peter O'Toole (b.1932), and Vanessa Redgrave (b.1937).

Significant 20th-century composers include Ralph Vaughan Williams (1872–1958); Sir William Walton (1902–83); Edward Benjamin Britten (Baron Britten,

1913–76); and, in popular music, John Winston Lennon (1940–80) and James Paul McCartney (b.1942) of the Beatles; and Andrew Lloyd Weber.

Notable British athletes include Sir Roger Bannister (b.1929), who on 6 May 1954 became the first person to run a mile in under four minutes.

Two natives of Northern Ireland—Betty Williams (b.1943), a Protestant, and Mairead Corrigan (b.1944), a Roman Catholic—received the Nobel Peace Prize (awarded in 1977) for their leadership of a peace movement in Ulster.

35 BIBLIOGRAPHY

Cannon, John and Ralph Griffiths. *The Oxford Illustrated History of the British Monarchy*. New York: Oxford University Press, 1988.

Halsey, A. H., ed. *British Social Trends since 1900: A Guide to the Changing Social Structure of Britain*. 2d ed. Basingstoke: Macmillan, 1988.

Jenkins, Philip. *A History of Modern Wales, 1536–1990*. New York: Longman, 1992.

Kearney, Hugh F. *The British Isles: A History of Four Nations*. Cambridge; New York: Cambridge University Press, 1989.

Lanting, Frans. "Falkland Islands Wildlife." *National Geographic*, March 1988, 413–422.

MacLean, Fitzroy. *Scotland: A Concise History*. New York: Thames and Hudson, 1993.

Nagel, Rob, and Anne Commire. "Alfred the Great." In *World Leaders, People Who Shaped the World*. Volume II: Europe. Detroit: U*X*L, 1994.

———. "Elizabeth I." In *World Leaders, People Who Shaped the World*. Volume II: Europe. Detroit: U*X*L, 1994.

———. "Mary, Queen of Scots." In *World Leaders, People Who Shaped the World*. Volume II: Europe. Detroit: U*X*L, 1994.

———. "Victoria." In *World Leaders, People Who Shaped the World*. Volume II: Europe. Detroit: U*X*L, 1994.

———. "William the Conqueror." In *World Lead-*

ers, *People Who Shaped the World*. Volume II: Europe. Detroit: U*X*L, 1994.

———. "Winston Churchill." In *World Leaders, People Who Shaped the World*. Volume II: Europe. Detroit: U*X*L, 1994.

Speck, W. A. *A Concise History of Modern Britain,* *1707–1975*. New York: Cambridge University Press, 1993.

Sutherland, D. *Scotland*. Chicago: Children's Press, 1985.

Sutherland, D. *Wales*. Chicago: Children's Press, 1987.

UNITED STATES OF AMERICA

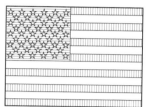

CAPITAL: Washington, D.C. (District of Columbia).

FLAG: The flag consists of 13 alternate stripes, 7 red and 6 white; these represent the 13 original colonies. Fifty 5-pointed white stars, representing the present number of states in the Union, are placed in 9 horizontal rows alternately of 6 and 5 against a blue field in the upper left corner of the flag.

ANTHEM: *The Star-Spangled Banner.*

MONETARY UNIT: The dollar ($) of 100 cents is a paper currency with a floating rate. There are coins of 1, 5, 10, 25, and 50 cents and 1 dollar, and notes of 1, 2, 5, 10, 20, 50, and 100 dollars. Although issuance of higher notes ceased in 1969, a limited number of notes of 500, 1,000, 5,000, and 10,000 dollars remain in circulation.

WEIGHTS AND MEASURES: The imperial system is in common use; however, the use of metrics in industry is increasing, and the metric system is taught in public schools throughout the United States. Common avoirdupois units in use are the avoirdupois pound of 16 ounces or 453.5924277 gram; the long ton of 2,240 pounds or 35,840 ounces; and the short ton, more commonly used, of 2,000 pounds or 32,000 ounces. (Unless otherwise indicated, all measures given in tons are in short tons.) Liquid measures: 1 gallon = 231 cubic inches = 4 quarts = 8 pints. Dry measures: 1 bushel = 4 pecks = 32 dry quarts = 64 dry pints. Linear measures: 1 foot = 12 inches; 1 statute mile = 1,760 yards = 5,280 feet. Metric equivalent: 1 meter = 39.37 inches.

HOLIDAYS: New Year's Day, 1 January; Birthday of Martin Luther King, Jr., 3d Monday in January; Presidents' Day, 3d Monday in February; Memorial or Decoration Day, last Monday in May; Independence Day, 4 July; Labor Day, 1st Monday in September; Columbus Day, 2d Monday in October; Election Day, 1st Tuesday after the 1st Monday in November; Veterans or Armistice Day, 11 November; Thanksgiving Day, 4th Thursday in November; Christmas, 25 December.

TIME: Eastern, 7 AM = noon GMT; Central, 6 AM = noon GMT; Mountain, 5 AM = noon GMT; Pacific (includes the Alaska panhandle), 4 AM = noon GMT; Yukon, 3 AM = noon GMT; Alaska and Hawaii, 2 AM = noon GMT; western Alaska, 1 AM = noon GMT.

1 LOCATION AND SIZE

Located in the Western Hemisphere on the continent of North America, the United States is the fourth-largest country in the world. Its total area, including Alaska and Hawaii, is 9,372,607 square kilometers (3,618,773 square miles). The continental United States has a total boundary length of 17,563 kilometers (10,913 miles).

Alaska, the 49th state, has an area of 1,477,267 square kilometers (570,374 square miles), with a total boundary length of 13,161 kilometers (8,178 miles). The 50th state, Hawaii, consists of islands in the Pacific Ocean with a total area of 16,636 square kilometers (6,423 square miles) and a combined coastline of 1,207 kilometers (750 miles).

2 TOPOGRAPHY

The northeastern coast, known as New England, is rocky, but along the rest of the eastern seaboard the Atlantic Coastal Plain rises gradually from the shoreline, merging with the Gulf Coastal Plain in Georgia. To the west is a plateau, bounded by the Appalachian Mountains, which extend from southwest Maine into central Alabama.

Between the Appalachians and the Rocky Mountains, more than 1,600 kilometers (1,000 miles) to the west, lies the vast interior plain of the United States. Its eastern reaches are bounded on the north by the Great Lakes—Lake Superior, Lake Michigan, Lake Huron, Lake Erie, and Lake Ontario—thought to contain about half the world's total supply of fresh water. The interior plain consists of two major divisions: the fertile Central Plains to the east and the drier Great Plains extending westward to the foothills of the Rocky Mountains. Running south through the center of the interior plain, and draining almost two-thirds of the area of the continental United States, is the Mississippi River.

The Continental Divide runs along the crest of the Rocky Mountains. The Rockies and the ranges to the west—the Sierra Nevada, the Coast, and Cascade ranges —are parts of a larger system of mountains that extends through the western part of Central and South America. Between the Rockies and the Pacific ranges lies a group of vast plateaus containing most of the nation's desert areas, known as the Great Basin. The coastal plains along the Pacific Ocean are narrow, and in many places the mountains plunge directly into the sea. The greatest rivers of the far west are the Colorado in the south and the Columbia in the northwest.

Separated from the continental United States by Canada, the state of Alaska occupies the extreme northwest portion of North America. A series of steep mountain ranges separates the Pacific Ocean coast on the south from Alaska's broad central basin, bounded on the north by the Brooks Range, which slopes down gradually to the Arctic Ocean. The Yukon River flows from Canada in the east through the Central Basin to the Bering Sea in the west. The state of Hawaii consists of a group of Pacific islands formed by volcanoes rising sharply from the ocean floor. The largest of the islands, Hawaii, still has active volcanoes.

The lowest point in the United States is Death Valley in California, at 86 meters (282 feet) below sea level. At 6,194 meters (20,320 feet), Mt. McKinley in Alaska is the highest peak in North America. These topographic extremes show how unstable the Pacific Coast region is geologically. Major earthquakes caused great destruction in San Francisco in 1906 and Anchorage, Alaska, in 1964.

UNITED STATES OF AMERICA

LOCATION: Conterminous US: 66°57′ to 124°44′w; 24°33′ to 49°23′N. Alaska: 130°w to 172°28′E; 51° to 71°23′N. Hawaii: 154°48′ to 178°22′w 18°55′ to 28°25′N. **BOUNDARY LENGTHS:** Conterminous US: Canada, 6,416 kilometers (3,987 miles); Atlantic Ocean, 3,330 kilometers (2,069 miles); Gulf of Mexico coastline, 2,625 kilometers (1,631 miles); Mexico, 3,111 kilometers (1,933 miles); Pacific coastline, 2,081 kilometers (1,293 miles). Alaska: Arctic Ocean coastline, 1,706 kilometers (1,060 miles); Canada, 2,475 kilometers (1,538 miles); Pacific coastline, including the Bering Sea and Strait and Chukchi coastlines, 8,980 kilometers (5,580 miles). Hawaii: coastline, 1,207 kilometers (750 miles).

3 CLIMATE

The east coast is affected mostly by masses of air moving from west to east across the continent. Its climate is basically continental, with clear contrasts between seasons. However, because Florida has the Gulf of Mexico lying to its west, it experiences only moderate differences between summer and winter temperatures. Mean annual temperatures vary considerably between north and south, ranging from 11°C (51°F) in Boston to 24°C (76°F) in Miami. Annual rainfall is generally more than 100 centimeters (40 inches). The Gulf and South Atlantic states are often hit by severe tropical storms in late summer and early autumn.

The prairie lands in the middle of the country have more drought than heavy rainfall. The average midwinter temperature in the extreme north—Minnesota and North Dakota—is about −13°C (9°F) or less, while the average July temperature is 18°C (65°F). In the Texas prairie region to the south, January temperatures average 10–13°C (50–55°F) and July temperatures 27–29°C (80–85°F). Rainfall in this region is as low as 46 centimeters (18 inches).

The Great Plains are semiarid. Rainfall in the southern plains averages about 50 centimeters (20 inches) per year and in the northern plains about 25 centimeters (10 inches). The contrast between summer and winter temperatures is extreme throughout the Great Plains. Maximum summer temperatures of over 43°C (110°F) have been recorded, while the average minimum temperature for January is −19°C (−3°F).

The higher reaches of the Rockies and the other western ranges have an alpine climate. The climate of the Western desert region varies considerably from north to south. In New Mexico, Arizona, and southeastern California, mean annual rainfall ranges from 8 centimeters (3 inches) to 76 centimeters (30 inches), while some of the mountainous areas of central Washington and Idaho receive at least 152 centimeters (60 inches) of rain per year. Phoenix, Arizona, has a mean annual temperature of 22°C (71°F).

The Pacific coast has a maritime climate, with mild winters and moderately warm, dry summers. Los Angeles in the south has an average temperature of 13°C (56°F) in January and 21°C (69°F) in July; Seattle in the north has an average temperature of 4°C (39°F) in January and 18°C (65°F) in July. Precipitation ranges from an annual average of 4.52 centimeters (1.78 inches) at Death Valley in California (the lowest in the United States) to more than 356 centimeters (140 inches) in Washington's mountain regions.

Alaska has varied climatic conditions. The Aleutian Islands and the coastal panhandle strip have a moderate maritime climate. The interior is characterized by short, hot summers and long, bitterly cold winters. In the region bordering the Arctic Ocean a polar climate prevails, the soil hundreds of feet below the surface remaining frozen year-round.

Northeast ocean winds give Hawaii a mild, stable climate. The mean temperature in Honolulu is 23°C (73°F) in January and 27°C (80°F) in July. Rainfall is moderate—about 71 centimeters (28 inches) per year—but much greater in the mountains.

The lowest temperature recorded in the United States was −62°c (−79.8°F) in Alaska at Prospect Creek Camp on 23 January 1971; the highest, 57°c (134°F) in California at Greenland Ranch in Death Valley on 10 July 1913. The record annual rainfall is 1,468 centimeters (578 inches) on Maui in Hawaii in 1950.

4 PLANTS AND ANIMALS

At least 7,000 species and subspecies of native United States plants have been categorized. Wildflowers bloom in all areas, from the seldom-seen blossoms of rare desert cacti to the hardiest alpine species. The eastern forests contain a mixture of softwoods and hardwoods that includes pine, birch, maple, and hickory. The central hardwood forest—still an important timber source—contains oak, ash, and walnut among others. Tupelo, pecan, and sycamore are found in the southern forest that stretches along the coast of the Gulf of Mexico into the eastern half of Texas. The forest along the Pacific Ocean coast is spectacular with its enormous redwoods and Douglas firs. In the southwest are saguaro (giant cactus), yucca, candlewood, and the Joshua tree.

Mesquite grass covers parts of west Texas, southern New Mexico, and Arizona. Short grass may be found in the highlands of the latter two states, while tall grass covers large portions of Texas and Louisiana. The Western desert supports sagebrush, creosote, and—near the Great Salt Lake and in Death Valley—saltbrush. Coniferous forests are found on the

Photo credit:CT Department of Economic Development.

A seal relaxing under the sun's rays at the Mystic Marinelife Aquarium in Connecticut.

lower mountain slopes. The central part of the Yukon Basin in Alaska is also a region of softwood forests, while the rest of the state is heath or tundra. Hawaii has extensive forests of bamboo and ferns.

An estimated 1,500 species and subspecies of mammals are found in the continental United States. Among the larger game animals are the white-tailed deer, moose, mountain goat, black bear, and grizzly bear. The Alaskan brown bear often reaches a weight of 540–635 kilograms (1,200–1,400 pounds). Some 25 important furbearers are common, including the muskrat, red and gray foxes, mink, raccoon, and beaver. The American buffalo (bison), millions of which once roamed the plains, is now found only on select reserves.

Year-round and migratory birds abound. Loons, wild ducks, and wild geese are found in lake country; terns, gulls, sandpipers, and other seabirds live along the coasts. Wrens, owls, hummingbirds, sparrows, woodpeckers, swallows, and finches appear in large numbers, along with the robin, cardinal, Baltimore oriole, and various blackbirds. Wild turkey, ruffed grouse, and ring-necked pheasant (introduced from Europe) are popular game birds.

Lakes, rivers, and streams are full of trout, bass, perch, carp, catfish, and pike. Sea bass, cod, snapper, and flounder are abundant along the coasts, along with such shellfish as lobster, shrimp, clams, oysters, and mussels. Four poisonous snakes survive, of which the rattlesnake is the most common. Alligators appear in southern waterways, and the Gila monster makes its home in the southwest.

5 ENVIRONMENT

The Environmental Protection Agency (EPA), created in 1970, is the main government agency responsible for control of air and noise pollution, water and waste management, and control of toxic substances.

Landmark federal laws protecting the environment include the Clean Air Act Amendments of 1970 and 1990, controlling automobile and electric utility emissions; and the Endangered Species Act of 1973, protecting wildlife near extinction.

The most influential environmental lobbies and conservation groups (with 1991 membership) include the National Wildlife Federation (6,200,000); the National Audubon Society (600,000); the Sierra Club (565,000); and the Nature Conservancy (550,000). Greenpeace USA (1,500,000 members) has gained international attention by trying to stop whale and seal hunts.

Among the environmental movement's most notable successes have been the creation of recycling programs; the banning in the United States of the insecticide dichlorodiphenyltrichloroethane (DDT); the protection of more than 40 million hectares (100 million acres) of Alaska lands; and the gradual elimination of chlorofluorocarbon (CFC) production by the year 2000.

A continuing environmental problem is pollution of the nation's water by dumping of raw or partially treated sewage from major cities into United States waterways. In addition, runoffs of agricultural pesticides are deadly to fishing streams and very difficult to regulate. The amount of land suitable for farming has decreased due to erosion, depletion of the soil, and urbanization.

Facilities for solid waste disposal are still inadequate, and the United States nuclear industry has expanded without having a good way to dispose of radioactive wastes. Other environmental issues include acid rain (precipitation contaminated from burning coal); the contamination of homes by radon (a radioactive gas that is produced by the decay of underground deposits of radium and which can cause cancer); and the lack of available water in many western states due to over-population in naturally drier areas.

As of April 1993, the United States Fish and Wildlife Service listed 539 endangered species in the United States, including 292 plants and 150 threatened species, including 64 plants. The agency listed another 493 endangered and 38 threatened foreign species by international agreement. In 1991, state and federal governments spent $177 million on the protection of endangered species.

6 POPULATION

According to census figures for 1990, the population of the United States (including the 50 states and Washington, D.C.) was 248,709,873 (up from 226,542,580 in 1980), of whom 51.3% were female and 48.7% male. The population was estimated at 257,908,000 in mid-1993. The median age of the population increased from 16.7 years in 1820 to 22.9 years in 1900, and to 33.1 years in 1991. The United States Bureau of the Census projected a population of 275,327,023 for the year 2000. Population density varies greatly from region to region; the average is 26 persons per square kilometer (67 per square mile).

Suburbs have absorbed most of the shift in population distribution since 1950. In 1990 there were 8 cities with more than 1 million population each.

7 MIGRATION

Between 1840 and 1930, some 37 million immigrants, most of them Europeans, arrived in the United States. In 1924 a quota system was established that favored immigrants from northern and western Europe. The quota system was radically reformed in 1965 and abandoned in 1978, when all specific limits by nationality were replaced by a simple total limit of 290,000. A major 1990 overhaul of immigration laws raised the annual ceiling to 700,000.

Between 30 September 1991 and 30 September 1992, 511,769 immigrants entered the United States. Some 207,822 were from Asia, 228,741 from the Americas, 62,912 from Europe, 10,137 from Africa, and 2,157 from Pacific Island nations. The changes in immigration law have resulted in a sharp rise in the number of Asian immigrants (primarily Chinese, Filipinos, Indians, Japanese, and Koreans), of whom 2,738,157 entered the country during 1981–90, as compared with 153,249 during the entire decade of the 1950s.

Between 1975 and 1978, following the defeat of the American-backed Saigon government in South Vietnam, several hundred thousand Vietnamese refugees came to the United States. Under the Refugee Act of 1980, a limit to the number of refugees allowed to enter the United States is set annually. In 1992, 123,010 immigrants were admitted under the various refugee acts, 61,631 from the former Soviet Union. More than 500,000 Cubans were living in southern Florida by 1980,

Photo credit: Oklahoma Tourism Photo by Fred W. Marvel.

American Indian Exposition, Anadarko, Oklahoma.

when another 125,000 Cuban refugees arrived.

In November 1986, Congress passed a bill allowing illegal aliens who had lived and worked in the United States since 1982 the opportunity to become permanent residents. By the end of fiscal year 1992, 2,650,000 persons had become permanent residents under this bill. In 1994 the number of illegal alien residents was estimated at 3,850,000, of whom 1,600,000 were believed to be in California.

The major migratory trends within the United States in the twentieth century have been an exodus of southern blacks to the cities of the north and midwest, especially

after World War I (1914–18); a shift of whites from central cities to surrounding suburbs since World War II (after 1945); and, also during the post–World War II period, a massive shift from the north and east to the south and southwest.

8 ETHNIC GROUPS

The majority of the population of the United States is of European origin. The largest groups in 1990 trace their ancestry to the United Kingdom (31,391,758), Germany (45,583,922), and Ireland (22,721,252). Many Americans have mixed ancestries. Major racial and national minority groups include blacks (either of United States or Caribbean parentage), Chinese, Filipinos,

Japanese, Mexicans, and other Spanish-speaking peoples of the Americas. Whites comprised 83.9% of the United States population in 1990; blacks, 12.3%; Asians and Pacific Islanders, 3%; Native Americans (Amerindians—more commonly known as Indians, Eskimos, and Aleuts), 0.8%. Responding to a census question that cut across racial lines, 9% of Americans in 1990 described themselves as of Hispanic origin.

In 1990, according to the official census count, there were 1,959,234 Amerindians in the United States, found mostly in the southwestern states of Oklahoma, Arizona, New Mexico, and California. The black population in 1992 was estimated at 31,439,000. More than three out of four black Americans live in cities. In New York City, which had the largest number of black residents (2,102,512) in 1990, 28.7% of the population was black.

Included in the population of the United States in 1990 were 7,226,986 persons who are of Asian and Pacific descent, chiefly Chinese, 1,648,696; Filipino, 1,419,711; Japanese, 866,160; Indian, 786,694; Korean, 797,304; and Vietnamese, 593,213. The Japanese population of Hawaii accounted in 1990 for 23.6% of the state's residents. As of March 1990 there were 22,354,000 Hispanic Americans, of whom 60.4% were of Mexican ancestry, 12.2% Puerto Rican, and 4.7% Cuban.

9 LANGUAGES

The primary language of the United States is English, enriched by words borrowed from the languages of Indians and immigrants, mostly European.

The 1990 census recorded that of 229,875,493 Americans five years of age or over, 198,101,862 spoke only English at home; the remaining 31,773,631 spoke a language other than English. The principal foreign languages and their speakers were as follows: Spanish, 17,310,043; French, 1,920,621; German, 1,544,793; Chinese, 1,316,956; and Italian, 1,307,068. Refugee immigration has greatly increased the number of foreign-language speakers from Latin America and Asia.

Educational problems raised by the presence of large numbers of non-English speakers led to the passage in 1976 of the Bilingual Educational Act, allowing children to study basic courses in their first language while they learn English. A related school issue is that of black English, a Southern dialect variant that is spoken by many black students now in northern schools.

10 RELIGIONS

United States religious traditions are predominantly Judeo-Christian, and most Americans identify themselves as Protestants (of various denominations), Roman Catholics, or Jews. As of 1990, there were 255,173 places of worship with 137,064,509 members; about half of the total population belongs to a Judeo-Christian religious group.

The largest Christian denomination is the Roman Catholic Church, with 53,385,998 members in 22,441 parishes in 1990. Immigration from western Europe and the Caribbean accounts for the large number of

Roman Catholics in the Northeast, Northwest, and some parts of the Great Lakes region. Hispanic traditions and more recent immigration from Mexico and other Latin American countries account for the historical importance of Roman Catholicism in California and throughout the southwest. Jewish immigrants settled first in the Northeast, where the largest Jewish population remains; in 1990, 1,843,240 Jews lived in New York out of an estimated total of 5,982,529 American Jews.

As of 1990, United States Protestant groups had at least 77,695,982 members. By far the nation's largest Protestant group, the Southern Baptist Convention, had 18,940,682 members in 1990; the American Baptist Churches in the USA claimed a membership of some 1,873,731. A concentration of Methodist groups extends westward in a band from Delaware to eastern Colorado; the largest of these groups, the United Methodist Church, had 11,091,032 members in 1990.

Lutheran denominations, reflecting in part the patterns of German and Scandinavian settlement, are most highly concentrated in the north-central states, especially Minnesota and the Dakotas. Two Lutheran synods, the Lutheran Church in America and the American Lutheran Church merged in 1987 to form the Evangelical Lutheran Church in America. In June 1983, the two major Presbyterian churches, the northern-based United Presbyterian Church in the USA and the southern-based Presbyterian Church in the US, formally merged as the Presbyterian Church (USA), ending a division that began with the Civil War.

Other Protestant denominations and their estimated memberships in 1990 were the Episcopal Church, 2,445,286; Church of Christ, 1,681,013; and the United Church of Christ (Congregationalist), 1,993,459. One Christian group, the Church of Latter-day Saints (Mormon), which claimed 3,540,820 members in 1990, was organized in New York in 1830 and, since migrating westward, has played a leading role in Utah's political, economic, and religious life. During the 1970s and early 1980s there was a rise in the fundamentalist, evangelical, and Pentecostal movements.

Many native Americans continue to follow their traditional religions. Several million Muslims, Eastern Orthodox Christians, followers of various Asian religions, a number of small Protestant groups, and a sizable number of cults also participate in United States religious life. The 1980s and 1990s have seen the rise of feminist spirituality, New Age, earth-centered, and Neo-Pagan movements.

11 TRANSPORTATION

The United States has well-developed systems of railroads, highways, inland waterways, oil pipelines, and domestic airways. Despite an attempt to encourage more people to travel by train through the development of a national network (Amtrak) in the 1970s, rail transport has continued to experience heavy financial losses. In 1992, over 38 million people rode on Amtrak. Railroads carried

1,581,871,847 tons of cargo through 23,316,176 rail-carloads handled in 1991.

The most widely used form of transportation is the automobile, and the extent and quality of the United States road-transport system are the best in the world. Over 190.3 million vehicles—a record number—were registered in 1992, including more than 144.2 million passenger cars and some 46.1 million trucks and buses. In 1992, 31% of the world's motor vehicles were registered in the United States, down from 36% in 1985. The United States has a vast network of public roads, whose total length as of 31 December 1992 was 6,277,859 kilometers (3,901,715 miles).

Major ocean ports or port areas are New York, Philadelphia, Baltimore, Norfolk, New Orleans, Houston, and the San Francisco Bay area. The inland port of Duluth on Lake Superior handles more freight than all but the top-ranking ocean ports. In 1991, the United States had the tenth-largest registered merchant shipping fleet in the world (by gross registered tons). The total American merchant fleet, including government-owned vessels, was 619 ships (with a total of 15,466,000 gross registered tons) in 1991.

In 1983, the United States had 96 certified air carriers, more than double the number in 1978 when the Airline Deregulation Act was passed. Passengers carried by the airlines in 1992 totaled 473 million. The United States in 1992 had 17,846 airports, of which 5,545 were public. An estimated 198,475 general aviation aircraft flew a total of 30,055,000 hours in 1991.

12 HISTORY

Origins

The first Americans—distant ancestors of the American Indians—probably crossed the Bering Strait from Asia at least 12,000 years ago. By the time Christopher Columbus came to the New World (as America was known) in 1492 there were probably about 2 million Native Americans living in the land that was to become the United States.

The Spanish established the first permanent settlement at St. Augustine in the future state of Florida in 1565, and another in New Mexico in 1599. During the early seventeenth century, the English founded Jamestown in present-day Virginia (1607) and Plymouth Colony in present-day Massachusetts (1620). The Dutch and Swedish also established settlements in the seventeenth century, but the English eventually took over settlement of the east coast except for Florida, where the Spanish ruled until 1821. In the southwest, California, Arizona, New Mexico, and Texas also were part of the Spanish empire until the nineteenth century.

The American Revolution

The colonies enjoyed a large measure of self-government until the end of the French and Indian War (1745–63), which resulted in the loss of French Canada to the British. To prevent further troubles with the Indians, the British government in 1763 prohibited the American colonists from settling beyond the Appalachian Mountains. The British also enacted a series of tax measures which the colonists

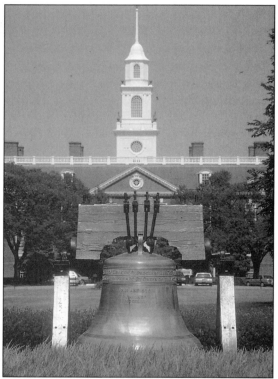

Photo credit: Delaware Tourism Office.

Liberty bell in front of Legislator Hall, in Dover, the state capital of Delaware.

protested, setting off a struggle between colonial and British authority.

A series of conflicts led to the colonists' decision to separate from British rule and set up their own independent government. George Washington was appointed commander-in-chief of the new American army, and on 4 July 1776, the 13 American colonies adopted the Declaration of Independence. The American Revolution was officially begun.

British and American forces met in their first organized encounter near Boston on 17 June 1775. Numerous battles up and down the east coast followed. The entry of France into the war on the American side eventually tipped the balance. On 19 October 1781, the British commander, Charles Cornwallis, surrendered his army at Yorktown, Virginia. American independence was acknowledged by the British in a treaty of peace signed in Paris on 3 September 1783.

The Beginnings of American Government

The first constitution uniting the 13 original states—the Articles of Confederation—denied Congress power to raise taxes or regulate commerce, and many of its authorized powers required the approval of a minimum of nine states. In 1787 Congress passed the Northwest Ordinance, providing for the establishment of new territories on the frontier. In that same year, a convention assembled in Philadelphia to revise the articles. The convention adopted an altogether new document, the present Constitution of the United States, which greatly increased the powers of the central government at the expense of the states.

This document was ratified by the states with the understanding that it would be amended to include a bill of rights guaranteeing certain fundamental freedoms. These freedoms—including the rights of free speech, press, and assembly, freedom from unreasonable search and seizure, and the right to a speedy and public trial by an impartial jury—are assured by the first ten amendments to the constitution, known as the "Bill of Rights," adopted on 5 December 1791. The constitution did recognize slavery, and did not provide for universal suffrage. On 30 April 1789 George Washington was inaugurated as the first president of the United States.

The Federalist Party, to which Washington belonged, was opposed to the French Revolution (1789), while the Democratic-Republicans (an anti-Federalist party led by Thomas Jefferson) supported it. This division of the nation's leadership was the beginning of the two-party system, which has been the dominant characteristic of the United States political scene ever since.

Westward Expansion

In 1803, President Thomas Jefferson purchased the Louisiana Territory from France, including all the present territory of the United States west of the Mississippi drained by that river and its tributaries. Exploration and mapping of the new territory, particularly through the expeditions of Meriwether Lewis and William Clark, began almost immediately.

To make room for the westward expansion of European American settlement, the federal government in 1817 began a policy of forcibly resettling the Indians. They were moved to what later became known as Indian Territory (now Oklahoma); those Indians not forced to move were restricted to reservations. This "removal" of native Americans to make way for European American settlement was a form of genocide (the deliberate destruction of a whole race, culture, or group of people).

The Missouri Compromise (1820) provided for admission of Missouri into the

Photo credit: Travel Montana/P. Fugleberg.

Lewis and Clark monument at Fort Benton in Montana.

Union as a slave state but banned slavery in territories to the west that lay north of 36°30´. And in 1823 President James Monroe declared the Western Hemisphere closed to further colonization by European powers.

Development of Farming and Industry

Farming expanded with westward migration. The cotton gin, invented by Eli Whitney in 1793, greatly simplified cotton production, and the growing textile industry in New England and Great Britain needed a lot of cotton. So the South remained an agricultural society based mostly on a one-crop economy. Large numbers of field hands were required for cotton farming, and black slavery became a significant part of the southern economy.

The successful completion of the Erie Canal (1825), linking the Great Lakes with the Atlantic, began a canal-building boom. Railroad building began in earnest in the 1830s, and by 1840 about 3,300 miles (5,300 kilometers) of track had been laid.

New States and the Slavery Question

In 1836, United States settlers in Texas revolted against Mexican rule and established an independent republic. Texas was admitted to the Union as a state in 1845. War with Mexico over a boundary dispute led in 1848 to the addition of California and New Mexico to the growing nation. A dispute with Britain over the Oregon Territory was settled in 1846 by a treaty that established the 49th parallel as the boundary with Canada.

Westward expansion increased the conflict over slavery in the new territories. The Kansas-Nebraska Act of 1854 repealed the Missouri Compromise and left the question of slavery in the territories to be decided by the settlers themselves. Finally, the election of Abraham Lincoln to the presidency in 1860 led strong supporters of slavery to decide to secede from the United States altogether.

The Civil War

Between December 1860 and February 1861, the seven states of the Deep South—South Carolina, Mississippi, Florida, Alabama, Georgia, Louisiana, and Texas—withdrew from the Union and formed a separate government. They were known as the Confederate States of America, under the presidency of Jefferson Davis. On 12 April 1861, the Confederates opened fire on Fort Sumter in the harbor of Charleston, South Carolina, beginning the United States Civil War. Arkansas, North Carolina, Virginia, and Tennessee quickly joined the Confederacy.

For the next four years, war raged between the Confederate and Union forces, largely in southern territories. An estimated 360,000 men in the Union forces lost their lives, including 110,000 killed in battle. Confederate dead were estimated at 250,000, including 94,000 killed in battle. The North, with more fighters and resources, finally won. With much of the South in Union hands, Confederate General Robert E. Lee surrendered to Union General Ulysses S. Grant at Appomattox Courthouse in Virginia on 9 April 1865.

The Post-Civil War Era

President Lincoln's Emancipation Proclamation of 1863 was the first step in freeing some four million black slaves. Their liberation was completed soon after the war's end by amendments to the Constitution. Five days after General Lee's surrender, Lincoln was assassinated by John Wilkes Booth. During the Reconstruction era (1865–77), the defeated South was governed by Union Army commanders. The resulting bitterness of southerners toward northern Republican rule, which gave blacks the rights of citizens, including the right to vote, lasted for years afterward. By the end of the Reconstruction era, whites had reestablished their political domination over blacks in the southern states and had begun to enforce rules of segregation that lasted for nearly a century.

Outside the South, the age of big business dawned. Pittsburgh, Chicago, and New York emerged as the nation's great industrial centers. The American Federation of Labor, founded in 1886, established a nationwide system of organized labor that remained dominant for many decades. During this period, too, the woman's rights movement began to organize to fight for the right to vote. It took women until 1920 to win their constitutional right of suffrage.

The 1890s marked the closing of the United States frontier for settlement and the beginning of United States overseas expansion. (Alaska had already been acquired from Russia for $7.2 million in 1867.) In 1898, at its own request, Hawaii was annexed as a territory by the United States. In the same year, as a result of the Spanish-American War, the United States added the Philippines, Guam, and Puerto Rico to its territories. A newly independent Cuba became a United States near-protectorate until the 1950s. In 1903, the United States leased the Panama Canal Zone and started construction of a 68-kilometer (42-mile) canal, completed in 1914.

World War I to World War II

United States involvement in World War I marked the country's emergence as one of the great powers of the world. By late 1917, when United States troops joined the Allied forces in the fighting on the western front, the European armies were approaching exhaustion. American intervention may well have been a key element in the eventual victory of the Allies. Fighting ended with the armistice (truce) of 11 November 1918. President Wilson played an active role in drawing up the 1919 Versailles peace treaty.

The 1920s saw a major business boom, followed by the great stock market crash of October 1929, which ushered in the longest and most serious economic depression the country had ever known. The election of Franklin D. Roosevelt, in March 1933, began a new era in United States history, in which the federal government took a much greater role in the nation's economic affairs. Relief measures were instituted, work projects established, and the federal Social Security program was set up. The National Labor Relations Act established the right of employees' organizations to bargain collectively with employers.

Following German, Italian, and Japanese aggression, World War II broke out in Europe during September 1939. In 1940, Roosevelt, ignoring a tradition dating back to Washington that no president should serve more than two terms, ran again for reelection. He easily defeated his Republican opponent, Wendell Willkie.

The United States was brought actively into the war by the Japanese attack on the Pearl Harbor naval base in Hawaii on 7 December 1941. United States forces waged war across the Pacific, in Africa, in Asia, and in Europe. Germany was successfully invaded in 1944 and conquered in May 1945. After the United States dropped the world's first atomic bombs on Hiroshima and Nagasaki in Japan, the Japanese surrendered in August.

Korean War and Civil Rights Movement

The United States became an active member of the new world organization, the United Nations, during President Harry S Truman's administration. In 1949 the North Atlantic Treaty Organization (NATO) established a defensive alliance among a number of West European nations and the United States. Following the North Korean attack on South Korea on 25 June 1950, the United Nations Security Council decided that members of the United Nations should go to the aid of South Korea. United States naval, air, and ground forces were immediately sent by President Truman. An undeclared war followed, which eventually was ended by a truce signed on 27 June 1953.

During President Dwight D. Eisenhower's administration, the United States Supreme Court's decision in *Brown v. Board of Education of Topeka* (1954) outlawed segregation of whites and blacks in public schools. In the early 1960s, sit-ins, freedom rides, and similar expressions of nonviolent resistance by blacks and their sympathizers—known collectively as the Civil Rights Movement—led to the end of some segregation practices.

In the early 1960s, during the administration of President Eisenhower's Demo-

cratic successor, John F. Kennedy, the Cold War heated up as Cuba, under the regime of Fidel Castro, aligned itself with the Soviet Union. In October 1962, President Kennedy successfully forced a showdown with the Soviet Union over Cuba in demanding the withdrawal of Soviet-supplied missiles from the nearby island. On 22 November 1963, President Kennedy was assassinated while riding in a motorcade through Dallas, Texas. Hours later, Vice President Lyndon B. Johnson was inaugurated president. President Johnson's ambitious "Great Society" program sought to ensure black Americans' rights in voting and public housing, to give the underprivileged job training, and to provide persons 65 and over with hospitalization and other medical benefits.

The Vietnam War and Watergate

In 1965, President Johnson sent American combat troops to support anti-Communist forces in South Vietnam and ordered United States bombing raids on Communist North Vietnam. But American military might was unable to defeat the Vietnamese guerrillas, and the American people were badly divided over continuing the undeclared war.

Under President Richard M. Nixon (elected in 1968), the increasingly unpopular and costly war continued for four more years before a ceasefire was finally signed on 27 January 1973 and the last American soldiers were withdrawn. Two years later, the South Vietnamese army collapsed, and the North Vietnamese Communist regime united the country. In 1972, President Nixon opened up relations with the People's Republic of China, which had been closed to Westerners since 1949. He also signed a strategic arms limitation agreement with the Soviet Union. (Earlier, in July 1969, American technology had achieved a national triumph by landing the first astronaut on the moon.)

The Watergate scandal began on 17 June 1972 with the arrest of five men associated with Nixon's reelection campaign during a break-in at Democratic Party headquarters in the Watergate office building in Washington, D.C. Although Nixon was reelected in 1972, further investigations by the press and by a Senate investigating committee revealed a pattern of political "dirty tricks" and illegal wire-tapping and other methods of spying on his opponents throughout his first term. The House voted to begin impeachment proceedings. On 9 August 1974, Nixon became the first president to resign the office. The American people's trust in their government leaders was seriously damaged.

The Reagan Era

Gerald R. Ford was appointed in October 1973 to succeed ousted Vice President Spiro T. Agnew. Less than a month after taking office, President Ford granted a full pardon to Nixon for any crimes he may have committed as president. Ford's pardon of Nixon probably contributed to his narrow defeat by a Georgia Democrat, Jimmy Carter, in 1976. During 1978–79, President Carter convinced the Senate to pass treaties ending United States sovereignty over the Panama Canal Zone. He also mediated a peace agreement between

Israel and Egypt, signed at the Camp David, Maryland, retreat in September 1978. But an economic recession and a prolonged quarrel with Iran over more than 50 United States hostages seized in Tehran on 4 November 1979 caused the American public to doubt his leadership. Exactly a year after the hostages were taken, former California governor Ronald Reagan defeated Carter in the 1980 presidential election. The hostages were released on 20 January 1981, the day of Reagan's inauguration.

President Reagan used his popularity to push through significant policy changes. He made cuts in income tax and more than doubled the military budget between 1980 and 1989, which resulted in a doubling of the national debt. In an effort to balance the federal budget, Reagan cut welfare and Medicare benefits, reduced allocations for food stamps, and slashed the budget of the Environmental Protection Agency.

Reagan's appointment of Sandra Day O'Connor as the first woman justice of the Supreme Court was widely praised and won unanimous confirmation from the Senate. Protests were raised, however, about his decisions to help the government of El Salvador in its war against leftist rebels, to aid groups in Nicaragua trying to overthrow the leftist Sandinista government in their country, and to send American troops to Grenada in October 1983 to overthrow a leftist government there.

Mount Rushmore, Black Hills, South Dakota.

Presidents Bush and Clinton

Reagan was succeeded in 1988 by his vice president, George Bush. President Bush used his personal relationships with foreign leaders to bring about peace talks between Israel and its Arab neighbors, to encourage a peaceful unification of Germany, and to negotiate significant arms cuts with the Russians. Bush sent 400,000 American soldiers to lead the way in forming a multinational coalition to oppose Iraq's invasion of Kuwait in 1990. The multinational forces destroyed Iraq's main force within seven months.

One of the biggest crises that the Bush administration encountered was the collapse of the savings and loan industry in the late 1980s. The federal government was forced by law to rescue the savings and loan banks, under the Federal Savings and Loan Insurance Corporation (FSLIC), costing taxpayers over $100 billion.

In the 1992 presidential election, Democrat Bill Clinton, governor of Arkansas, defeated Bush, winning 43% of the vote to Bush's 38% and third party candidate Ross Perot's 18%. Clinton's major achievements since becoming president have included passage of a budget designed to raise revenue and thereby lower the deficit, which had ballooned during the Reagan and Bush years. Clinton also persuaded Congress to approve the North American Free Trade Agreement (NAFTA), which removed or reduced tariffs on most goods moving across the borders of the United States, Canada, and Mexico.

13 FEDERAL GOVERNMENT

The Constitution of the United States, signed in 1787, is the nation's governing document. In the first ten amendments to the Constitution, ratified in 1791 and known as the Bill of Rights, certain rights are guaranteed to United States citizens. In all, there have been 26 amendments to the Bill of Rights, including the 13th Amendment (1865) which banned slavery, and the 19th (1920), which gave women the right to vote. Suffrage is universal beginning at age 18.

The United States has a federal form of government, with the distribution of powers between federal and state governments constitutionally defined. The legislative powers of the federal government rest in Congress, which consists of the House of Representatives and the Senate. There are 435 members of the House of Representatives. Each state is given a number of representatives in proportion to its population. Representatives are elected for two-year terms in every even-numbered year. The Senate consists of two senators from each state, elected for six-year terms. One-third of the Senate is elected in every even-numbered year.

A bill that is passed by both houses of Congress in the same form is then given to the president, who may sign it or veto (reject) it. The president must be a citizen born in the United States, at least 35 years old, and must have been a resident of the United States for 14 years. Under the 22nd Amendment to the Constitution, adopted in 1951, a president may not be elected more than twice.

The vice president, elected at the same time and on the same ballot as the president, serves as president of the Senate. The vice president assumes the power and duties of the presidency on the president's removal from office or as a result of the president's death, resignation, or inability to perform his duties. Both the president and the vice president can be removed from office after impeachment by the House and conviction at a Senate trial for "treason, bribery, or other high crimes and misdemeanors."

The president nominates and, with the approval of the Senate, appoints ambassadors, consuls, and all federal judges, including the justices of the Supreme Court. As commander in chief, the president is ultimately responsible for the management of the land, naval, and air forces, but the power to declare war belongs to Congress. The president conducts foreign relations and makes treaties with the advice and consent of the Senate. No treaty is binding unless it wins the approval of two-thirds of the Senate. The president's independence is also limited by the House of Representatives, where all money bills originate.

The president also appoints his cabinet, subject to Senate confirmation. The cabinet consists of the secretaries who head the departments of the executive branch. As of 1995, the executive branch included the following cabinet departments: Agriculture, Commerce, Defense, Education, Energy, Health and Human Services, Veterans' Affairs, Housing and Urban Development, Interior, Justice, Labor, State, Transportation, and Treasury.

Each state is divided into counties, municipalities, and special districts such as those for water, education, sanitation, highways, parks, and recreation. There are more than 3,000 counties in the United States and more than 19,000 municipalities, including cities, villages, towns, and boroughs.

14 POLITICAL PARTIES

Two major parties, Democratic and Republican, have dominated national, state, and local politics since 1860. Minority parties have been formed at various periods in American political history, but none has had any real national impact. The most successful minority party in recent decades was that of Texas billionaire Ross Perot in 1992. Independent candidates have won state and local office, but no candidate has won the presidency without major party backing.

Traditionally, the Republican Party is more sympathetic to business interests and gets greater support from business than does the Democratic Party. A majority of blue-collar workers, by contrast, have generally supported the Democratic Party, which favors more lenient labor laws, particularly as they affect labor unions. Republicans promote private business and an increased role for state government, while Democrats generally support greater federal government participation and regulatory authority.

In 1984 Geraldine A. Ferraro, a Democrat, became the first female vice-presidential nominee of a major United States political party. As of 1994, 7 women served in the United States Senate, 22 women held seats in the United States House of Representatives, and 4 women occupied state governorships. Also in 1984, presidential candidate Jesse L. Jackson was the first black ever to win a plurality in a state primary election. As of 1993, the United States had 8,015 black elected officials, including the mayors of some of the nation's largest cities. One black woman, Carol Moseley-Braun, won election to the Senate in 1992, becoming the first black senator. There were 38 blacks in the House. The House also had 17 Hispanics as of 1993.

15 JUDICIAL SYSTEM

The Supreme Court, established by the United States Constitution, is the nation's highest judicial body, consisting of the chief justice of the United States and eight associate justices. All justices are appointed for life by the president with the approval of the Senate.

The Supreme Court acts as an appeals court for federal district courts, circuit courts of appeals, and the highest courts in the states. The Supreme Court also exercises the power of judicial review, determining the constitutionality of any state laws, state constitutions, congressional statutes, and federal regulations that are specifically challenged.

The United States Congress establishes all federal courts lower than the Supreme Court. On the lowest level and handling the most federal cases are the district courts—numbering 94 in 1986, including one each in Puerto Rico, Guam, the Virgin Islands, the Northern Mariana Islands, and the District of Columbia. District courts have no appeals jurisdiction; their decisions may be carried to the courts of appeals, organized into 13 circuits. For most cases, this is usually the last stage of appeal, except where the court rules that a statute of a state conflicts with the Constitution of the United States, with federal law, or with a treaty. Special federal courts include the Court of Claims, Court of Customs and Patent Appeals, and Tax Court.

State courts operate independently of the federal judiciary. Most states have a court system that begins on the lowest level with a justice of the peace and includes courts of general trial jurisdiction and appeals courts. At the highest level of the system is a state supreme court. The court of trial jurisdiction (sometimes called the county or superior court) has both original and appeals jurisdiction; all criminal cases and some civil cases are tried in this court. The state supreme court interprets the constitution and the laws of the state.

16 ARMED FORCES

The armed forces of the United States of America in 1993 numbered 1.9 million on active duty and 1.7 million in the Ready Reserve. The Standby and Retired Reserve includes about 200,000 experienced officers and members who can be recalled in a national emergency. Membership in all of these forces is voluntary and has been since 1973 when the draft expired at the end of the Vietnam War. However, all male citizens must still register for the draft at age 18. The active duty force includes 212,600 women.

The United States Army numbers 674,800 soldiers (77,700 women) on active duty, divided roughly between 7 heavy (armored or mechanized) divisions, 6 light (infantry airborne, airmobile) divisions, 5 independent brigades, 2 armored cavalry regiments, 7 aviation brigades, and 17 air defense battalions. The Army National Guard numbers 443,150 (32,200 women) and the Army Reserve 680,900 (121,000 women).

The United States Navy (546,650; 55,100 women) combines three combat elements: air, surface, and subsurface. The navy has 87 nuclear-powered attack submarines with 1 configured for special operations. The Marine Corps (193,000; 8,800 women) trains for a wide range of maneuvers.

The United States Air Force (499,300; 71,000 women) operates 3,500 aircraft. Air Force personnel manage the United States radar and satellite early-warning and intelligence effort. The Air Force Reserve and Air National Guard (roughly 200,000 active reserves) provide a wide range of flying and support units.

About one-third of active duty personnel are assigned to overseas stations (one to three years) or serve in air, naval, and ground units that serve short tours on a

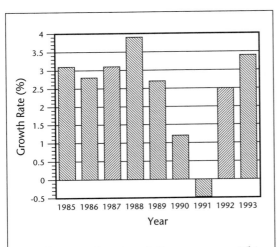

Yearly growth rate of the economy. This economic indicator tells by what percent the economy has increased or decreased when compared with the previous year.

strated during the 1973 Arab oil embargo, when serious fuel shortages developed in many sections of the country.

Industrial activity within the United States has been expanding southward and westward for much of the twentieth century, most rapidly since World War II. Louisiana, Oklahoma, and especially Texas are centers of industries based on petroleum refining; aerospace and other high technology industries are the basis of the new wealth of Texas and California, the nation's leading manufacturing state. The industrial heartland of the United States consists of Ohio, Indiana, Illinois, Michigan, and Wisconsin, with steelmaking and automobile manufacturing among the leading industries. The Middle Atlantic states (New Jersey, New York, and Pennsylvania) and the Northeast are also highly industrialized.

In 1990, the American economy fell into a recession. Output fell 1.6%, and 1.7 million jobs were cut. Unemployment rose from 5.2% in 1989 to 7.4% in 1992, falling to 6.4% in 1993. Recovery has come slowly.

Inflation is an ever-present factor in the United States economy, although the United States inflation rate tends to be lower than that of the majority of industrialized countries. Consumer prices rose 3.0% in 1993.

rotating basis. The United States has one battalion in Egypt and participates in four other peacekeeping missions. By the late 1980s, defense spending was around $300 billion a year and had increased roughly 30% over the decade. In the early 1990s, it had slipped back to the $250–$260 billion level, accounting for roughly 18% of federal spending.

17 ECONOMY

The United States probably has a greater variety and quantity of natural resources than any other nation, with the possible exception of the former Soviet Union. However, because of its vast economic growth, the United States depends increasingly on foreign sources for a long list of raw materials. American dependence on oil imports was dramatically demon-

18 INCOME

Total earned income increased by 4.9% from 1991 to 1992, rising from $3.1 trillion to $3.3 trillion. Nonfarm personal income grew by 5.1% during that time, from $4.8 trillion to $5.1 trillion. The gross domestic product (GDP) amounted to $5,951 billion in 1992 ($24,740 per person), for a real growth rate of 2.1%. The inflation rate in 1992 was 3%. According to the International Labor Organization (ILO), general consumer prices for goods rose by 65.6% between 1980 and 1992.

The median household income in 1992 was $33,769. Some 36.9 million persons from nearly 8 million families lived below the United States federal poverty level in 1992. Approximately 14.5% of all United States residents live in poverty; the proportion has steadily risen since 1973 but is still far below the 1959 level of 22.4%. By race, 33% of blacks in the United States were below the federal poverty level, comprising 29% of the total number of impoverished United States citizens.

19 INDUSTRY

Although the United States remains one of the world's top industrial powers, manufacturing no longer plays as dominant a role in the economy as it once did. Between 1979 and 1991, manufacturing employment fell from 21.8% to 16.2% of national employment. Throughout the 1960s, manufacturing accounted for about 29% of total national income; by 1987, the proportion was down to about 19%. The Midwest leads all other regions in heavy industry, including the manufacturing of automobiles, trucks, and other vehicles.

Leading manufacturing industries of durable goods in 1989 included non-electrical machinery, electric and electronic equipment, motor vehicles and equipment, and other transportation equipment. The principal manufacturing industries of nondurable goods in 1989 were chemicals and allied products, food, printing and publishing, and petroleum and coal products. Large corporations are dominant especially in areas such as steel, automobiles, pharmaceuticals, aircraft, petroleum refining, computers, soaps and detergents, tires, and communications equipment.

Advances in chemistry and electronics have revolutionized many industries through new products and methods. Industries that have been best able to make use of new technology have done well, and the economies of some states—in particular California and Massachusetts—are largely based on it. On the other hand, certain industries—especially clothing and steelmaking—have suffered from outmoded facilities that force the price of their products above the world market level.

In 1991, the United States was the world's second-leading steel producer (after Japan) at 79.7 million metric tons, but also the world's second-largest steel importer (after Germany) at 14.3 million metric tons. Employment in the steel industry has fallen from 521,000 in 1974 to 190,000 in 1992. Automobile manufacturing was another industry suffering in the 1980s: passenger car production fell from 7,098,910 in 1987 to 5,438,579 in 1991.

20 LABOR

The country's civilian and military labor force in 1992 numbered about

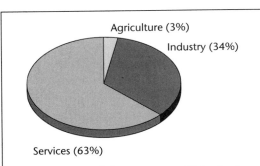

Agriculture (3%)

Industry (34%)

Services (63%)

Components of the economy. This pie chart shows how much of the country's economy is devoted to agriculture (includes forestry, hunting, and fishing), industry, or services.

117,600,000 persons. During 1992, a recession year, the unemployment rate reached 7.4%; the following year it fell to 6.4%. As of March 1991, services employed 29,575,248 people; retail trade, 19,600,024; manufacturing, 13,383,368; finance, insurance and real estate, 6,860,177; wholesale trade, 6,218,875; transportation and public utilities, 5,584,484; construction, 4,671,221; and agriculture 3,115,372. As of 1991, federal, state, and local governments employed 18,554,000 persons.

Earnings of workers vary considerably with type of work and section of country. The national average wage was $11.45 per hour for industrial workers in 1992. There were 39 national labor unions with over 100,000 members, the largest being the National Educational Association with 2,000,000 members. In 1990, 16.1% of the nonagricultural work force belonged to labor unions. The most important federation of organized workers in the United States is the American Federation of Labor–Congress of Industrial Organiza-

tions (AFL–CIO), whose affiliated unions had 14,100,000 members in 1992. In the mid-1990s, 19 states had right-to-work laws, forbidding forced union membership as a condition of employment.

21 AGRICULTURE

In 1992, the United States produced a huge share of the world's agricultural commodities, including soybeans, 52%; corn for grain (maize), 46%; cotton, 17%; oats, 13%; wheat, 12%; and tobacco, 10%.

About 15% of the total United States land area was actively used for crops in 1991; another 26% was grassland pasture. The total amount of farmland declined from 479 million hectares (1.18 billion acres) in 1959 to 397 million hectares (980 million acres) in 1991. The farm population, which comprised 35% of the total United States population in 1910, declined to 25% during the Great Depression of the 1930s and dwindled to 1.8% by 1991.

A remarkable increase in the use of farm machinery took place during and after World War II. Tractors, trucks, milking machines, grain combines, corn pickers, and pickup bailers became near-necessities in farming. In 1920 there was less than one tractor in use for every 400 hectares (1,000 acres) of cropland harvested; by 1991 there were 15. Two other elements essential to United States farm productivity are chemical fertilizers and irrigation.

Substantial quantities of corn, the most valuable crop produced in the United

Photo credit: Candace Cochrane, State of New Hampshire Tourism.

Maple sugaring is a popular activity as the sap begins to run in New Hampshire.

States, are grown in almost every state. Its yield and price are important factors in the economies of the regions where it is grown. In 1991, production figures for major crops (in thousands of metric tons) included corn (for grain) 240,774; wheat, 66,920; soybeans, 59,780; sorghum, 22,455; potatoes, 18,671; cotton, 9,211; oats, 4,276; and tobacco, 764.

22 DOMESTICATED ANIMALS

The livestock population at the end of 1992 included an estimated 99.5 million head of cattle (approximately 10.2% were milk cows), 57.7 million hogs, 10.7 million sheep and lambs, 1.4 billion chickens, and 90 million turkeys (35% of the world's total). Meat production in 1992 amounted to 30,876,000 metric tons, of which poultry accounted for 12,026,000 tons; beef, 10,607,000 tons; pork, 7,817,000 tons; and mutton and lamb, 158,000 tons. Some 4,175,700 metric tons of eggs were produced in 1992.

Milk production totaled 68,966,000 metric tons in 1992. United States butter production totaled 632,000 metric tons in 1992; in that year, the United States was the world's largest producer of cheese, with more than 3.3 million metric tons (23% of the world's total).

23 FISHING

The United States, which ranked sixth in the world in numbers of commercial fish caught in 1991, nevertheless imports far more fish and fishery products than it exports. The 1991 commercial catch was 5.5 million metric tons. Fish for food make up 74% of the catch, and nonfood fish (processed for fertilizer and oil), 26%. Alaska accounted for 58% of 1992 commercial fish caught.

Alaska pollock, amounting to 1.3 million metric tons (3.0 billion pounds), was the most important species in terms of quantity for 1992, followed by menhaden, salmon, flounder, crab, cod, and shrimp. Per person finfish and shellfish consumption (edible meat basis) was 6.7 kilograms (14.8 pounds) in 1992.

24 FORESTRY

United States forest and woodlands covered about 286.8 million hectares (708.8

million acres) in 1991. Major forest regions include the eastern, central hardwood, southern, Rocky Mountain, and Pacific coast areas. The National Forest System accounts for approximately 27% of the nation's forestland. As of 30 September 1992, the United States Forest Service managed 77.2 million hectares (191 million acres) of forest, including 13.8 million hectares (34 million acres) of designated wilderness.

Domestic production of roundwood during 1991 amounted to 495.8 million cubic meters (17,507 million cubic feet), of which softwoods accounted for roughly 80%. The United States, the world's second-leading producer of newsprint, produced 6.2 million metric tons in 1991. Other forest products in 1991 included 72.7 million metric tons of paper and paperboard (excluding newsprint), 58.9 million metric tons of wood pulp, 17.3 million cubic meters (611 million cubic feet) of plywood, and 6.8 million cubic meters (240 million cubic feet) of particleboard. Rising petroleum prices in the late 1970s caused an increase in the use of wood as home heating fuel, especially in the Northeast. Fuelwood and charcoal production amounted to 85.9 million cubic meters in 1991.

25 MINING

Rich in a variety of mineral resources, the United States is a world leader in the production of many important mineral commodities such as aluminum, cement, copper, pig iron, lead, molybdenum, phosphates, potash, salt, sulfur, uranium, and zinc. The leading mineral-producing states are: Texas, Louisiana, Oklahoma, and New Mexico, which are important for petroleum and natural gas; and Kentucky, West Virginia, and Pennsylvania, important for coal. Iron ore supports the nation's most basic nonagricultural industry, iron and steel manufacture.

In 1991, the United States ranked first in the mining of salt, phosphate, and elemental sulfur; second in lead, gold, and silver; third in uranium and nitrogen in ammonia; fourth in potash and cement; and sixth in iron ore. Selected mineral production (excluding fossil fuels) in 1991 (in tons) was as follows: cement, 69,853,000; iron ore, 56,596,000; phosphate, 48,096,000; salt, 35,943,000; nitrogen (in ammonia), 12,692,000; elemental sulfur, 10,816,000; potash, 1,749,000; and copper, 1,631,000. (Figures for salt and cement include Puerto Rico.) Silver production in 1991 was 1,848 tons; gold output was 320 tons.

26 FOREIGN TRADE

The United States led the world in value of exports and imports in 1992. Exports of domestic merchandise, raw materials, agricultural and industrial products, and military goods amounted in 1992 to nearly $420 billion. General imports were valued at over $520 billion, a record high, leaving a trade deficit of over $100 billion. One import category that grew rapidly between the late 1970s and the mid-1980s was telecommunications apparatus—mainly television sets and video cassette recorders from Japan—which increased by 900% between 1975 and 1985. Road vehicles accounted for nearly 14% of

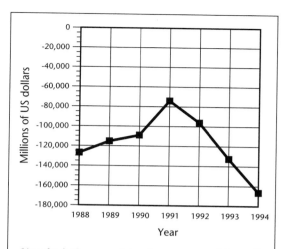

Yearly balance of trade measured in millions of US dollars. The balance of trade is the difference between what a country sells to other countries (its exports) and what it buys (its imports). If a country imports more than it exports, it has a negative balance of trade (a trade deficit). If exports exceed imports there is a positive balance of trade (a trade surplus).

imports in 1992. A rapidly growing export category was computers, which rose from $1.2 billion in 1970 to $30.9 billion in 1992.

Leading merchandise exports by value in 1992 (in billions) included: transportation equipment, $38.7; road vehicles, $37.9; electric machinery and parts, $37.4; office and automatic data processing machines, $31; miscellaneous manufactured articles, $23.3; industrial machinery and parts, $18.9; and power-generating machinery, $18.5.

Leading merchandise imports by value in 1992 (in billions) included: road vehicles, $74.5; electric machinery and parts, $39.7; office and automatic data process-ing machines, $36.4; apparel and clothing, $31.2; miscellaneous manufactured articles, $28.5; telecommunications and sound re-production equipment, $25.8; and power-generating machinery, $15.9.

Principal purchasers of United States exports in 1992 were Canada, Japan, Mexico, the United Kingdom, Germany, France, and Taiwan. Principal suppliers of imports to the United States were Canada, Japan, Mexico, Germany, Taiwan, the United Kingdom, and South Korea.

27 ENERGY AND POWER

The United States, with about 4.7% of the world's population, consumed 24.1% of the world's energy in 1991. Coal supplied about 55% of the energy used by electric utilities in 1992; nuclear sources, 22.7%; natural gas, 9.7%; waterpower, 8.4%; petroleum, 3.2%; and geothermal, wood, waste, wind, photovoltaic, and solar thermal energy, 1%.

In 1993 proved recoverable reserves of crude oil totaled an estimated 31.2 billion barrels; reserves of natural gas were about 4.7 trillion cubic meters (165 trillion cubic feet); and recoverable coal reserves amounted to 240,560 million tons (47% anthracite and bituminous). Mineral fuel production in 1992 included an estimated 607 million tons of hard coal and 295 million tons of lignite; 508.2 billion cubic meters (17.9 trillion cubic feet) of natural gas; and 416.6 million tons of crude oil (second after Saudi Arabia).

In 1991, public utilities and private industrial plants generated 2.8 trillion kilowatt hours of electricity. In 1992, nuclear-powered plants generated 618.8 billion kilowatt hours of electricity. Because of cost and safety problems, the future of the nuclear power industry in the United States came into doubt in the late 1980s.

During the 1980s, attention was focused on the development of solar power, synthetic fuels, geothermal resources, and other energy technologies. The federal government promoted energy conservation measures such as mandatory automobile fuel-efficiency standards and tax incentives for home insulation.

28 SOCIAL DEVELOPMENT

Social welfare programs in the United States depend on both the federal government and the state governments for resources and administration. The old age, survivors', disability, and Medicare (health) programs are administered by the federal government. Unemployment insurance, dependent child care, and a variety of other public assistance programs are state administered, although the federal government contributes to all of them through grants to the states.

In 1990, 13,285,000 Americans received $18.5 billion under the Aid to Families with Dependent Children (AFDC) program. The Food and Nutrition Service of the United States Department of Agriculture oversees several food assistance programs, including the food stamp program, school lunch and breakfast programs, and nutrition programs for the elderly.

The present Social Security program differs greatly from that created by the Social Security Act of 1935. Since 1939, Congress has attached a series of amendments to the program, including provisions for workers who retire at age 62, widows, dependent children under 18 years of age, and children who are disabled prior to age 18. Disabled workers between 50 and 65 years of age are also entitled to monthly benefits. By 1983, Social Security benefits totaled $268.1 billion, paid to more than 40.6 million beneficiaries.

In January 1974, the Social Security Administration took on responsibility for helping the aged, blind, and disabled under the Supplemental Security Income program. In 1991, some 5,118,470 disabled Americans received over $18 billion in benefits. Medicare, another program administered under the Social Security Act, provides hospital insurance and voluntary medical insurance for persons 65 and over, with reduced benefits available at age 62. Medicare hospital insurance covered some 29,866,000 Americans in 1990. Medicaid is a program that helps the needy meet the costs of medical, hospital, and nursing-home care.

29 HEALTH

The United States health care system is among the most advanced in the world. In 1993, health expenditures were to have reached a projected $903.3 billion, and national health care spending is projected to rise to $1.6 trillion by 2000 ($5,712 per person). Medical facilities in the United States included 6,634 hospitals in 1991, with 1,202,000 beds. During the period 1988–93, there was an average of 1 doctor per 419 people. During 1991, the United States Census Bureau estimated that 35.4 million United States residents (14% of the population) were without any form of health insurance.

Life expectancy in 1992 was 76 years. Males could expect to live 72.3 years, females 79.0 years. By race and gender, white females had the highest average expected lifespan, with 79.7 years; next came black females, 73.9; white males, 73.2; and black males, 65.5.

Leading causes of death (with percent of total deaths) in 1992 were: heart disease (33.1%); cancer (23.9%); cerebrovascular diseases (6.6%); chronic obstructive pulmonary diseases (4.2%); accidents and adverse effects (4.0%); pneumonia and influenza (3.5%); diabetes mellitus (2.3%); human immunodeficiency virus (HIV) infection (1.5%); suicide (1.4%); and homicide and legal intervention (1.2%).

Other leading causes of death in 1992 included chronic liver disease and cirrhosis, nephritis, and arteriosclerosis. About 20% of all deaths in the United States were attributed to cigarette smoking in 1990. First identified in 1981, HIV infection and AIDS (acquired immune deficiency syndrome) have spread rapidly; by 1992, there were just under 250,000 AIDS cases reported in the United States.

30 HOUSING

The housing resources of the United States far exceed those of any other country, with 102,264,000 housing units as of April 1990, 91,946,000 of which were occupied. Construction of housing following World War II set a record-breaking pace; 1986 was the 38th successive year during which construction of more than one million housing units was begun.

After 1986, housing starts dropped for five years in succession, hitting 1,014,000 in 1991 and then climbing to 1,200,000 in 1992. Most dwellings are one-family houses. Perhaps the most significant change in the housing scene has been the shift to the suburbs made possible by the widespread ownership of automobiles.

31 EDUCATION

The literacy rate is estimated to be 98% (males, 97% and females, 98%). Education is compulsory in all states and a responsibility of each state and local government. Generally, formal schooling begins at the age of 6 and continues up to age 17. Government spending on education (state and federal) was $280,713 million in 1988–89.

Elementary schooling is from grade 1 to grade 8. High schools cover grades 9 through 12. Colleges include junior or community colleges, offering two-year associate degrees; regular four-year colleges and universities; and graduate or professional schools.

In 1990, public elementary schools had 27 million students, while private elementary schools had 4 million; there were 14 million students in public secondary schools and 1 million students in private ones. In the same year, public colleges had

10.7 million students, while private college enrollment was 2.97 million. In 1991–92, there were 3,500 two-year and four-year colleges and universities. Persons 25 years old and over completing college accounted for 21% of those graduating in 1992, compared with 11% in 1970.

32 MEDIA

All major electronic communications systems are privately owned but regulated by the Federal Communications Commission. In 1990, 97.8% of all United States households had telephones. In 1993, broadcasting stations on the air comprised 11,420 radio stations (both AM and FM) and, as of 1 May 1993, 1,541 television stations. In 1993, 98% of all American households owned at least one TV set. The expanding cable television industry, with 11,385 cable systems as of 1993, served 57.6 million subscribers.

In 1992 there were 1,570 daily newspapers in the United States. The following newspapers reported average daily circulations of one million or more in 1991: *The Wall Street Journal* (1,795,448); *USA Today* (1,418,477); *The Los Angeles Times* (1,177,253); and *The New York Times* (1,110,562). *The Washington Post* (1991 circulation 791,289), which gained national recognition for its coverage of the Watergate affair in the early 1970s, is another influential daily newspaper.

The two general circulation magazines that appealed to the largest audiences were *Reader's Digest*, 16,258,476, and *TV Guide*, 14,498,341. *Time* and *Newsweek* were the leading news magazines, with a weekly circulation of 4,203,991 and

Photo credit: The Wagner Perspective.

Bullriding at The Cheyenne Frontier Days rodeo in Wyoming, the largest professional outdoor rodeo in the world.

3,240,131 respectively. In 1992, 44,528 books were published in the United States.

33 TOURISM AND RECREATION

Foreign visitors to the United States numbered approximately 42,723,000 in 1991. Of these visitors, 44% came from Canada, 18% from Mexico, 18% from Europe, and 12% from Eastern Asia and the Pacific. In 1991, travelers to the United States from all foreign countries spent $45.5 billion. There were 3,080,000 hotel rooms with 5,544,000 beds. With a few exceptions, such as Canadians entering from the Western Hemisphere, all visitors to the United States are required to have passports and visas.

The United States had a total of 49 national parks as of August 1987. Among the most striking scenic attractions in the United States are the Grand Canyon in Arizona; Carlsbad Caverns in New Mexico; Yosemite National Park in California; Yellowstone National Park in Idaho, Montana, and Wyoming; Niagara Falls, partly in New York; and the Everglades in Florida.

Historical attractions include the Liberty Bell and Constitution Hall in Philadelphia; the Statue of Liberty in New York City; the White House, the Capitol, and the monuments to Washington, Jefferson, and Lincoln in Washington, D.C.; the Williamsburg historical restoration in Virginia; the Alamo in San Antonio, Texas; and Mt. Rushmore in South Dakota.

Among many other popular tourist attractions are the movie and television studios in Los Angeles; the cable cars in San Francisco; casino gambling in Las Vegas, Nevada, and in Atlantic City, New Jersey; the Grand Ole Opry in Nashville, Tennessee; the many jazz clubs of New Orleans; and such amusement parks as Disneyland (Anaheim, California) and Walt Disney World (near Orlando, Florida). For amount and variety of entertainment—theater, movies, music, dance, and sports—New York City has few rivals.

Americans' recreational activities range from the major spectator sports—professional baseball, football, basketball, ice hockey, soccer, horse racing, and college football and basketball—to home gardening. Participant sports are a favorite form of recreation, including jogging, tennis, and golf. Skiing is a popular recreation in New England and the western mountain ranges. Sailing, power boating, and rafting are popular water sports. In 1994, the United States hosted the World Cup Soccer Championship. A number of Winter and Summer Olympics have been held in the United States in the past, and the 1996 Summer Olympics are scheduled to be held in Atlanta, Georgia.

34 FAMOUS AMERICANS

Political and Military Figures

Printer, inventor, scientist, and statesman, Benjamin Franklin (1706–90) was America's outstanding figure of the colonial period. George Washington (1732–99), military leader in the American Revolution and first president of the United States, is known as the father of his country. Chief author of the Declaration of Independence and third president was Thomas Jefferson (1743–1826). His leading political opponents were John Adams (1735–1826), second president; and Alexander Hamilton (b.West Indies, 1755–1804), first secretary of the treasury. James Madison (1751–1836), a leading figure in drawing up the United States Constitution, served as fourth president.

Abraham Lincoln (1809–65) led the United States through its most difficult period, the Civil War, in the course of which he issued the Emancipation Proclamation. Jefferson Davis (1808–89) served as the only president of the short-lived Confederacy. Among the foremost presidents of the 20th century have been Nobel Peace Prize winner Theodore Roosevelt (1858–1919); Woodrow Wilson (1856–1924), who led the nation during World War I; and Franklin Delano Roosevelt (1882–1945), elected to four terms spanning the Great Depression and World War II. The presidents during the 1961–95 period were John Fitzgerald Kennedy (1917–63), Lyndon Baines Johnson (1908–73), Richard Milhous Nixon (1913–94), Gerald Rudolph Ford (b.1913), Jimmy Carter (James Earl Carter, Jr., b.1924), Ronald Wilson Reagan (b.1911), George Herbert Walker Bush (b.1924), and Bill Clinton (William Jefferson Clinton, b.1946).

Outstanding military leaders of the Civil War were Union general Ulysses Simpson Grant (1822–85), who later served as the eighteenth president; and Confederate general Robert Edward Lee (1807–70). Douglas MacArthur (1880–1964) commanded the United States forces in Asia during World War II, oversaw the postwar occupation and reorganization of Japan, and directed United Nations forces in the first year of the Korean conflict. Dwight D. Eisenhower (1890–1969) served as supreme Allied commander during World War II, later becoming the thirty-fourth president.

John Marshall (1755–1835), chief justice of the United States from 1801 to 1835, established the power of the Supreme Court through the principle of judicial review. Other important chief justices included Earl Warren (1891–1974), whose period as chief justice from 1953 to 1969 saw important decisions on desegre-

gation, reapportionment, and civil liberties. Prominent associate justices included Oliver Wendell Holmes (1841–1935) and Louis Dembitz Brandeis (1856–1941).

Native American chiefs renowned for their resistance to white invasion were Tecumseh (1768–1813), Geronimo (1829?–1909), Sitting Bull (1831?–90), and Crazy Horse (1849?–77). Historical figures who have become part of American folklore include pioneer Daniel Boone (1734–1820); silversmith, engraver, and patriot Paul Revere (1735–1818); frontiersman David "Davy" Crockett (1786–1836); scout and Indian agent Christopher "Kit" Carson (1809–68); William Frederick "Buffalo Bill" Cody (1846–1917); and the outlaws Jesse Woodson James (1847–82) and Billy the Kid (William H. Bonney, 1859–81).

Inventors and Scientists

Outstanding inventors were Robert Fulton (1765–1815), who developed the steamboat; Samuel Finley Breese Morse (1791–1872), who invented the telegraph; and Elias Howe (1819–67), who invented the sewing machine. Alexander Graham Bell (b.Scotland, 1847–1922) invented the telephone. Thomas Alva Edison (1847–1931) was responsible for hundreds of inventions, among them the incandescent electric lamp, the phonograph, and a motion picture camera and projector. Two brothers, Wilbur Wright (1867–1912) and Orville Wright (1871–1948), designed, built, and flew the first successful motor-powered airplane. Amelia Earhart (1898–1937) and Charles Lindbergh (1902–74) were aviation pioneers. Pioneers in the space program include John Glenn (b.1921), the first American astronaut to orbit the earth; and Neil Armstrong (b.1930), the first man to set foot on the moon.

Outstanding botanists and naturalists include George Washington Carver (1864–1943), known especially for his work on industrial applications for peanuts; and John James Audubon (1785–1851) who won fame as an ornithologist and artist.

Albert Abraham Michelson (b.Germany, 1852–1931) measured the speed of light and became the first of a long line of United States Nobel Prize winners. The theory of relativity was conceived by Albert Einstein (b.Germany, 1879–1955), generally considered one of the greatest minds in the physical sciences. Enrico Fermi (b.Italy, 1901–54) created the first nuclear chain reaction and contributed to the development of the atomic and hydrogen bombs. Also prominent in the splitting of the atom were J. Robert Oppenheimer (1904–67) and Edward Teller (b.Hungary, 1908). Jonas Edward Salk (1914–95) developed an effective vaccine for polio, and Albert Bruce Sabin (1906–93) contributed oral, attenuated live-virus polio vaccines.

Noah Webster (1758–1843) was the outstanding American dictionary author, and Melvil Dewey (1851–1931) was a leader in the development of library science. Also important in the social sciences has been anthropologist Margaret Mead (1901–78).

Social Reformers

Social reformers of note include Frederick Douglass (Frederick Augustus Washington Bailey, 1817–95), a prominent abolitionist; Elizabeth Cady Stanton (1815–1902) and Susan Brownell Anthony (1820–1906), leaders in the women's suffrage movement; Clara Barton (1821–1912), founder of the American Red Cross; Eugene Victor Debs (1855–1926), labor leader and an outstanding organizer of the Socialist movement in the United States; Jane Addams (1860–1935), a pioneer in settlement house work; Margaret Higgins Sanger (1883–1966), pioneer in birth control; and Martin Luther King, Jr. (1929–68), a central figure in the black civil rights movement and winner of the Nobel Peace Prize in 1964.

Religious leaders include Roger Williams (1603–83), an early advocate of religious tolerance in the United States; Jonathan Edwards (1703–58), New England preacher and theologian; Joseph Smith (1805–44), founder of the Church of Jesus Christ of Latter-day Saints (Mormon), and his chief associate, Brigham Young (1801–77); and Mary Baker Eddy (1821–1910), founder of the Christian Science Church.

Literary Figures

The first American author to be widely read outside the United States was Washington Irving (1783–1859). James Fenimore Cooper (1789–1851) was the first popular American novelist. The writings of two men of Concord, Massachusetts—Ralph Waldo Emerson (1803–82) and Henry David Thoreau (1817–62)—influenced philosophers, political leaders, and ordinary men and women in many parts of the world. The novels and short stories of Nathaniel Hawthorne (1804–64) explore New England's Puritan heritage. Herman Melville (1819–91) wrote the novel *Moby-Dick,* a symbolic work about a whale hunt that has become an American classic. Mark Twain (Samuel Langhorne Clemens, 1835–1910) is the best-known American humorist.

Other leading novelists of the later 19th and early 20th centuries were Henry James (1843–1916), Edith Wharton (1862–1937), Stephen Crane (1871–1900), Willa Cather (1873–1947), and Sinclair Lewis (1885–1951), first American winner of the Nobel Prize for literature (1930). Later Nobel Prize–winning United States novelists include William Faulkner (1897–1962) in 1949; Ernest Hemingway (1899–1961) in 1954; John Steinbeck (1902–68) in 1962; Saul Bellow (b.Canada, 1915), in 1976; and Isaac Bashevis Singer (b.Poland, 1904–91) in 1978. Among other noteworthy writers are James Thurber (1894–1961), Francis Scott Key Fitzgerald (1896–1940), Elwyn Brooks White (1899-1985), Richard Wright (1908–60), Eudora Welty (b.1909), James Baldwin (1924–87), Toni Morrison (b.1931), and John Updike (b.1932).

Noted American poets include Henry Wadsworth Longfellow (1807–82), Edgar Allan Poe (1809–49), Walt Whitman (1819–92), Emily Dickinson (1830–86), and Robert Frost (1874–1963). Allen Ginsberg (b.1926), Maya Angelou (b. 1928), and Sylvia Plath (1932–63) are among the best-known poets since World War II. Carl Sandburg (1878–1967) was a noted poet, historian, novelist, and folklorist. The foremost United States playwrights include Eugene (Gladstone) O'Neill (1888–1953), who won the Nobel Prize for literature in 1936; Tennessee Williams (Thomas Lanier Williams, 1911–83); and Arthur Miller (b.1915). Neil Simon (b.1927) is among the nation's most popular playwrights.

Artists

Two renowned painters of the early period were John Singleton Copley (1738–1815) and Gilbert Stuart (1755–1828). Outstanding 19th-century painters were James Abbott McNeill Whistler (1834–1903) and John Singer Sargent (b.Italy, 1856–1925). More recently, Edward Hopper (1882–1967), Georgia O'Keeffe (1887–1986), Norman Rockwell (1894–1978), and Andrew Wyeth (b.1917) have achieved wide recognition.

Sculptors of note include Alexander Calder (1898–1976), Louise Nevelson (b.Russia, 1899–1988), and Isamu Noguchi (1904–88). Frank Lloyd Wright (1869–1959) was the country's most famous architect. Contemporary architects of note include Richard Buckminster Fuller (1895–1983) and Ieoh Ming Pei (b.China, 1917). The United States has produced many fine photographers, notably Mathew B. Brady (1823?–96), who documented the Civil War in pictures; Alfred Stieglitz (1864–1946); and Margaret Bourke-White (1904–71).

Entertainment Figures

The first great American "showman" was Phineas Taylor Barnum (1810–91). Outstanding figures in the motion picture industry are Sir Charles Spencer "Charlie" Chaplin (b.England, 1889–1978), Walter Elias "Walt" Disney (1906–66), and George Orson Welles (1915–85). Sir Alfred Hitchcock (b.England, 1899–1980) was a famous motion picture director; George Lucas (b.1944), Steven Spielberg (b.1947), and Spike Lee (b.1957) have achieved remarkable popular success with their films, as has Woody Allen (Allen Konigsberg, b.1935).

World-famous American actors and actresses include Humphrey Bogart (1899–1957); Clark Gable (1901–60); Cary Grant (Alexander Archibald Leach, b.England, 1904–86); John Wayne (Marion Michael Morrison, 1907–79); Judy Garland (Frances Gumm, 1922–69); Marlon Brando (b.1924); Marilyn Monroe (Norma Jean Mortenson, 1926–62); Jane Fonda (b.1937); and Dustin Hoffman (b.1937). Among other great entertainers are W. C. Fields (William Claude Dukenfield, 1880–1946); Jack Benny (Benjamin Kubelsky, 1894–1974); Fred Astaire (Fred Austerlitz, 1899–1987); Bob (Leslie Townes) Hope (b.England, 1903); Frank (Francis Albert) Sinatra (b.1915); Elvis Aaron Presley (1935–77); and Barbra (Barbara Joan) Streisand (b.1942).

Composers and Musicians

The songs of Stephen Collins Foster (1826–64) have achieved folk-song status. Among the foremost composers are Edward MacDowell (1861–1908), Aaron Copland (1900–90), and Leonard Bernstein (1918–90). Leading composers of popular music are John Philip Sousa (1854–1932), George Michael Cohan (1878–1942), George Gershwin (1898–1937), Woody Guthrie (1912–67), Stephen Joshua Sondheim (b.1930), Paul Simon (b.1941), and Bob Dylan (Robert Zimmerman, b.1941). Prominent in the blues tradition are Leadbelly (Huddie Ledbetter, 1888–1949), Bessie Smith (1898?–1937), and Muddy Waters (McKinley Morganfield, 1915–83). Leading jazz figures include the composers Scott Joplin (1868–1917), Edward Kennedy "Duke" Ellington (1899–1974), and William "Count" Basie (1904–84), and performers Louis Armstrong (1900–1971), Billie Holiday (Eleanora Fagan, 1915–59), John Birks "Dizzy" Gillespie (b.1917), and Charlie "Bird" Parker (1920–55).

Many foreign-born musicians have enjoyed personal and professional freedom in the United States. Principal among them were pianists Arthur Rubinstein (b.Poland, 1887–1982) and Vladimir Horowitz (b.Russia, 1904–89), and violinists Jascha Heifetz (b.Russia, 1901–87) and Isaac Stern (b.USSR, 1920).

Singers Marian Anderson (1897–1993), Leontyne Price (b.1927), and Beverly Sills (Belle Silverman, b.1929) have achieved international acclaim. Martha Graham (1893–1991) pioneered in modern dance.

Sports Figures

Among the many noteworthy sports stars are baseball's Tyrus Raymond "Ty" Cobb

(1886–1961) and George Herman "Babe" Ruth (1895–1948); football's Jim Brown (b.1936); and golf's Mildred "Babe" Didrikson Zaharias (1914–56). Billie Jean (Moffitt) King (b.1943) starred in tennis; Joe Louis (Joseph Louis Barrow, 1914–81) and Muhammad Ali (Cassius Marcellus Clay, b.1942) in boxing; Wilton Norman "Wilt" Chamberlain (b.1936) and Michael Jordan (b.1963) in basketball; Mark Spitz (b.1950) in swimming; Eric Heiden (b.1958) in speed skating; and Jesse Owens (1913–80) in track and field.

35 BIBLIOGRAPHY

Barone, Michael. *The Almanac of American Politics*. Washington, D.C.: National Journal, 1992.

Bennett, Lerone. *Before the Mayflower: A History of Black America*. 6th ed. New York: Penguin, 1993.

Hart, James David, ed. *Oxford Companion to American Literature*. New York: Oxford University Press, 1983.

Harvard Encyclopedia of American Ethnic Groups. Cambridge: Harvard University Press, 1980.

Josephy, Alvin M., Jr. *Now that the Buffalo's Gone: A Study of Today's American Indians*. Norman, Okla.: Univ. of Oklahoma Press, 1984.

Morison, Samuel Eliot. *The Oxford History of the American People*. New York: New American Library, 1972.

Nagel, Rob, and Anne Commire. "Abraham Lincoln." In *World Leaders, People Who Shaped the World*. Volume III: North and South America. Detroit: U*X*L, 1994.

———. "Benjamin Franklin." In *World Leaders, People Who Shaped the World*. Volume III: North and South America. Detroit: U*X*L, 1994.

———. "Crazy Horse." In *World Leaders, People Who Shaped the World*. Volume III: North and South America. Detroit: U*X*L, 1994.

———. "Eleanor Roosevelt." In *World Leaders, People Who Shaped the World*. Volume III: North and South America. Detroit: U*X*L, 1994.

———. "Franklin D. Roosevelt." In *World Leaders, People Who Shaped the World*. Volume III: North and South America. Detroit: U*X*L, 1994.

———. "Frederick Douglas." In *World Leaders, People Who Shaped the World*. Volume III: North and South America. Detroit: U*X*L, 1994.

———. "George Washington." In *World Leaders, People Who Shaped the World*. Volume III: North and South America. Detroit: U*X*L, 1994.

———. "Harriet Tubman." In *World Leaders, People Who Shaped the World*. Volume III: North and South America. Detroit: U*X*L, 1994.

———. "John F. Kennedy." In *World Leaders, People Who Shaped the World*. Volume III: North and South America. Detroit: U*X*L, 1994.

———. "Malcolm X." In *World Leaders, People Who Shaped the World*. Volume III: North and South America. Detroit: U*X*L, 1994.

———. "Martin Luther King, Jr." In *World Leaders, People Who Shaped the World*. Volume III: North and South America. Detroit: U*X*L, 1994.

———. "Robert E. Lee." In *World Leaders, People Who Shaped the World*. Volume III: North and South America. Detroit: U*X*L, 1994.

———. "Roger Williams." In *World Leaders, People Who Shaped the World*. Volume III: North and South America. Detroit: U*X*L, 1994.

———. "Sitting Bull." In *World Leaders, People Who Shaped the World*. Volume III: North and South America. Detroit: U*X*L, 1994.

———. "Susan B. Anthony." In *World Leaders, People Who Shaped the World*. Volume III: North and South America. Detroit: U*X*L, 1994.

———. "Thomas Jefferson." In *World Leaders, People Who Shaped the World*. Volume III: North and South America. Detroit: U*X*L, 1994.

———. "Thomas Paine." In *World Leaders, People Who Shaped the World*. Volume III: North and South America. Detroit: U*X*L, 1994.

———. "Thurgood Marshall." In *World Leaders, People Who Shaped the World*. Volume III: North and South America. Detroit: U*X*L, 1994.

———. "Ulysses S. Grant." In *World Leaders, People Who Shaped the World*. Volume III: North and South America. Detroit: U*X*L, 1994.

Stein, R. *The United States of America*. Chicago: Children's Press, 1994.

Tocqueville, Alexis de. *Democracy in America*. New York: A. Knopf, 1994.

URUGUAY

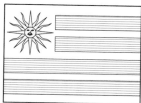

Oriental Republic of Uruguay
República Oriental del Uruguay

CAPITAL: Montevideo.

FLAG: The flag, approved in 1830, has four azure blue horizontal stripes on a white background; on a white canton is a golden sun, alternately straight and wavy. This "Sun of May" symbolizes Uruguay's independence.

ANTHEM: *Himno Nacional,* which begins "Orientales, la patria o la tumba" ("Easterners [Uruguayans], our country or death").

MONETARY UNIT: The Uruguayan peso (UP), of 100 centésimos replaced the new peso in 1993 at the rate of UP1=1,000 new pesos. There are coins of 10, 20, and 50 centésimos and 1, 2, 5, and 10 new pesos, and notes of 1, 5, 10, 20, and 50 Uruguayan pesos. UP1 = $0.2133 ($1 = UP4.6880).

WEIGHTS AND MEASURES: The metric system is the legal standard, but some traditional measures are also used.

HOLIDAYS: New Year's Day, 1 January; Epiphany, 6 January; Landing of the 33, 19 April; Labor Day, 1 May; Battle of Las Piedras, 18 May; Birthday of Artigas, 19 June; Constitution Day, 18 July; Independence Day, 25 August; Columbus Day, 12 October; All Souls' Day, 2 November; Blessing of the Waters, 8 December; Christmas Day, 25 December.

TIME: 9 AM = noon GMT.

1 LOCATION AND SIZE

The second-smallest South American country, Uruguay is situated in the southeastern part of the continent. It has an area of 176,220 square kilometers (68,039 square miles), slightly smaller than the state of Washington. Uruguay has a total boundary length of 2,063 kilometers (1,282 miles). Uruguay's capital city, Montevideo, is located in the southern part of the country on the Atlantic coast.

2 TOPOGRAPHY

Southern Uruguay consists mostly of rolling plains and is an eastward extension of the pampas (grass-covered plain) of Argentina. The Atlantic coastline is fringed with tidal lakes and sand dunes. Low, unbroken stretches of level land line the banks of the two border rivers, the Uruguay and the Rio de la Plata. The northern section is broken by occasional highlands (*cuchillas*), alternating with broad valleys. The highest point in the country, near Montevideo, is 501 meters (1,644 feet) above sea level. The most noteworthy features of the northwest landscape are the highlands known as Cuchilla de Haedo. The Cuchilla Grande runs northeastward from the southern region to the Brazilian border.

3 CLIMATE

The climate is temperate; the average temperatures are 15°C (59°F) in June and 25°C (77°F) in January. Rainfall is evenly distributed throughout the year; it averages about 109 centimeters (43 inches), varying from 97 centimeters (38 inches) in Montevideo to nearly 127 centimeters (50 inches) farther north. Frost is virtually unknown.

4 PLANTS AND ANIMALS

Uruguay is primarily a grass-growing land, and the vegetation is essentially a continuation of the Argentine pampas (grass-covered plain). Forest areas are relatively small. The most useful hardwoods are algarobo, guayabo, quebracho, and urunday; other hardwoods include arazá, coronilla, espinillo, lapacho, lignum vitae, and nandubay. The acacia, alder, aloe, eucalyptus (imported from Australia), ombú, poplar, and willow are common softwoods. Palms are native to the valleys. Rosemary, myrtle, scarlet-flowered ceibo, and mimosa are common. Most of the valleys are covered with aromatic shrubs, and the rolling hills with white and scarlet verbena.

Large animals have practically disappeared from the eastern regions. The carpincho (water hog), fox, deer, nutria, otter, and small armadillo roam the northern foothills. On the pampas are the hornero (ovenbird), quail, partridge, and crow. The avestruz (a small ostrich similar to the Argentine rhea), swan, and royal duck are found at lagoons.

Fish include pompano, salmon, and corvina. The principal reptiles are cross vipers and tortoises. Seals are found on Lobos Island, near Punta del Este.

5 ENVIRONMENT

Air pollution is a problem, particularly in the larger population centers. Its primary sources are industry and an energy plant in Brazil. Pollution from mining and industrial sources threatens the nation's water supply; 95% of the nation's rural dwellers do not have pure water.

The nation's cities produce 0.5 million tons of solid waste per year; 40% of the urban population does not have adequate waste disposal facilities. As of 1994, 5 of Uruguay's mammal species and 11 of its bird species were endangered, and 14 types of plants were threatened with extinction.

6 POPULATION

According to the 1985 census, the population of Uruguay was 2,955,241. It was estimated at 3,179,000 in 1994. A population of 3,274,000 was projected for the year 2000. In 1985, 44% of the population lived in Montevideo. The estimated population density is 18 persons per square kilometer (47 per square mile).

7 MIGRATION

There were 103,002 foreign-born people in 1985. Immigration came to 1,471 in 1990. Substantial emigration by Uruguayans for political or economic reasons occurred during the mid-1970s and early 1980s. Official figures suggest that about 180,000 Uruguayans left between 1963 and 1975 and 150,000 between 1975 and 1985. Most of them were young and, on average, better educated than the total population. Argentina was the main destination.

8 ETHNIC GROUPS

The inhabitants of Uruguay are primarily (about 88%) white and of European origin, mostly Spanish and Italian; a small percentage is descended from Portuguese, English, and other Europeans. Mestizos (mixed white and Amerindian lineage) represent 8% of the population, and blacks and mulattoes (mixed black and white) about 4%.

9 LANGUAGES

Spanish is the official language. Uruguayan Spanish, like Argentine Spanish, has been somewhat modified by the Italians who migrated in large numbers to both countries.

10 RELIGIONS

Uruguay is the only Latin American nation that approaches religious diversity. Contrasting with the 90% formal Roman Catholic affiliation in other Latin American countries, only 78% of Uruguayans identified themselves as Roman Catholics in 1993. Many claimed no church membership. Only 3% of the population was Protestant, and there were some 24,000 Jews in 1990.

11 TRANSPORTATION

Four main lines connect the western and northern areas with Montevideo. In 1991 there were 3,005 kilometers (1,867 miles)

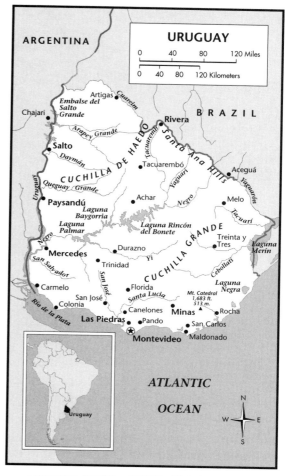

LOCATION: 30°06′ to 35°02′s; 53°05′ to 59°29′w.
BOUNDARY LENGTHS: Brazil, 1,003 kilometers (623 miles); Atlantic coastline, 565 kilometers (351 miles); Argentina, 495 kilometers (308 miles). **TERRITORIAL SEA LIMIT:** 200 miles.

of standard-gauge, government-owned track. Highways have surpassed railroads as the principal means of transport for passengers and freight. In 1991 there were 49,900 kilometers (31,007 miles) of roads. In 1992, there were 350,000 motor vehicles, two-thirds of which were passenger cars.

Contrasting modes of transportation in Colonia, Uruguay.

Montevideo is the major Uruguayan port. There are some 1,600 kilometers (994 miles) of inland waterways, of which the most important are the Río de la Plata and the Uruguay. There were four vessels in the merchant fleet in 1991, with gross registered tons of 59,000. Carrasco, an airport outside Montevideo, is used by most international carriers and serviced 821,000 passengers in 1991.

12 HISTORY

In the sixteenth century, the native Charrúa Indians drove off the few Spanish expeditions that landed on the east bank of the Uruguay river. By 1680, when Portuguese from Brazil founded Colonia do Sacramento as a rival to Buenos Aires, Uruguay became a focal point for Spanish-Portuguese rivalry.

Montevideo was founded in 1726, and Uruguay became part of the viceroyalty of La Plata, which the Spaniards established in Buenos Aires in 1776. During the Napoleonic Wars, the British invaded the region of La Plata and captured Buenos Aires and Montevideo (1806–7), but they were forced out in 1807. After Buenos Aires refused to give Uruguay autonomy, the Uruguayan national hero, José Gervasio Artigas, declared Uruguay independent in 1815. A year later, Brazilians attacked Montevideo from the north, and, after four years of fighting, Uruguay was annexed to Brazil in 1821.

On 25 August 1825, Juan Antonio Lavalleja issued a declaration of independence. After a three-year fight, a peace treaty signed on 28 August 1828 guaranteed Uruguay's independence. During the following period of political turmoil and civil war, the two political parties around which Uruguayan history has traditionally revolved, the Colorados (reds) and the Blancos (whites), were founded.

The nineteenth century was largely a struggle between the two factions. Some measure of national unity was achieved in the 1860s. In 1865, Uruguay allied with Brazil and Argentina to defeat Paraguay in the Paraguayan War (1865–70), also known as the War of the Triple Alliance. The administrations of José Batlle y Ordóñez (1903–7, 1911–15) marked the nation's period of greatest progress. Batlle initiated Uruguay's famed social welfare system, funded primarily by earnings of beef and wool in foreign markets.

After World War II (1939–45), the Colorados ruled, except for an eight-year period from 1958–66. During the administration of President Jorge Pacheco Areco (1967–72) Uruguay entered a period of crisis. Economic and political instability stemming from the decline of wool revenues resulted in the emergence of Uruguay's National Liberation Movement, popularly known as the Tupamaros. A well-organized Marxist (communist) guerrilla movement, the Tupamaros mounted a campaign of kidnapping, assassination, and bank robbery.

Their activities, coupled with the worsening economic situation, aggravated Uruguay's political uncertainty. Gradually, the military assumed a greater role in government and by 1973 was in control of the system, crushing the Tupamaros by the end of that year. The military retained control of the country until 1981, suspending the constitution and, in 1976, naming a new president, Aparicio Méndez Manfredini. In 1979, Amnesty International estimated the number of political prisoners at 6,000.

In September 1981, a "transitional" president, Georgio Álvarez Armellino, was installed, and the moderate government of Colorado candidate Julio María Sanguinetti Cairolo took office in March 1985.

The new government released all political prisoners, declared amnesty for former military and police leaders, and initiated talks between employers and union leaders to reduce social tension. However, slow progress on the economic front led to the 1989 election of the Blanco candidate, Luis Alberto Lacalle. Lacalle has emphasized deficit reduction, reforms in education, labor, and the civil service, and the return of state enterprises to private ownership. However, these plans were dealt a serious blow in a 1993 election, when the public failed to ratify a set of proposals for liberalization.

13 GOVERNMENT

According to the constitutional revision of 1966, the Congress (or General Assembly) consisted of the 30-member Senate and the 99-member Chamber of Deputies. From

June 1973 until March 1985, Uruguay was ruled by executive decree, subject to veto by the military, with legislative functions carried out by the 25-member Council of State, appointed by the executive.

In March 1985, democracy was restored under President Sanguinetti; in July, the government set up a National Constituent Assembly to devise constitutional reforms that would be submitted to the electorate for ratification. Uruguay is divided into 19 departments (provinces).

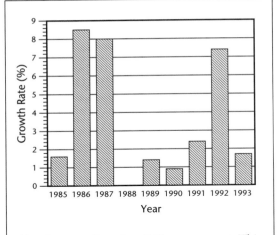

Yearly growth rate of the economy. This economic indicator tells by what percent the economy has increased or decreased when compared with the previous year.

14 POLITICAL PARTIES

Uruguay has Latin America's oldest two-party system. The Colorados (reds) and Blancos (whites), formed during the conflicts of the 1830s and 1840s, persisted into the 1990s. The Colorados are traditional Latin American liberals, representing urban business interest, and favoring limitation on the power of the Catholic Church. The Blancos (officially called the National Party) are conservatives, defenders of large landowners and the Church.

In 1989, Blanco candidate Lacalle took 37% of the vote. The Blancos also carried a plurality in each house of the legislature, followed respectively by the Colorados, the Broad Front and the "New Space" Coalition.

15 JUDICIAL SYSTEM

Below the Supreme Court are appeals courts and lower civil and criminal courts, justices of the peace, electoral and administrative courts, and an accounts court. A parallel military court system operates under its own procedure. When the Supreme Court hears cases involving the military, two military justices join the Court. Civilians are tried in the military court only in time of war or insurrection.

16 ARMED FORCES

The armed forces numbered 24,700 in 1993. The active army consists of volunteers between the ages of 18 and 45 who contract for one or two years of service.

The army numbered 17,200, organized in 4 regional divisions of 10 brigades; the navy (including naval air force and infantry) numbered 4,500 with 3 frigates and 8 patrol and coastal combatants. The air force had 3,000 men and 37 combat aircraft. Defense spending was $168 million in 1988.

17 ECONOMY

Uruguay's economy is based on the production and processing of agricultural commodities. In 1986, exports of wool and meat accounted for 39% of the total goods sold outside the country. After 1982 there was an uninterrupted fall in production, low levels of investment, high unemployment, and mounting inflation (74% in 1986).

The new government, in mid-1985, was able to negotiate new credit agreements with the International Monetary Fund (IMF) and creditor banks. An economic and financial program was initiated to reduce the government deficit and inflation. Some measure of success was achieved by 1987. There was strong economic growth in 1992. Tourism, in particular, contributed to the economy. Inflation in 1993 was 52.8%.

18 INCOME

In 1992, the gross national product (GNP) was $10,444 million at current prices, or about $3,830 per person. For the period 1985–92, the average inflation rate was 78.6%, resulting in a real growth rate in per person GNP of 2.9%.

19 INDUSTRY

Although foreign trade depends mainly on agricultural production, the production of industrial goods for domestic consumption is increasing, primarily in the fields of textiles, rubber, glass, paper, electronics, chemicals, cement, light metallurgical manufactures, ceramics, and beverages. World War II (1939–45) spurred the industrial growth of Uruguay, and now

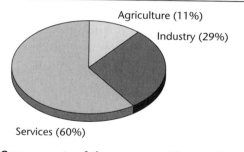

Components of the economy. This pie chart shows how much of the country's economy is devoted to agriculture (includes forestry, hunting, and fishing), industry, or services.

local industry supplies most of the manufactured products used. Most industry is concentrated in and around Montevideo.

20 LABOR

About 1,380,000 Uruguayans, or an estimated 44% of the population, were in the civilian labor force in 1992. In that same year, manufacturing and construction accounted for 28% of the labor force; agriculture, 5%; and services, 67%. The unemployment rate rose from 8.94% in 1991 to 9.03% in 1992.

The 8-hour day and 48-hour week were instituted in 1915. Civil servants and employees of state-run businesses and other public services have a 30-hour week. Unemployment and dismissal compensation, old age and liability pensions, workers' accident compensation, and family allowances are provided by law.

21 AGRICULTURE

About 77% of Uruguay's land area is devoted to stock raising and 7.4% to the cultivation of crops. In pasturage, large farms predominate, with farms of more than 1,000 hectares (2,500 acres) accounting for two-thirds of all farmland. Crops are grown mainly on small farms of less than 100 hectares (250 acres).

In 1992 production of Uruguay's principal crops (in thousands of tons) was as follows: rice, 622; sugarcane, 430; wheat, 265; barley, 214; sugar beets, 160; potatoes, 155; sorghum, 126; corn, 82; sunflowers, 41; oats, 26; and linseed, 4.

22 DOMESTICATED ANIMALS

Livestock is the basis of the economy. As of 1992, Uruguay surpassed Argentina and now has more sheep than any other South American country. The production costs of stock raising are low, and the quality of the product is generally high.

Uruguay is especially suited to the raising of sheep and cattle. In 1992 there were 9.5 million head of cattle, and slaughtered livestock amounted to 360,000 tons; about 82% was used for domestic consumption and 18% for export. Sheep (25.7 million in 1992) are raised mainly for wool. Other livestock in 1992 included 475,000 horses and 215,000 hogs. Milk production in 1992 reached 1,100,000 tons.

23 FISHING

Fishing underwent rapid growth in the 1970s. The government-promoted fishing industry made an average annual catch of 143,170 tons in 1991. Important sea fish are corvina negra (a kind of bass), mullet, sole, anchovy, mackerel, whiting, and

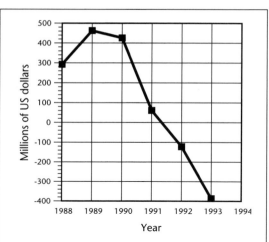

Yearly balance of trade measured in millions of US dollars. The balance of trade is the difference between what a country sells to other countries (its exports) and what it buys (its imports). If a country imports more than it exports, it has a negative balance of trade (a trade deficit). If exports exceed imports there is a positive balance of trade (a trade surplus).

shark. The finest freshwater fish is the dorado, a type of salmon. The southern coastal zone from Piriápolis to Punta del Este is considered one of the finest fishing areas in the world.

24 FORESTRY

Uruguay has some 669,000 hectares (1,653,000 acres) of forestland. About 8,200 hectares (20,300 acres) were reforested annually from 1981 to 1986. The principal species cultivated are eucalyptus and pine; domestic woods are used for windbreaks, fence posts, and firewood. Lumber suitable for building and construction is imported. Roundwood removals totaled 3,829,000 cubic meters in 1991.

Selected Social Indicators

These statistics are estimates for the period 1988 to 1993. For comparison purposes, data for the United States and averages for low-income countries and high-income countries are also given.

Indicator	Uruguay	Low-income countries	High-income countries	United States
Per capita gross national product†	**$3,830**	$380	$23,680	$24,740
Population growth rate	**0.6%**	1.9%	0.6%	1.0%
Population growth rate in urban areas	**0.9%**	3.9%	0.8%	1.3%
Population per square kilometer of land	**18**	78	25	26
Life expectancy in years	**72**	62	77	76
Number of people per physician	**513**	>3,300	453	419
Number of pupils per teacher (primary school)	**21**	39	<18	20
Illiteracy rate (15 years and older)	**4%**	41%	<5%	<3%
Energy consumed per capita (kg of oil equivalent)	**715**	364	5,203	7,918

† The gross national product (GNP) is the total dollar value of all goods and services produced by a country in a year. The per capita GNP is calculated by dividing a country's GNP by its population. The World Bank defines low-income countries as those with a per capita GNP of $695 or less. High-income countries have a per capita GNP of $8,626 or more. Less than 14% of the world's 5.5 billion people live in high-income countries, while almost 60% live in low-income countries.

> = greater than   < = less than

Sources: World Bank, *Social Indicators of Development 1995,* Baltimore: Johns Hopkins University Press, 1995. Central Intelligence Agency, *World Fact Book,* Washington, D.C.: Government Printing Office, 1994.

25 MINING

Mineral resources are limited and undeveloped. There are deposits of manganese, iron, lead, and copper, and in the Rivera Department, gold is mined in small quantities. More important are stones, such as the marble quarried for local use, limestone, granite, quartz, gypsum, and dolomite. Sand, common stone, and talcum are exported. Agates, opals, and onyx are found in Salto and Artigas.

26 FOREIGN TRADE

Uruguay traditionally relies on foreign sales of wool, hides, meat, and meat products for its export revenues, which have been increasing over the past several years. In 1992, exports kept rising, amounting to $1,702 million. Imports followed the same trend, totaling $1,941.2 million in 1992. Imports mostly grew in the consumer goods area. There was a greater concentration of regional trade (with Argentina and Brazil).

27 ENERGY AND POWER

Uruguay's power is provided by hydroelectric and diesel-generating plants. Uruguay's total electrical power output was 7,017 million kilowatt hours, of which

87% came from hydroelectric sources. In the mid-1970s, the government imposed a mandatory program to curb power consumption because of rising fuel import costs.

By a bilateral agreement signed with the United States, Uruguay is entitled to receive atomic equipment and to lease nuclear fuels. In 1991, the state-owned refinery at Montevideo processed 2.9 million barrels of distillate fuel oil, 2.6 million barrels of residual fuel oil, and 1.9 million barrels of gasoline. Consumption included 30,000 barrels per day of crude petroleum in 1992.

28 SOCIAL DEVELOPMENT

Uruguay has frequently been referred to as South America's first welfare state. The social reform movement began under the leadership of José Batlle y Ordóñez in the early 1900s. Social legislation now provides for a day of rest in every week (plus Saturday afternoon), holidays with pay, minimum wages, annual cash and vacation bonuses, family allowances, compensation for unemployment or dismissal, workers' accident compensation, retirement pensions for rural and domestic workers, old age and disability pensions, and special consideration for working women and minors. The state also provides care for children and mothers, as well as for the blind, deaf, and mute. Free medical attention is available to the poor, as are low-cost living quarters for workers.

The government's social security system is divided into six main funds: civil service and teachers, industrial and commercial, rural workers and domestic servants, family allowances, banking, and the professions.

In 1993, women made up about one third of the work force but tended to be concentrated in lower paying jobs. Nevertheless, many attend the national university and pursue professional careers.

29 HEALTH

The US Institute of Inter-American Affairs and the Uruguayan Ministry of Public Health created the Inter-American Cooperative Public Health Service, which built four health centers and clinics. The ratios of doctors and beds to the population are exceptionally good. For the period 1988–93, there was 1 doctor per 513 people. In 1990 there were 4.6 hospital beds per 1,000 people (about 15,000 beds). Total health care expenditures in 1990 were $383 million.

For the region, life expectancy is high (72 years in 1992); infant mortality is low. The major causes of death are heart diseases, cancer, and digestive disorders. Degenerative diseases rank higher as a cause of death in Uruguay than in most other Latin American countries. In 1992, 82% had access to health care services.

30 HOUSING

The housing situation is more favorable in Uruguay than in most Latin American countries. The National Institute of Low-Cost Housing builds low-cost dwellings for low-income workers and pensioners. In 1985, 98% of all housing units were made of durable materials including stone masonry, wood, zinc, or concrete. Of all housing units, 92% had private toilet facilities and 74% had water piped indoors.

31 EDUCATION

Adult illiteracy is approximately 4% (males, 3.4%, and females, 4.1%), among the lowest in Latin America. Elementary education, which lasts six years, is compulsory. Secondary education is in two stages of three years each. In 1991 there were 2,413 primary schools, with 15,747 teachers and 340,789 students. There were 276,482 students in secondary and technical schools. Enrollment at all institutions of higher learning was 73,660.

32 MEDIA

The state owns the telegraph and telephone services. In 1991 there were 528,674 telephones, most of them in the metropolitan Montevideo area. Uruguay in 1991 had 110 radio stations and 33 television stations. The number of radio receivers was about 1,880,000 in 1991; the number of television sets was 720,000.

In 1991, Uruguay had 33 daily newspapers, with a combined circulation of more than 694,000. Major Montevideo dailies, with their 1991 circulations included *El Diario* (170,000); *El País* (65,000); *La Mañana* (40,000); and *La Republica* (25,000).

33 TOURISM AND RECREATION

Tourism, one of Uruguay's major enterprises, enjoys government support. The state owns many hotels along the coast,

Photo credit: Mary A. Dempsey

Beloved Palacio Salvo on Montevideo's Plaza de Independencia.

including some of the more sophisticated resorts in South America. Montevideo has been promoted as the "city of roses" because of its many parks and gardens. In 1991, 1,509,962 tourists visited Uruguay, 68% from Argentina and 9% from Brazil.

The most popular sport in Uruguay is soccer; there is an intense rivalry between supporters of the two major teams, the Peñarol and the Nacional. Other popular sports include basketball, cycling, tennis, pelota (handball), golf, and water sports.

34 FAMOUS URUGUAYANS

The national hero of Uruguay is José Gervasio Artigas (1764–1850), who led the fight for independence against Brazil and Portugal. Juan Antonio Lavalleja (1786?–1853) directed the uprising that established Uruguay's independence in 1828. One of Uruguay's greatest citizens was José Batlle y Ordóñez (1856–1929), who served twice as president of the country.

Eduardo Acevedo Díaz (1851–1924) won fame as the writer of a gaucho (South American cowboy) novel, *Soledad* (1894). Horacio Quiroga (1878–1937) is regarded as one of Latin America's foremost short-story writers. The poets Julio Herrera y Reissig (1875–1910) and Juana de Ibarbourou (1895–1979) have attained a devoted audience beyond the borders of Uruguay. The painter Juan Manuel Blanes (1830–1901) is best known for his *Episode of the Yellow Fever*. Eduardo Fabini (1883–1951) is Uruguay's best-known composer.

35 BIBLIOGRAPHY

Finch, Martin. *Uruguay.* Santa Barbara, Calif.: Clio, 1989.

Hudson, Rex A., and Sandra W. Meditz, eds. *Uruguay, a Country Study.* 2d ed. Washington, D.C.: Dept. of the Army, 1992.

UZBEKISTAN

Republic of Uzbekistan
Uzbekiston Respublikasi

CAPITAL: Tashkent (Toshkent).

FLAG: Horizontal bands of blue (top), white, and green separated by narrow red bands; white crescent moon and twelve stars on the blue band.

MONETARY UNIT: The som is the official currency, introduced when Uzbekistan left the ruble zone in November 1993.

WEIGHTS AND MEASURES: The metric system is used.

HOLIDAYS: Independence Day, 1 September.

TIME: 5 PM = noon GMT.

1 LOCATION AND SIZE

Uzbekistan, a republic of the former Soviet Union, is located in central Asia bordering the Aral Sea, between Kazakhstan and Turkmenistan. Comparatively, it is slightly larger than the state of California, with a total area of 447,400 square kilometers (172,742 square miles). Uzbekistan's boundary length totals 6,221 kilometers (3,866 miles). Its capital city, Tashkent, is located in the eastern part of the country.

2 TOPOGRAPHY

Uzbekistan consists of mostly flat to rolling sandy desert with dunes. A valley lies in the east surrounded by mountainous Tajikistan and Kyrgyzstan. The Aral Sea lies in the northwest. There is semiarid grassland in the east.

3 CLIMATE

Temperatures in the desert can reach upwards of 32°C (90°F). In the capital city of Tashkent the mean temperature is 32°C (90°F) in the summer and 3°C (37°F) in January. There is very little rainfall in the country.

4 PLANTS AND ANIMALS

Uzbekistan, a republic of the former Soviet Union, suffered damage to its environment by the Soviet agricultural programs of the 1950s. Due to its excessive use of irrigation, the Amu Dar'ya and Syr Dar'ya rivers run dry in places. Half of the Aral Sea is now a dry lake bed, and the land is poisoned from the overuse of fertilizer. Much of the country is devoid of animal life.

5 ENVIRONMENT

Uzbekistan's main environmental problems are soil salt content, land pollution, and water pollution. Chemicals used in farming contribute to the pollution of the soil, and the nation's forestlands are dwindling. The country's water supply also suffers from toxic chemical pollutants. The nation's cities produce 45.8 million tons of solid waste per year.

In 1994, 20 of Uzbekistan's mammal species were endangered and 38 of its bird species were threatened with extinction.

6 POPULATION

The population of Uzbekistan was estimated at 23,089,261 in 1995 and projected at 25,224,000 for the year 2000. Tashkent, the capital, had an estimated population of 2,094,000 in 1990.

7 MIGRATION

About 30,000 people fled to Uzbekistan in 1993 to escape the civil war in Tajikistan, but only some of them were allowed to stay.

8 ETHNIC GROUPS

In 1989, 71.4% of the population was Uzbek. Russians constituted 8.4%; Tajiks, 4.7%; Kazakhs, 4.1%; Tatars, 2.4%; Karakapaks, 2.1%; and Crimean Tatars, 1%.

9 LANGUAGES

Uzbek, the state language, was the most widely spoken non-Slavic tongue in the former Soviet Union. It is a Turkic language.

10 RELIGIONS

Ethnic Uzbeks mostly belong to the Hanafi School of Sunni Islam, but the Wahhabi sect has flourished in recent years. Uzbekistan had a significant Jewish population of some 93,000 in the early 1990s.

11 TRANSPORTATION

Uzbekistan has about 3,460 kilometers (2,150 miles) of railroad and 78,400 kilometers (48,700 miles) of highways. The Zeravshan River is the largest inland waterway.

12 HISTORY

Independent states existed in present-day Uzbekistan in the first millenium BC. The territory was conquered by Alexander the Great in 329–327 BC. After a series of other conquests, Arabs won control of the region in the eighth century and introduced Islam.

Genghis Khan's Mongols invaded in 1219, and a series of Mongol kingdoms ruled Uzbekistan. In the sixteenth century, the region was divided into separate principalities. Bukhara (Bukhoro) was conquered by Persia in 1740, and soon afterwards by the Mangyt dynasty, which ruled until 1920. In the early nineteenth century the Kokand Khanate (kingdom ruled by a khan, or local chieftain) grew powerful in the eastern part of present day Uzbekistan.

Concern about British expansion in India and Afghanistan led eventually to Russian conquest, which began in the 1860s and ended in the 1880s, when Uzbekistan became part of Turkestan, with Bukhara (Bukhoro) administered as a separate emirate (Islamic territory) under Russian protection.

During the Bolshevik revolution of 1917–20, the Muslim Congress attempted to form an Autonomous Government of Turkestan. Red Army (communist) forces

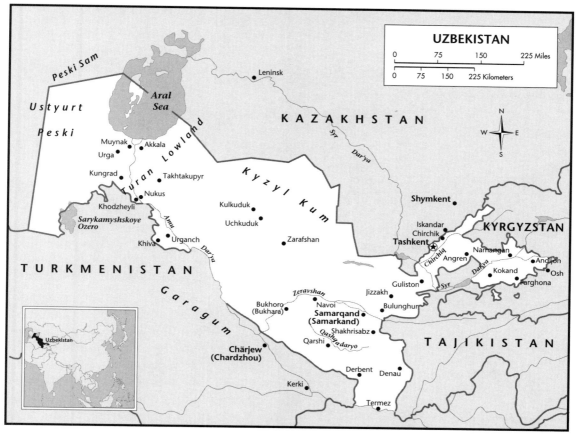

LOCATION: 41°0′N; 64°0′E. **BOUNDARY LENGTHS:** Afghanistan, 137 kilometers (85 miles); Kazakhstan, 2,203 kilometers (1,369 miles); Kyrgyzstan, 1,099 kilometers (683 miles); Tajikistan, 1,161 kilometers (722 miles); Turkmenistan, 1,621 kilometers (1,007 miles).

intervened savagely, but armed resistance continued as late as 1924. The Uzbek Soviet Socialist Republic was created in 1925. Under the leadership of long-time leader S. Rashidov, Uzbekistan was politically conservative during the 1970s and early 1980s. In the mid-1980s, considerable fraud was discovered in the cotton industry.

In March 1990, Islam Karimov was elected to the newly created post of presi-dent by the Uzbek Supreme Soviet. Uzbekistan declared independence on 1 September 1991.

13 GOVERNMENT

The executive branch consists of the president and his appointed prime minister and Cabinet of Ministers. The legislative branch consists of a single-chamber Supreme Soviet of 150 seats. The judicial branch is appointed by the president.

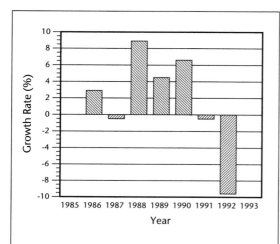

Yearly growth rate of the economy. This economic indicator tells by what percent the economy has increased or decreased when compared with the previous year.

sures toward establishing a market economy have been more cautious than in many other post-Soviet countries. Uzbekistan adopted its own currency, the som, in late 1993.

18 INCOME

In 1992, Uzbekistan's gross national product (GNP) was $18,377 million at current prices, or about $970 per person. For the period 1985–92 the average inflation rate was 61.7%.

19 INDUSTRY

Soft goods (mainly cotton, wool, and silk fiber) and processed foods (including cottonseed oil, meat, dried fruit, wines, and tobacco) accounted for about 39% and 13% of industrial production respectively in 1990.

Heavy industry contributes about 41% of the country's industrial production. Uzbekistan's machinery industry is the primary producer of machines and heavy equipment in central Asia. Around 21,100 tractors were produced in 1991. The country's total steel production equalled 0.9 million tons; rolled ferrous metal manufactures totaled 0.8 million tons.

14 POLITICAL PARTIES

The ruling National Democratic Party is the renamed Communist Party.

15 JUDICIAL SYSTEM

There are three levels of courts: district courts (people's courts) at the lowest level, regional courts, and the Supreme Court.

16 ARMED FORCES

Uzbekistan has a significant army in place; in addition, it has about 1,000 internal security forces.

17 ECONOMY

Uzbekistan has one of the lowest per capita incomes in Central Asia. The world's third largest cotton producer, it is evolving from a mainly agricultural economy to include more industry. Government mea-

20 LABOR

The labor force was estimated at over 7.9 million. Agriculture engaged 29% of the labor force in 1991; personal services, 30%; mining, utilities, and manufacturing, 18%; construction, 11%; trade, 7%; and other sectors, 5%.

21 AGRICULTURE

Uzbekistan is the world's third-largest producer of cotton, accounting for 25% of world supply in 1992. Rice, wheat, barley, and corn are important grain crops. In 1992, over 2.1 million tons of cereal grains were produced.

22 DOMESTICATED ANIMALS

The livestock population in 1992 included 9,200,000 sheep, 5,100,000 cattle, 34,000,000 chickens, 900,000 goats, and 700,000 pigs. Meat production that year totaled 510,000 tons. Wool production was estimated at 26,000 tons.

23 FISHING

Fishing occurs mainly in the eastern valley between Kazakhstan and Tajikistan.

24 FORESTRY

Commercial forestry is not a significant part of the economy.

25 MINING

Copper, lead-zinc, and molybdenum are mined, as well as gold and fluorspar.

26 FOREIGN TRADE

Among the former Soviet republics, Russia is the dominant trade partner. Trade involves mainly the export of light industry products and machinery along with the import of food items, light industry products, and chemicals. The United Kingdom, Belgium, and Germany were the country's leading foreign export markets in 1992; Switzerland, China, and Turkey were its largest suppliers.

27 ENERGY AND POWER

Uzbekistan is the third-largest producer of natural gas in the Commonwealth of Independent States (CIS). In 1992, production totaled 40.3 billion cubic meters (1,425 billion cubic feet). About 50,000 barrels of oil per day are produced. In 1992, electricity production came to 54,100 million kilowatt hours.

28 SOCIAL DEVELOPMENT

The state cares for and educates orphans and other children deprived of parental guardianship. Traditional customs decree that women generally marry young and confine their activities to the home.

29 HEALTH

The average life expectancy is 69 years. During the period 1988–93, Uzbekistan had 1 doctor for every 281 people. There were 12.4 hospital beds per 1,000 people. Total health care expenditures in 1990 were $2,388 million.

30 HOUSING

In 1990, Uzbekistan had 12.1 square meters of housing space per persons. As of 1 January 1991, 204,000 households (or 11.5%) were on waiting lists for housing.

31 EDUCATION

The estimated adult literacy rate in 1990 was 97%, with men estimated at 98.5% and women at 96%. In recent years, there has been an increased emphasis on teaching Uzbek literature, culture, and history. There are three universities: Tashkent State University; Nukus State University; and Samarkland Alisher Naroi State Uni-

Selected Social Indicators

These statistics are estimates for the period 1988 to 1993. For comparison purposes, data for the United States and averages for low-income countries and high-income countries are also given.

Indicator	Uzbekistan	Low-income countries	High-income countries	United States
Per capita gross national product†	**$970**	$380	$23,680	$24,740
Population growth rate	**2.3%**	1.9%	0.6%	1.0%
Population growth rate in urban areas	**2.7%**	3.9%	0.8%	1.3%
Population per square kilometer of land	**48**	78	25	26
Life expectancy in years	**69**	62	77	76
Number of people per physician	**281**	>3,300	453	419
Number of pupils per teacher (primary school)	**n.a.**	39	<18	20
Illiteracy rate (15 years and older)	**3%**	41%	<5%	<3%
Energy consumed per capita (kg of oil equivalent)	**2,033**	364	5,203	7,918

† The gross national product (GNP) is the total dollar value of all goods and services produced by a country in a year. The per capita GNP is calculated by dividing a country's GNP by its population. The World Bank defines low-income countries as those with a per capita GNP of $695 or less. High-income countries have a per capita GNP of $8,626 or more. Less than 14% of the world's 5.5 billion people live in high-income countries, while almost 60% live in low-income countries.

n.a. = data not available   > = greater than   < = less than

Sources: World Bank, *Social Indicators of Development 1995,* Baltimore: Johns Hopkins University Press, 1995. Central Intelligence Agency, *World Fact Book,* Washington, D.C.: Government Printing Office, 1994.

versity. In 1990, all higher level institutions had a total of 340,900 students.

32 MEDIA

Radio Tashkent broadcasts in Uzbek, English, Urdu, Hindi, Farsi, Arabic, and Uighur. There is also a television station. In 1990 there were 279 newspapers and 93 periodicals.

33 TOURISM AND RECREATION

Uzbekistan tourist attractions include the Islamic cities of Samarkand, Bukhara, Khiva, and Kokand.

34 FAMOUS UZBEKISTANIS

Islam A. Karimov has been president of Uzbekistan since October 1992. Abdullah Quaisi wrote the historical novels *Days Gone By* and the *Scorpion from the Pulpit*, published in the 1920s.

35 BIBLIOGRAPHY

Critchlow, James. *Nationalism in Uzbekistan: A Soviet Republic's Road to Sovereignty.* Boulder, Colo.: Westview Press, 1991.

Gippenreiter, Vadim Evgenevich. *Fabled Cities of Central Asia: Samarkand, Bukhara, Khiva.* New York: Abbeville Press, 1989.

Uzbekistan. Minneapolis: Lerner, 1993.

VANUATU

Republic of Vanuatu

[French:] *République de Vanuatu* [Bislama:] *Ripablik blong Vanuatu*

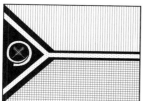

CAPITAL: Port-Vila.

FLAG: Red and green sections are divided horizontally by a gold stripe running within a black border and widening at the hoist into a black triangle on which is a pig's tusk enclosing two crossed yellow mele leaves.

ANTHEM: *Yumi, Yumi, Yumi (We, We, We).*

MONETARY UNIT: As of 1 January 1981, the vatu (VT) replaced at par value the New Hebridean franc as the national currency. There are coins of 100 vatu and notes of 100, 500, 1,000, and 5,000 vatu. VT1 = $0.0084 (or $1 = VT119.29).

WEIGHTS AND MEASURES: The metric standard is used.

HOLIDAYS: New Year's Day, 1 January; May Day, 1 May; Independence Day, 30 July; Assumption, 15 August; Constitution Day, 5 October; National Unity Day, 29 November; Christmas Day, 25 December; Family Day, 26 December. Movable religious holidays include Good Friday, Easter Monday, and Ascension.

TIME: 11 PM = noon GMT.

1 LOCATION AND SIZE

Vanuatu is an irregular Y-shaped chain of some 80 South Pacific islands, with a total land area of about 14,760 square kilometers (5,699 square miles)—slightly larger than the state of Connecticut—and a total coastline of 2,528 kilometers (1,571 miles). The island chain is about 800 kilometers (500 miles) long.

Vanuatu's capital city, Port-Vila, is located on the island of Éfaté.

2 TOPOGRAPHY

The islands are of coral and volcanic origin; there are active volcanoes on several islands, including Ambrym, Loopévi, and Tanna. Mt. Tukosméra is one of the highest peaks at 1,084 meters (3,556 feet). Most of the islands are forested and mountainous, with narrow coastal strips.

3 CLIMATE

Average midday temperatures in Port-Vila range from 25°C (77°F) in winter to 29°C (84°F) in summer. Humidity averages about 74%, and rainfall on Éfaté is about 230 centimeters (90 inches) a year.

4 PLANTS AND ANIMALS

Despite its tropical forests, Vanuatu has a limited number of plant and animal species. The region is rich in sea life, with more than 4,000 species of marine mollusks.

5 ENVIRONMENT

Urban water is polluted due to inadequate sanitation systems. The logging industry threatens the forests and contributes to the problem of soil erosion. Coral reefs, homes to the country's marine life, are threatened by harmful fishing methods. The green sea and hawksbill turtles are endangered species.

6 POPULATION

The census of May 1989 established a total population of 142,419; estimated population in 1995 was 169,000. As of May 1989, the population of the capital, Port-Vila, on Éfaté, was 19,311.

7 MIGRATION

Adverse economic conditions have encouraged emigration to Fiji, New Zealand, and the United States.

8 ETHNIC GROUPS

Nearly 95% of the total population is of Melanesian origin. Minority groups include Europeans, mostly French, and other Pacific Islanders.

9 LANGUAGES

More than 100 languages and dialects are spoken in Vanuatu. Melanesian, the principal language, is related to Fijian and New Caledonian speech. Pidgin English, known as Bislama or Bichelama, is recognized by the constitution as the common language, although English and French are also official languages.

10 RELIGIONS

About 80% of the population is considered to be Christian; other Vanuatuans follow native traditional religions.

11 TRANSPORTATION

In 1991 there were 1,027 kilometers (638 miles) of roads and 7,000 registered motor vehicles, including 4,200 passenger cars.

The chief airports are Bauerfield, on Éfaté, and Pekoa, on Espiritu Santo. Air Vanuatu, the national airline operated by Ansett Airlines of Australia, maintains regular service to Australia. Port-Vila and Luganville are the chief seaports. As of 1 January 1992, there were 109 ships in the Vanuatuan merchant fleet, with a total capacity of 1.8 million gross registered tons.

12 HISTORY

The British Captain James Cook discovered, named, and charted most of the southern New Hebrides islands, as Vanuatu was known, in 1774. The next century brought British and French missionaries, planters, and traders.

A joint Anglo-French naval commission was established in 1887 to protect the lives and interests of the islanders. In 1906, the Anglo-French Condominium (joint rule by nations) was established, largely to settle land claims.

In 1975, a representative assembly replaced the nominated advisory council under which the New Hebrides had been governed. Two years later, the National Party *(Vanua'aku Pati)* demanded independence, and self-government was agreed on for 1978, to be followed by a 1980 referendum on independence.

In May 1980, however, a dissident French-speaking group, based on Espiritu Santo, attempted to break away and declare an independent government. This attempt was suppressed by the presence of British and French troops sent to Luganville on 24 July, although no shots were fired. The soldiers remained until Vanuatu's formal declaration of independence on 30 July 1980. They were then replaced, at the new government's request, by forces from Papua New Guinea, who were assisted by the local police in putting down the rebellion.

Since independence, Vanuatu has been the only South Pacific nation to follow a nonaligned foreign policy. In January 1987 it signed a controversial fishing agreement with the former Soviet Union.

13 GOVERNMENT

Vanuatu is an independent republic within the Commonwealth of Nations. The head of state is the president (Ati George Sokomanu since 1980); the head of government is the prime minister (Father Walter Lini since 1979). The single-chamber legislature consists of 46 members elected by universal adult suffrage to four-year terms. Vanuatu is divided into four administrative districts.

14 POLITICAL PARTIES

The Union of Moderate Parties *(UMP, Maxime Carlot)* is the largest single party in the legislature. Its coalition partner in

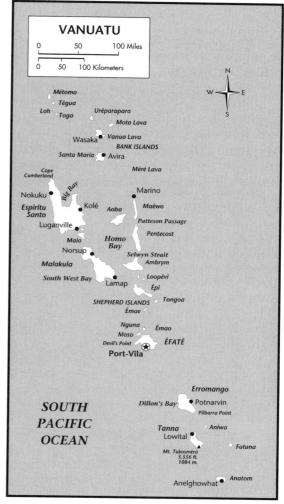

LOCATION: 13° to 21°s; 166° to 171°E. **TOTAL COASTLINE:** 2,528 kilometers (1,571 miles). **TERRITORIAL SEA LIMIT:** 12 miles.

governing is the National United Party (NUP). In opposition are the Vanua'aku Pati (VPÑ—Our Land Party), Melanesian Progressive Party (MPP), National United Party (NUP), and Fren Melanesian Party (FMP).

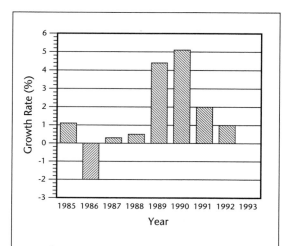

Yearly growth rate of the economy. This economic indicator tells by what percent the economy has increased or decreased when compared with the previous year.

15 JUDICIAL SYSTEM

The constitution establishes a Supreme Court, with a chief justice and three other judges, as well as an appeals court.

16 ARMED FORCES

Vanuatuan cadets train in Papua New Guinea for a mobile defense force under the direction of the Australian Ministry of Defense.

17 ECONOMY

Agriculture supports about 75% of the population, but the service industry is playing an increasingly important role in the economy. The absence of personal and corporate income taxes have made Vanuatu an offshore financial center.

18 INCOME

In 1992, Vanuatu's gross national product (GNP) was $189 million at current prices, or about $1,230 per person. For the period 1985–92 the average inflation rate was 6.3%, resulting in a real growth rate in per person GNP of 0.5%.

19 INDUSTRY

Industries include fish freezing, meat canning, sawmilling, and the production of furniture, soft drinks, and fabricated aluminum goods. Native crafts include basketry, canoe building, and pottery.

20 LABOR

About 80% of the people are engaged in peasant labor either for survival or production of commercial crop, such as copra. For persons engaged in government, port work, construction, and certain other jobs, the terms of employment, wages, and union membership are set by legislation.

21 AGRICULTURE

While most crops, including yams, taro, manioc, sweet potato, and breadfruit, are raised for local consumption, cash crops like copra (dried coconut meat), cocoa, and coffee have been increasingly important. Production of copra totaled 27,000 tons in 1992.

22 DOMESTICATED ANIMALS

Hogs and fowl form part of the village economy. Vanuatu is ideal for cattle, and large numbers are raised on plantations; in 1992 there were 131,000 head of cattle.

23 FISHING

Fishing is currently focused on domestic consumption. Vanuatu's fish exports totaled only $19,000 in 1990.

24 FORESTRY

Sawlog and veneer log exports were 39,000 cubic meters in 1991.

25 MINING

Vanuatu has few known minerals, although gold deposits have recently been discovered.

26 FOREIGN TRADE

Copra (dried coconut meat) accounted for 37% of total exports in 1990, beef for 23%, cocoa 15%, and timber 6%. Vanuatu's main trade partners are Australia, France, the Netherlands, and New Zealand.

27 ENERGY AND POWER

Electricity production totaled 26 million kilowatt hours in 1991.

28 SOCIAL DEVELOPMENT

The extended family system ensures that no islanders starve, while church missions and the social development section of the Education Ministry concentrate on rural development and youth activities. A provident fund system provides lump-sum benefits for old age, disability, and death. Women are just beginning to emerge from traditional cultural roles.

29 HEALTH

Malaria is the most serious of the country's diseases, which also include leprosy, tuberculosis, filariasis, and venereal diseases. Life expectancy averages 66 years. Medical care is provided by 94 hospitals, health centers, and clinics. The country had 15 physicians in 1991.

30 HOUSING

In urban areas only the emerging middle class can afford government-built housing. Other migrants to the towns buy plots of land and build cheap shacks of corrugated iron and waste materials, principally near Port-Vila and Luganville. The vast majority of villagers still build their own homes from local materials.

31 EDUCATION

The overall literacy rate is 60%. Primary education is available for almost all children except in a few remote tribal areas. In 1992, there were 272 primary schools with 852 teachers and 26,267 students. General secondary schools had 220 teachers and 4,269 students.

32 MEDIA

The weekly government newspaper, *The Vanuatu Weekly,* appears in English, French, and Bislama. In 1991, it had a circulation of 2,000. Radio Vanuatu broadcasts daily in English, French, and Bislama. In 1991 there were 3,240 telephones, 45,000 radios, and 1,000 television sets.

Selected Social Indicators

These statistics are estimates for the period 1988 to 1993. For comparison purposes, data for the United States and averages for low-income countries and high-income countries are also given.

Indicator	Vanuatu	Low-income countries	High-income countries	United States
Per capita gross national product†	$1,230	$380	$23,680	$24,740
Population growth rate	2.7%	1.9%	0.6%	1.0%
Population growth rate in urban areas	3.6%	3.9%	0.8%	1.3%
Population per square kilometer of land	13	78	25	26
Life expectancy in years	66	62	77	76
Number of people per physician	8,080	>3,300	453	419
Number of pupils per teacher (primary school)	31	39	<18	20
Illiteracy rate (15 years and older)	40%	41%	<5%	<3%
Energy consumed per capita (kg of oil equivalent)	280	364	5,203	7,918

† The gross national product (GNP) is the total dollar value of all goods and services produced by a country in a year. The per capita GNP is calculated by dividing a country's GNP by its population. The World Bank defines low-income countries as those with a per capita GNP of $695 or less. High-income countries have a per capita GNP of $8,626 or more. Less than 14% of the world's 5.5 billion people live in high-income countries, while almost 60% live in low-income countries.

> = greater than   < = less than

Sources: World Bank, *Social Indicators of Development 1995*, Baltimore: Johns Hopkins University Press, 1995. Central Intelligence Agency, *World Fact Book*, Washington, D.C.: Government Printing Office, 1994.

33 TOURISM AND RECREATION

The number of tourist arrivals reached 39,784 in 1991; of these, 53% were from Australia and 18% from New Zealand. There were 536 hotel rooms. Popular recreations include marine sightseeing, deep-sea fishing, and sailing.

34 FAMOUS VANUATUANS

Father Walter Hayde Lini (b.1943), ordained as an Anglican priest in 1970, has been the major political force in Vanuatu since independence.

35 BIBLIOGRAPHY

Douglas, Norman. *Vanuatu: A Guide*. Sydney: Pacific Publications, 1987.

Lini, Walter. *Beyond Pandemonium: From the New Hebrides to Vanuatu*. Wellington: Asia Pacific Books, 1981.

MacClancy, Jeremy. *To Kill a Bird with Two Stones: A Short History of Vanuatu*. Port-Vila: Vanuatu Cultural Center, 1981.

VATICAN

The Holy See (State of the Vatican City)
Santa Sede (Stato della Cittá del Vaticano)

FLAG: The flag consists of two vertical stripes, yellow at the hoist and white at the fly. On the white field, in yellow, are the crossed keys of St. Peter, the first pope, surmounted by the papal tiara (triple crown).

ANTHEM: *Pontifical March* (no words).

MONETARY UNIT: In 1930, after a lapse of 60 years, the Vatican resumed issuance of its own coinage—the lira (L)—but it agreed to issue no more than 300 million lire in any year. There are coins of 10, 20, 50, 100, and 500 lire. Italian notes are also in use. The currencies of Italy and the Vatican are mutually convertible. L1 = $0.0006 (or $1 = L1,611.3).

WEIGHTS AND MEASURES: The metric system is in use.

HOLIDAYS: Roman Catholic religious holidays; the coronation day of the reigning pope; days when public consistory is held.

TIME: 1 PM = noon GMT.

1 LOCATION AND SIZE

Located within Rome, Vatican City is the smallest state in Europe and in the world. It is a roughly triangular area of 44 hectares (108.7 acres) lying near the west bank of the Tiber River and to the west of the Castel Sant'Angelo. The Vatican area comprises the following: St. Peter's Square; St. Peter's Basilica, the largest Christian church in the world, to which the square serves as an entrance; an area comprised of administrative buildings and Belvedere Park; the pontifical palaces; and the Vatican Gardens, which occupy about half the acreage.

A number of churches and palaces outside Vatican City itself—including the Lateran Basilica and Palace in the Piazza San Giovanni—are under its jurisdiction, as are the papal villa and its environs at Castel Gandolfo, 24 kilometers (15 miles) southeast of Rome, and an area at Santa Maria di Galeria where a Vatican radio station was established in 1957.

2 TOPOGRAPHY

Vatican City lies on a slight hill not far from the Tiber River.

3 CLIMATE

Winters are mild, and although summer temperatures are high during the day, the evenings are cold. Temperatures in January average 7°C (45°F); in July, 24°C (75°F).

4 PLANTS AND ANIMALS

The gardens are famous for their fine collection of orchids and other exotic plants.

Vatican City, being entirely urban, does not have distinctive native animals.

5 ENVIRONMENT

The environment of Vatican City is similar to that of Rome (*see Italy*).

6 POPULATION

The resident population is estimated at about 1,000. About 600 inhabitants have citizenship, including the pope, cardinals resident in Rome, diplomats of the Vatican, and Swiss Guards.

7 MIGRATION

Does not apply.

8 ETHNIC GROUPS

Although the citizenry of the Vatican includes cardinals and other clergymen from all parts of the world, most of the inhabitants are Italian. The members of the Swiss Guard are a notable exception.

9 LANGUAGES

Italian is the official language of Vatican City, but Latin is the official language of the Holy See (the seat of the pope's jurisdiction as spiritual leader) and is employed for most papal encyclicals (letters) and other formal pronouncements. As the ordinary working language, Italian is in greater use.

10 RELIGIONS

Vatican City is the center of the worldwide organization of the Roman Catholic Church and the seat of the pope. Roman Catholicism is the official religion and the primary business of the state itself.

11 TRANSPORTATION

Vatican City is easily reached by the public transportation system of Rome. It has its own railroad station, with 850 meters (2,789 feet) of track, and a helicopter landing pad.

12 HISTORY

Since the time of St. Peter, regarded by the Catholic Church as the first pope, Rome has been the seat of the popes, except in periods of great turbulence, when they were forced to take refuge elsewhere, most notably in Avignon, France, from 1309 to 1377.

The State of the Vatican City and the places over which the Vatican now exercises jurisdiction are the sole remnants of the States of the Church, or Papal States. At various times, beginning in 755, these states included large areas in Italy and, until the French Revolution, even parts of southern France. Most of the papal domain fell into the hands of King Victor Emmanuel II in 1860 in the course of the unification of Italy. By 1870, Pope Pius IX, supported by a garrison of French troops, retained rule over only the besieged city of Rome and a small territory surrounding it. When the French troops withdrew to take part in the Franco-Prussian War, the walls of Rome were broken through by Italian forces on 20 September, and the city fell. On 2 October, following a referendum, the city was annexed to the kingdom of Italy and made the national capital.

In May 1871, the Italian government passed a Law of Guarantees, which

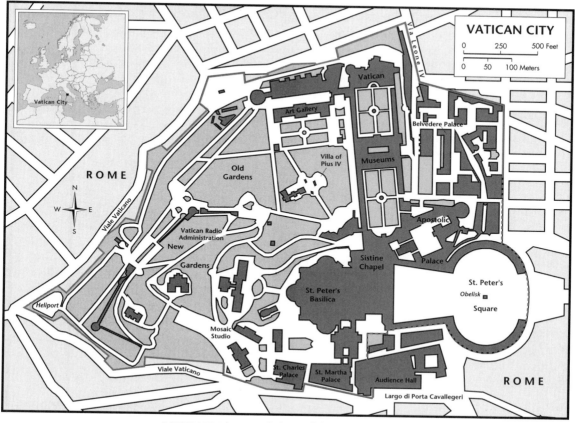

BOUNDARY LENGTHS: Italy, 3.2 kilometers (2 miles).

attempted to define the relationship between the Italian kingdom and the papacy (popes's rule). The enactment declared the safety of the pope, guaranteed him full liberty in his religious functions and in the conduct of diplomatic relations; awarded an annual indemnity (payment to compensate for the income lost when the Papal States were annexed), and provided the pope the right of jurisdiction over the Vatican and the papal palaces. Pius IX refused to accept the law or the money allowance; he and his successors chose to become "prisoners of the Vatican." Until 1919, Roman Catholics were prohibited by the papacy from participating in the Italian government.

The so-called Roman Question was brought to an end by the conclusion on 11 February 1929 of three treaties between the Vatican and Italy. One treaty recognized the full sovereignty of the Vatican and established its territorial extent. Another treaty established the Roman Catholic Church as the state church of

Italy. The remaining treaty awarded the Vatican financial reparations to settle all financial claims against Italy for annexing the Papal States. In 1962–65, the Vatican was the site of the Second Vatican Council, the first worldwide council in almost a century. Convened by Pope John XXIII and continued under Paul VI, the Council resulted in modernization of the Church's role in spiritual and social matters.

On 13 May 1981, Pope John Paul II was wounded in Vatican Square by a Turkish gunman, who is serving a life sentence for this action. The alleged accomplices, three Bulgarians and three Turks, were acquitted of conspiracy in the assassination attempt on 29 March 1986 because of lack of evidence. The treaties of 1929 were superseded in 1984 by a new agreement under which the pope retains temporal authority over Vatican City but Roman Catholicism is no longer Italy's state religion. In December 1993, the Vatican and the Israeli government concluded a mutual recognition agreement.

13 GOVERNMENT

The pope is simultaneously the absolute sovereign of the State of the Vatican City and the head of the Roman Catholic Church throughout the world. Since 1984, the pope has been represented by the cardinal secretary of state in the civil governance of Vatican City. In administering the government of the Vatican, the pope is assisted by the Pontifical Commission for the State of the Vatican City. Religious affairs are governed under the pope's direction by a number of ecclesiastical bodies known collectively as the Roman Curia. Much of the work of the Roman Curia is conducted by offices called sacred congregations, each headed by a cardinal appointed for a five-year period.

Under the Pontifical Commission are the following: a central council (heading various administrative offices); the directorships of museums, technical services, economic services (including the postal and telegraph systems), and medical services; the guard; the Vatican radio system and television center; the Vatican observatory; and the directorship of the villa at Castel Gandolfo, the traditional summer residence of popes.

A pope serves from his election until death. On his decease, the College of Cardinals meets to choose a successor from among themselves. The usual method is to vote on the succession; in this case, the cardinal who receives two-thirds plus one of the votes of those present is declared elected. As of 15 August 1987, the members of the College of Cardinals numbered 140, of whom 36 were over 80 years old.

14 POLITICAL PARTIES

Does not apply.

15 JUDICIAL SYSTEM

A tribunal rules on ordinary legal matters occurring within Vatican territory. Criminal cases are tried in Italian courts. There are three tribunals at the Vatican for religious cases. The Apostolic Penitentiary determines questions of penance and absolution from sin. The Roman Rota deals principally with marital issues but is also competent to handle appeals from any

Photo credit: Corel Corporation.

The detailed front of St. Peter's Church in the Vatican City.

decisions of lower ecclesiastical courts. In exceptional cases, the Supreme Tribunal of the Apostolic Signature hears appeals from the Rota.

16 ARMED FORCES

The papal patrol force now consists only of the Swiss Guard, who walk their posts in picturesque striped uniforms supposedly designed by the artist Michelangelo (1475–1564). The force was founded in 1506 and is recruited from several Roman Catholic cantons of Switzerland. It now numbers approximately 100 members. There is also a civilian security force, which protects Vatican personnel and property and the art treasures owned by the Church.

17 ECONOMY

The Vatican, being essentially an administrative center, is dependent for its support on the receipt of charitable contributions, the fees charged those able to pay for the services of the congregations and other ecclesiastical bodies, and interest on investments. Funds are also raised from the sale of stamps, religious literature, and mementos, and from museum admissions.

18 INCOME

Income in 1992 was estimated at $92 million.

19 INDUSTRY

A studio in the Vatican produces mosaic work, and a sewing establishment produces uniforms. There is a large printing plant, the Vatican Polyglot Press.

20 LABOR

The labor force consists mainly of priests, who serve as consultants and counselors; about 3,000 laborers, who live outside the Vatican; the guards; the nuns, who do administrative work as well as the cooking, cleaning, laundering, and tapestry repair; and the cardinals, archbishops, bishops, and other higher dignitaries. Some ecclesiastical (church) officials live outside Vatican City and commute from the secular (not religious) city. The Association of Vatican Lay Workers, a trade union, has 1,800 members.

21 AGRICULTURE

Does not apply.

22 DOMESTICATED ANIMALS

Does not apply.

23 FISHING

Does not apply.

24 FORESTRY

Does not apply.

25 MINING

Does not apply.

26 FOREIGN TRADE

Does not apply.

27 ENERGY AND POWER

Electric power is supplied by Italy, but the Vatican's generating plant had a capacity of 5,000 kilowatts in 1990.

28 SOCIAL DEVELOPMENT

Celibacy (abstention from sexual intercourse) is required of all Roman Catholic clergy, except permanent deacons. The Church upholds the concept of family planning through traditional methods, such as abstinence, but resolutely opposes such "artificial methods" as contraceptive pills and devices, as well as abortion and sterilization. Five important papal encyclicals (letters)—*Rerum Novarum* (1870), *Quadragesimo Anno* (1931), *Mater et Magistra* (1961), *Pacem in Terris* (1963), and *Laborem Exercens* (1981)—have enunciated the Church position on matters of workers' rights and social and international justice.

29 HEALTH

The health services directorate, under the Pontifical Commission for the Vatican City State, is responsible for health matters.

30 HOUSING

Information is not available.

31 EDUCATION

The Vatican is a major center for higher Roman Catholic education, especially of the clergy being trained for important positions. Adult literacy is 100%. About

65 papal educational institutions are scattered throughout Rome; some of the more important (all prefixed by the word "Pontifical") are the Gregorian University, the Biblical Institute, the Institute of Oriental Studies, the Lateran Athenaeum, the Institute of Christian Archaeology, and the Institute of Sacred Music. There were a total of 11,681 students in 1991 with 1,584 teaching staff in all higher level institutions.

32 MEDIA

The state maintains its own telegraph and postal facilities and has a 2,000-line automatic telephone exchange. Radio Vatican operates three AM and four FM stations. Programs in 34 languages are broadcast regularly. The Vatican Television Center, founded in 1983, produces and distributes religious programs.

Vatican City is an important center for publishing. A semiofficial newspaper of wide fame, *L'Osservatore Romano,* is published daily, with an estimated 1990 circulation of 70,000 copies. The Vatican has also publishes *L'Osservatore della Domenica,* an illustrated weekly, and the *Acta Apostolicae Sedis (Record of the Apostolic See)* on a monthly basis, as well as papal encyclicals (letters) and other official papers. An annual, the *Annuario Pontificio,* is issued as a record of the Vatican and the Roman Catholic hierarchy. The international Religious Press Service distributes news of missionary activity. In 1990, 47 periodicals were published, with a total circulation of 57,000. The book publishers for the Vatican are the Vatican Editions, the Vatican Apostolic Library, and the Vatican Polyglot Press (*Tipografia Poliglotta Vaticana*). In 1991, there were 196 titles published.

33 TOURISM AND RECREATION

The Vatican is regularly visited by tourists in Rome, as well as by pilgrims attracted by the jubilees (festivals) proclaimed by the pope every 25 years and by other special occasions. While there are no public accommodations in the Vatican, special inexpensive facilities are often arranged in Rome for pilgrims. No passport or identification is needed ordinarily for admission to the public parts of the Vatican.

34 FAMOUS POPES

Among those who greatly increased the secular (non-religious) power of the papacy were St. Gregory I (the Great, 540?–604), pope from 590 to 604, who also was influential in matters of doctrine and missionary work; St. Gregory VII (Hildebrand, 1020?–1085), pope from 1073 to 1085, who engaged in conflict with Holy Roman Emperor Henry IV, who was forced to do public penance at the village of Canossa, but who later drove the pope out of Rome; and Alexander VI (Rodrigo Lanzol y Borja, b. Spain, 1431?–1503), pope from 1492 to 1503, who also divided colonial territories in the New World between Spain and Portugal.

The most significant 19th-century pope was Pius IX (Giovanni Maria Mastai-Ferretti, 1792–1878), pope from 1846 to 1878, who lost the Papal States to the kingdom of Italy and convened the First

Vatican Council (1869–70). John XXIII (Angelo Giuseppe Roncalli, 1881–1963), pope from 1958 to 1963, made history by convening the Second Vatican Council (1962–65) and by strongly defining the position of the Church on problems of labor and social progress (in his encyclical *Mater et Magistra* of June 1961). His greatest achievement was generally considered to be his eighth encyclical, *Pacem in Terris*, a profound plea for peace, in which he hailed the United Nations as a defender of human rights.

Paul VI (Giovanni Battista Montini, 1897–1978), pope from 1963 to 1978, continued Pope John's effort to attain unity of the Christian world. On 4 October 1965, he addressed the United Nations General Assembly, appealing for world peace and international cooperation. John Paul II (Karol Wojtyla, b.1920), was elevated to the papacy on 16 October 1978. This former archbishop of Krakow was not only the first Polish pope but also the first non-Italian pope since the Renaissance. Despite suffering severe wounds in a 1981 assassination attempt, John Paul II has continued to travel widely. To the dismay of Jewish and other leaders, John Paul II granted Austrian President Kurt Waldheim (b.1918) an audience in June 1987, despite accusations that Waldheim had taken part in war crimes during World War II when he was an officer in the German army.

35 BIBLIOGRAPHY

Bull, George. *Inside the Vatican*. New York: St. Martin's, 1983.

Martin, Malachi. *Vatican*. New York: Harper & Row, 1986.

McDowell, Bart. *Inside the Vatican*. Washington, D.C.: National Geographic Society, 1991.

Packard, Jerrold M. *Peter's Kingdom: Inside the Papal City*. New York: Scribner, 1985.

Wynn, Wilton. *Keepers of the Keys*. New York: Random House, 1988.

VENEZUELA

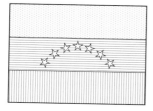

Republic of Venezuela
República de Venezuela

CAPITAL: Caracas.

FLAG: The national flag, adopted in 1930, is a tricolor of yellow, blue, and red horizontal stripes. An arc of seven white stars on the blue stripe represents the seven original states.

ANTHEM: *Himno Nacional,* beginning "Gloria al bravo pueblo" ("Glory to the brave people").

MONETARY UNIT: The bolívar (B) is a paper currency of 100 céntimos. There are coins of 5, 25, and 50 céntimos and 1, 2, and 5 bolívars, and notes of 5, 10, 20, 50, 100, 500, and 1,000 bolívars. B1 = $0.0087 (or $1 = B114.721).

WEIGHTS AND MEASURES: The metric system is the legal standard.

HOLIDAYS: New Year's Day, 1 January; Declaration of Independence and Day of the Indian, 19 April; Labor Day, 1 May; Army Day and Anniversary of the Battle of Carabobo, 24 June; Independence Day, 5 July; Bolívar's Birthday, 24 July; Civil Servants Day, 4 September; Columbus Day, 12 October; Christmas, 25 December; New Year's Eve, 31 December. Movable holidays are Carnival (Monday and Tuesday before Ash Wednesday), Holy Thursday, Good Friday, and Holy Saturday. Numerous other bank holidays and local festivals are observed.

TIME: 8 AM = noon GMT.

1 LOCATION AND SIZE

Venezuela, located on the northern coast of South America, covers an area of 912,050 square kilometers (352,144 square miles), slightly more than twice the size of the state of California. It has a total boundary length of 7,609 kilometers (4,729 miles). There are 72 offshore islands. Venezuela's capital city, Caracas, is located in the northern part of the country on the Caribbean Sea coast.

2 TOPOGRAPHY

Venezuela has four principal geographical divisions. In the north emerges a low extension of the Andes mountain chain; to the west lies the hot basin of Lake Maracaibo (Lago Maracaibo); to the southeast spread the great plains (*llanos*) and forests; and south of the Orinoco River lie the unoccupied and largely unexplored Guiana Highlands, accounting for about half the country's total area. The Orinoco River, which is more than 2,900 kilometers (1,800 miles) long, drains four-fifths of Venezuela. There are more than 1,000 other rivers.

Outstanding geographical features include Angel Falls (979 meters/3,212 feet high) in the Guiana Highlands of southeastern Venezuela, the highest waterfall in the world, and Bolívar Peak, the highest

Photo credit: Mary A. Dempsey

Beach at Puerto La Cruz, Venezuela.

parched. The temperate and cold regions are located above elevations of 1,830 meters (6,000 feet). There is perpetual snow on several peaks of the mountain chain, Cordillera de Mérida.

4 PLANTS AND ANIMALS

The natural vegetation of the tropical zone varies from the rainforest regions of the lower Lake Maracaibo Basin to the grasslands of the llanos. The subtropical zone was originally almost covered by a luxuriant forest and is now the nation's principal agricultural region. In the temperate region, wild vegetation is sparse and scrubby. In the higher altitudes, from about 2,740 to 4,880 meters (9,000 to 16,000 feet), vegetation becomes even thinner. Above 3,050 meters (10,000 feet), the only vegetation seen is the espeletia, similar to the century plant, which grows to a height of 1.8–2.1 meters (6–7 feet).

The wild animals of Venezuela are abundant because of their relative isolation from human disturbance. The forests are populated with tapirs, sloths, anteaters, and a variety of monkeys. In the mountains are puma, margay, vampire bats, and deer. Semiwild horses, donkeys, and cattle are found in the plains. The forests are rich in tropical birds such as the cacique, crested coquette, heron, umbrella bird, manakin, cock-of-the-rock, parrot, macaw, and aigrette. Aquatic fowl include the pelican, heron, flamingo, and a muscovy duck weighing up to 9.1 kilograms (20 pounds). More than 32 species of eagles are found in Venezuela. There are numerous reptiles, including the rattlesnake, coral snake, bushmaster, anaconda,

peak in Venezuela (5,007 meters/16,427 feet).

3 CLIMATE

Although Venezuela lies entirely within the torrid zone, generally there are four climatic regions, based mainly on altitude. In the tropical region, mean annual temperatures range from 24° to 35°C (75° to 95°F). In the subtropical region, where Caracas is situated, the means range from 10° to 25°C (50° to 77°F). During the wet season (May to October), the llanos and forest areas are swampy, green, and lush. Upon the advent of the dry season, the same areas become dry, brown, and

LOCATION: 0°35′ to 12°11′N; 60°10′ to 73°25′W. **BOUNDARY LENGTHS:** Total coastline, 2,816 kilometers (1,750 miles); Guyana, 743 kilometers (462 miles); Brazil, 2,000 kilometers (1,243 miles); Colombia, 2,050 kilometers (1,274 miles). **TERRITORIAL SEA LIMIT:** 12 miles.

and boa. Crocodiles are found in the lowland rivers. Fish, shellfish, tortoises, and sand tortoises are also plentiful.

5 ENVIRONMENT

Power plants, industry, and transportation vehicles contribute to air pollution; Venezuela's waterways have been polluted by untreated industrial wastes and by mining activity. In the 1980s, the nation lost 1,000 square miles of forest land per year. In the Andes mountain area, Venezuela loses up to 300 tons of soil per hectare (120 tons per acre) due to land erosion by rivers. Pressing environmental problems led the government in 1976 to establish the Ministry of Environment and Renewable Natural Resources. Measures designed to prevent forest depletion include suspension of logging permits and a large-scale afforestation program.

In 1994, 19 of the nation's mammal species and 34 bird species were endangered, as well as 106 plant types. As of 1987, endangered species in Venezuela included the tundra peregrine falcon, giant otter, and five species of turtle.

6 POPULATION

The last census, taken in 1990, placed the total population of Venezuela at 18,105,265. A population of 23,622,000 was projected for the year 2000. Venezuela is one of the least densely populated countries in the Western Hemisphere with an estimated population density of 22 persons per square kilometer (56 per square mile). In 1990, 84.1% of the population was urban. In 1990 Caracas, the capital, had a population of 1,822,465.

7 MIGRATION

In the decades immediately before and after World War II (1939–45), nearly 500,000 Europeans—mostly from Italy, Spain, and Portugal—came to Venezuela. By 1990, however, only 5.7% of the resident population was of foreign birth. In 1989 there were 18,893 immigrants and 9,643 emigrants. An estimated 300,000 illegal immigrants, most of them Colombians, were living in Venezuela in 1985. Internal migration in the 1980s was chiefly eastward from the far northwest.

8 ETHNIC GROUPS

The original inhabitants of Venezuela were Amerindians, mainly Caribs and Arawaks. The bulk (about 68%) of the present population is mestizo (mixed race); an estimated 21% is unmixed white, 8–10% black, and 2% Amerindian.

9 LANGUAGES

The official language is Spanish, with marked regional variations.

10 RELIGIONS

In 1993, an estimated 92.1% of the population was Roman Catholic. In 1987, there were about 350,000 Protestants, 200,000 tribal religionists, 122,000 Afro-American spiritists, and 20,000 Jews.

11 TRANSPORTATION

The most important mode of domestic cargo and passenger transport is shipping over the country's more than 16,000 kilometers (9,900 miles) of navigable inland waterways. In 1991, the merchant fleet had 62 vessels of over 1,000 gross tons, for a total of 824,000 gross registered tons. Puerto Cabello handles the most cargo, and Maracaibo is the main port for oil shipments.

Highway and railroad construction is both costly and dangerous because of the rough mountainous terrain in the areas of dense population. Nevertheless, the government has undertaken massive highway construction projects throughout the country. By 1991, Venezuela had 22,780 kilometers (14,155 miles) of paved highway. In 1992 there were 1,532,572 passenger cars and 449,135 commercial vehicles in Venezuela.

Venezuela's two railroads carry mostly freight. There were 542 kilometers (337 miles) of track in 1991. Much of the equipment is out of date, and the linking of lines is difficult because of the different gauges in use. In the early 1980s, the government planned to build a 3,900-kilometer (2,420-mile) railroad network by the end of the decade; however, the financial crisis that began in 1983 has scaled the program down to 2,000 kilometers (1,200 miles) over 20 years.

Cities and towns of the remote regions are linked principally by air transportation. Venezuela has three main airlines, the government-owned Aerovías Venezolanas S.A. (AVENSA), Línea Aeropostal Venezolana (LAV), and Venezolana Internacional de Aviación, S.A. (VIASA). Of the 61 commercial airports 7 are international. The government has expanded Simón Bolívar International Airport at Maiquetía, near Caracas, to accommodate heavy jet traffic.

12 HISTORY

Venezuela received its name, meaning "Little Venice," from Alonso de Ojeda, who sailed into the Gulf of Venezuela (Golfo de Venezuela) in August 1499 and was reminded of the Italian city by the native huts built on stilts over the water. Except for a brief period of control by German commercial interests, Venezuela was a colonial territory of Spain.

Under the Spanish, eastern Venezuela was governed under the audiencia (region

Photo credit: Anne Kalosh

Venezuelans pause for a snack at a shrine on a trail in the Andes.

under a royal court) of Santo Domingo, and the western and southern regions became a captaincy-general under the viceroyalty of Peru. Settlement of the colony was hampered by constant wars with the Amerindians, which did not stop until after a smallpox epidemic in 1580. In 1717, the western and southern provinces were incorporated into the viceroyalty of New Granada, and in 1783, the area of present-day Venezuela became a captaincy-general of Caracas.

Beginning in 1811, Venezuela struggled for independence from Spain for 10 years, first under Francisco de Miranda, then led by Simón Bolívar. The end of the Venezuelan war of independence came with Bolívar's victory in June 1821. Under Bolívar's leadership, Gran Colombia (Greater Colombia) was formed from Colombia, Ecuador, and Venezuela, with Bolívar as its president and military dictator.

In 1830, Venezuela seceded from Gran Colombia. A period of civil wars lasted from 1846 to 1870, when Antonio Guzmán Blanco assumed power. After this, Venezuela was ruled by dictatorships for nearly a century. When Cipriano Castro, who ruled from 1899 to 1908, refused to repay Venezuela's international loans, Germany, Great Britain, and Italy sent gunboats to blockade the Venezuelan coast. During the dictatorship of Juan Vicente Gómez (1908–35), agriculture was developed and oil was discovered, making Venezuela one of the richest countries in Latin America. Oil concessions attracted American, British, and Dutch companies, initiating an era of oil wealth that continues today.

After the death of Gómez, Venezuela began to move toward democracy. The first free election for president in Venezuelan history was held in 1947, and Rómulo Gallegos, a distinguished novelist and candidate of Democratic Action (Acción Democrática—AD), was elected overwhelmingly. However, Gallegos was replaced by a military junta, followed by another dictatorship in the 1950s. Venezuela took its last steps toward full democracy in 1958, when Rómulo Betancourt was chosen president. Venezuela has had fair and free elections ever since.

The Betancourt government (1959–64) instituted modest financial and agricultural reforms, built schools, and eliminated illiteracy. In spite of attempts by the military to return to power, and the activities of pro-Castro guerrillas, the AD was reelected in December 1964, when Raúl Leoni won the presidency over five other candidates. In 1968, Venezuela passed another test of democracy by transferring power peacefully from AD to the opposition Social Christian Party.

In 1979, Venezuela received a rude awakening when demand for oil dropped, threatening the foundations of its economic and political systems. The crisis climaxed with the devaluation of the national currency, the bolívar, which dropped to one-third of its previous value against the dollar. Venezuelan consumers responded angrily, and the early 1980s were years of unrest. In the elections of December 1983, the AD returned to power behind presidential candidate Jaime Lusinchi.

While the economy floundered through the 1980s, the government maintained public confidence by stressing a "social pact" with guarantees of housing, education, and public health. Some progress has been made in boosting non-oil exports, particularly in agriculture and mining. The 1988 elections brought back Carlos Andrés Pérez, who had been elected president 15 years earlier. When Pérez removed government subsidies on a number of consumer goods, including gasoline, prices rose and Caracas was rocked by rioting on a scale not seen since 1958. The military was called in to quell the disturbances, but when the trouble finally died down, thousands had been killed or injured.

In 1992 Venezuela was shocked by two military coup attempts, and Pérez was suspended from office on embezzlement and theft allegations. In the regularly scheduled presidential elections of December 1993, Venezuelans chose former president Rafael Caldera, who ran under a coalition of four parties. Even though Venezuela remained one of the wealthiest countries in Latin America, its government is increasingly unstable.

13 GOVERNMENT

Venezuela is a republic governed under the constitution of 23 January 1961, which stresses social, economic, and political rights. The president is elected by direct popular vote for a five-year term. Presidential duties include the selection and removal of cabinet ministers and all other administrative officers and employees of the national government, as well as the appointment of state governors.

The president is commander-in-chief of the armed forces, directs foreign affairs, and may make and ratify international treaties, conventions, and agreements. He may veto legislation, but a two-thirds majority of Congress can override it. There is no vice-president, and if the president cannot complete a term of office, the Congress, meeting in joint session, must select a new president by secret vote.

The Congress has two chambers, a 47-member Senate and 200-seat Chamber of Deputies. Both houses are elected concurrently with the president for five-year terms. A bill may be introduced in either house but must be passed by both in order to become law. There is compulsory adult voting at age 18.

Venezuela is divided into 21 states, 1 federal territory, the Federal District, and 72 offshore islands. The states are subdivided into 156 districts and 613 municipalities.

14 POLITICAL PARTIES

Since 1958, the dominant force in Venezuelan politics has been the Democratic Action Party (Acción Democrática—AD), formed from the nationalist and democratic-socialist faction of the socialist movement. The most recent development from the left has been the emergence of the Movement for Socialism (Movimiento al Socialismo—MAS), which took 10% of the vote for the Chamber of Deputies in 1988.

The right has been characterized by small parties, some of which have been able to form coalitions with larger parties to achieve some success within the system. COPEI is a center-right Christian Democratic party that has succeeded as an opposition party to the AD, occasionally taking advantage of splits in the AD's governing coalition or within the AD itself.

Agreements between AD and COPEI in 1970 and 1973 called for cooperation in appointive posts, so that the competition has been controlled. AD and COPEI have dominated the system since, although the recent election of Caldera as the candidate of a four-party coalition suggests a movement away from the two-party arrangement.

15 JUDICIAL SYSTEM

The Supreme Court, which organizes and directs the other courts and tribunals of the republic, is the nation's highest tribunal, and there is no appeal of its decisions. It can declare a law, or any part of a law or any regulation or act of the president unconstitutional. The Court determines whether there are grounds for the trial of the president, a member of Congress, members of the Court itself, or certain executive officials.

The lower branches of the judiciary include courts of appeal and direct courts, whose judges and magistrates are appointed by the Supreme Court. Each state has its own supreme court, superior court, district courts, and municipal courts. The territories have civil and military judges. The jury system is not used.

16 ARMED FORCES

Venezuela's armed forces are professional and well equipped. In principle, all male Venezuelans 18 years of age are required to serve two years (or 30 months in the navy) and then to remain in the reserve until the age of 45. In practice, however, many males, including workers in essential occupations, students, and heads of households, are exempted from service.

Total armed strength in 1993 was 75,000, including 23,000 volunteers in the Fuerzas Armados de Cooperacion, an internal security force. The army had 34,000 regulars, including 6 infantry divi-

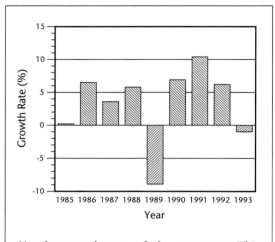

Yearly growth rate of the economy. This economic indicator tells by what percent the economy has increased or decreased when compared with the previous year.

sions and 12 specialized brigades, and 2,000 airmen. The navy had 11,000 members, including 6,000 marines; naval strength included 2 submarines and 6 frigates. The air force had 7,000 personnel, 102 combat aircraft, and 30 armed helicopters. Defense expenditures in 1991 were $1.95 billion.

17 ECONOMY

For over 40 years the economy has been completely dominated by the petroleum industry; in the mid-1980s, oil exports accounted for 90% of all export value. Weakening world oil prices contributed to economic stagnation in the 1980s, when Venezuela had difficulty meeting its payments on short-term loans accumulated by state-owned enterprises.

After severe adjustments during 1989 and 1990, the main economic indicators improved considerably in 1991 and 1992. Growth was led by the oil industry, due mainly to the Persian Gulf War. Inflation remained stubbornly high at 38% in 1993. The healthiest areas of the economy are trade, transportation, communications, manufacturing, and construction.

18 INCOME

In 1992, Venezuela's gross national product (GNP) was $58,901 million at current prices, or approximately $2,840 per person. For the period 1985–92 the average inflation rate was 35.8%, resulting in a real growth rate in per person GNP of 1.1%.

19 INDUSTRY

Although much of Venezuela's petroleum is exported in crude form, petroleum refining is a major industry. Petroleum products amounted to 327.7 million barrels in 1985. The steel industry produced 3 million tons of steel in 1985. Other industries include shipbuilding, automobile production (149,902 vehicles in 1986), and fertilizer manufacture.

Valencia is a major new industrial center. A second major industrial development scheme has made Ciudad Guayana the hub of a vast industrial area with a 160-kilometers (100-miles) radius. There is a steel mill with a yearly capacity of 750,000 tons, and a bauxite-processing plant. The manufacturing sector suffered from a recession in 1989, but was recovering at a steady rate during the next four years. It grew at more than 10% in 1992.

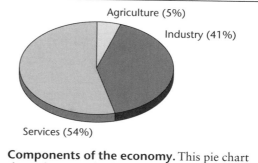

Components of the economy. This pie chart shows how much of the country's economy is devoted to agriculture (includes forestry, hunting, and fishing), industry, or services.

20 LABOR

Venezuela's economically active population in 1991 was 7,417,929. The distribution of employment among major economic areas was as follows: services, 33.5%; trade, restaurants, and hotels, 20.9%; manufacturing, 16.3%; agriculture, 11.3%; construction, 9.2%; transportation and communications, 5.7%; mining and quarrying, 1%; and other areas, 2.1%. The unemployment rate was 9.5% at the end of 1991. In 1992, about 25% of the labor force was unionized.

The constitution provides for a minimum wage, the right to strike, and the right of labor to organize into unions. Labor laws include provisions for an 8-hour day, a paid vacation of at least 15 workdays a year, compulsory profit sharing, severance pay, death and disability payments, medical services, and social security.

Photo credit: Anne Kalosh

Picking coffee beans at Mt.Mochima national Park near Pto, La Cruz, Venezuela.

21 AGRICULTURE

Venezuela does not have the rich soil of many other Latin American countries. In 1992, 3,905,000 hectares (9,649,000 acres), or 4.4% of the total land area, were used for temporary or permanent crops. The most highly developed agricultural region is a lake basin west of Caracas and inland from Puerto Cabello. The principal crop of this area is coffee.

The main field crops are sugarcane, rice, corn, and sorghum; and the chief fruits are bananas, plantains, oranges, coconuts, and mangoes. The most important agricultural items for industrial use are cotton, tobacco, and sisal. Two varieties of tobacco grow in Venezuela, black and Virginia blond; the latter is used for the most part to make certain popular brands of American cigarettes under license. Sisal is grown and widely used to make cordage and bags for sacking grains and coffee. Thin strings of the fiber are also employed in hammocks, household bags, doormats, hats, and sandals.

Agricultural production in 1992 (in thousands of tons) included sugarcane, 6,700; bananas, 1,215; corn, 904; rice, 595; sorghum, 528; plantains, 510; oranges, 440; potatoes, 215; cotton, 24; tobacco, 15; and sisal, 9.

22 DOMESTICATED ANIMALS

Since colonial days, cattle raising has been the dominant livestock industry in Venezuela. Chiefly *criollos*, or Spanish longhorns, the cattle are raised on unfenced ranges. Venezuela's livestock population in 1992 included 1,727,000 hogs, 1,530,000 goats, and 525,000 sheep and significant herds of cattle. Egg production in 1992 was 122,265 tons, and the milk output fell to 1,485,000 tons. Beef production increased from 147,000 tons in 1963 to 361,000 tons in 1992. In the same year, pork production was 102,000 tons; goat meat, 7,000 tons; mutton, 2,000 tons; and poultry, 415,000 tons.

23 FISHING

With its 2,816 kilometers (1,750 miles) of open coast, Venezuela has vast fishing potential. Fish and fish products currently play a relatively minor role in Venezuela's international trade, but fish are extremely important domestically. Venezuela has the highest per person fish consumption in Latin America, about three times that of the United States. Some of the main fishing areas are La Guaira, and the Isla de Margarita–Carúpano area. The total catch in 1991 was 352,835 tons, up from 284,235 tons in 1986.

24 FORESTRY

Partly because of the remoteness of forest areas, exploitation of Venezuela's high-quality wood is underdeveloped. Forest land is misused by small farmers, who clear land for farming by burning trees without replacing them. The greatest concentration of forests lies south of the Orinoco. Cedar and mahogany are the principal trees cut; rubber, dividivi, mangrove bark, tonka beans, oil-bearing palm nuts, and medicinal plants are also produced. Roundwood output was about 1.3 million cubic meters in 1991.

25 MINING

Principal mineral commodities are aluminum, cement, diamonds, ferroalloys, gold, and iron ore. The most important metal mined in Venezuela is iron. Iron ore production was an estimated 21.2 million tons in 1991. Gold, the first metal found in Venezuela, reached its production peak in 1890. Production was 7,700 kilograms in 1990, but fell by 43% to 4,215 kilograms in 1991. In the same year, diamond production fell to an estimated 213,557 carats. At 1,992,448 tons, bauxite production reached a new high in 1991.

Other minerals extracted are sulfur, gypsum, limestone, salt (produced as a government monopoly), granite, clay, and phosphate rock. Minerals known to exist but not yet exploited are manganese (with deposits estimated at several million tons), mercury, nickel, magnesite, cobalt, mica, cyanite, and radioactive materials.

26 FOREIGN TRADE

Imports have been increasing in recent years. Total imports amounted to $13.0 billion in 1993. Venezuela's principal imports were machinery and transport equipment, chemicals, construction material, and agricultural products. The country's major suppliers included the United States (47.7%), Germany (6.1%), Italy (4.7%), Brazil (4.1%) and other countries (29.6%).

Merchandise exports totaled $14.4 billion in 1993, mainly composed of petroleum and petroleum products, aluminum, steel, iron ore, coal, gold, coffee, and cocoa.

After several years of negotiations, the Group of Three (Colombia, Mexico, and Venezuela) signed a free-trade agreement. The agreement went into effect on 1 January 1995 and committed the countries to lift most trade restrictions over a 10-year period.

27 ENERGY AND POWER

With vast petroleum deposits, extensive waterways, and an abundance of natural gas, Venezuela possesses great electric power potential. In 1991, total electrical power generation was an estimated

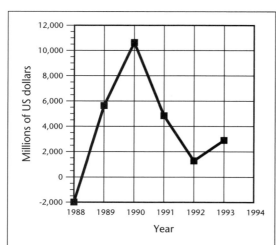

Yearly balance of trade measured in millions of US dollars. The balance of trade is the difference between what a country sells to other countries (its exports) and what it buys (its imports). If a country imports more than it exports, it has a negative balance of trade (a trade deficit). If exports exceed imports there is a positive balance of trade (a trade surplus).

57,150 million kilowatt hours. Venezuela was the world's sixth-largest oil producer in 1992, when proven oil reserves were estimated at 63 billion barrels. Petroleum production rose to an estimated 2,500,000 barrels per day in 1993. The output of natural gas was an estimated 25,700 million cubic meters in 1992. Proven reserves totaled 3.6 trillion cubic meters in 1992.

28 SOCIAL DEVELOPMENT

The social security system covers medical care, maternity benefits, disability, retirement and survivors' pensions, burial costs, and a marriage bonus. In July 1982, a reform of the Venezuelan civil code extended women's rights. Women comprise roughly half the student body of most universities, and have advanced in many professions, but women are still underrepresented in political and economic life.

29 HEALTH

Despite strenuous government efforts in the field of public health, Venezuela does not have enough physicians for its booming population. In 1992 there were 639 people per physician, with a nurse-to-doctor ratio of 0.5. Total health care expenditures were $1,747 million in 1990.

Great strides have been made in improving public health conditions. The infant mortality rate, 50.2 per 1,000 live births in 1971, fell to 20 in 1992. Life expectancy averages 72 years. Venezuela is virtually free of malaria, typhoid, and yellow fever. To maintain this status, the Department of Health and Social Welfare continues its drainage and mosquito control programs. It also builds aqueducts and sewers in towns of fewer than 5,000 persons. In 1991, 89% of the population had access to safe water, and 92% had adequate sanitation.

30 HOUSING

During 1977–81, the public sector built 167,325 housing units, and private business built 71,922. In 1981, the government introduced new low-interest housing loans, but that policy did not prevent a housing slump that persisted from 1982 through 1986 as a result of the general recession; housing units built by the public sector in 1986 totaled 91,666. The

Selected Social Indicators

These statistics are estimates for the period 1988 to 1993. For comparison purposes, data for the United States and averages for low-income countries and high-income countries are also given.

Indicator	Venezuela	Low-income countries	High-income countries	United States
Per capita gross national product†	**$2,840**	$380	$23,680	$24,740
Population growth rate	**2.5%**	1.9%	0.6%	1.0%
Population growth rate in urban areas	**3.0%**	3.9%	0.8%	1.3%
Population per square kilometer of land	**22**	78	25	26
Life expectancy in years	**72**	62	77	76
Number of people per physician	**639**	>3,300	453	419
Number of pupils per teacher (primary school)	**23**	39	<18	20
Illiteracy rate (15 years and older)	**7%**	41%	<5%	<3%
Energy consumed per capita (kg of oil equivalent)	**2,369**	364	5,203	7,918

† The gross national product (GNP) is the total dollar value of all goods and services produced by a country in a year. The per capita GNP is calculated by dividing a country's GNP by its population. The World Bank defines low-income countries as those with a per capita GNP of $695 or less. High-income countries have a per capita GNP of $8,626 or more. Less than 14% of the world's 5.5 billion people live in high-income countries, while almost 60% live in low-income countries.

> = greater than   < = less than

Sources: World Bank, *Social Indicators of Development 1995,* Baltimore: Johns Hopkins University Press, 1995. Central Intelligence Agency, *World Fact Book,* Washington, D.C.: Government Printing Office, 1994.

total number of housing units in 1992 was 3,384,000.

31 EDUCATION

Venezuela has made considerable progress in education in recent years. The rate of literacy is approximately 93%. Public education from kindergarten through university is free, and education is compulsory for children aged 7 through 13. Approximately 20% of the national budget is assigned to education.

After nine years of elementary school, children attend two to three years of secondary school. In 1990–1991, there were 4,052,947 students enrolled in elementary schools; 281,419 in secondary schools; and 550,030 in colleges and universities.

There are 17 universities, both national and private, including the University of Venezuela, Los Andes University, Simón Bolívar University, and the Open University. Over 74 institutes of higher learning, colleges, and polytechnic institutes exist where students pursue at least 180 different fields or professions.

32 MEDIA

Venezuela is covered by a network of telephone, telegraph, and radiotelephone services and is also served by international cable and radiotelephone systems. In 1991 there were 1,749,325 telephones in use. There were 204 radio stations in 1991 and 63 television stations, and an estimated 8,820,000 radios and 3,200,000 television sets were in use.

Leading Venezuelan newspapers (all published in Caracas) with their 1991 circulations include *Diario Ultimas Noticias* (285,000), *Meridiano* (200,000), *El Nacional* (155,000), *El Mundo* (150,000), *Diario 2001* (130,000), and *El Universal* (125,000).

33 TOURISM AND RECREATION

Since the early 1970s, Venezuela has sought foreign investors for the construction, rehabilitation, and management of top-ranking hotels. The number of foreign visitors in 1991 was an estimated 598,328. Of these, 335,016 came from the Americas and 254,885 from Europe. There were 68,063 hotel rooms with a 69.6% occupancy rate, and tourism receipts totaled $365 million.

Tourist attractions include Angel Falls, the world's highest waterfall; the many memorials to Simón Bolívar; numerous beach resorts; and the duty-free shopping and superb water sports facilities of the Isla de Margarita. Cultural life in the national capital offers, among other attractions, the Ballet Nuevo Mundo de Caracas. The most popular sports are baseball, soccer (called football), bullfight-ing, cockfighting, horse racing, and water-related activities.

34 FAMOUS VENEZUELANS

No one in Venezuelan history is as well known, both nationally and internationally, as the great "Liberator" of the South American revolution, Simón Bolívar (1783–1830), renowned for his military genius and his ability to lead and to inspire. Simón Rodríguez (1771–1854), called the "American Rousseau," was the leading liberal scholar of the prerevolutionary period.

Teresa Carreño (1853–1917) won world fame as a concert pianist. The first painter of note in Venezuela was Juan Llovera (1785–1840). Important Venezuelan painters of the 19th century were Martín Tovar y Tovar (1828–1902) and Arturo Michelena (1863–98).

The outstanding pioneer of Venezuelan science was José María Vargas (1786–1854).

35 BIBLIOGRAPHY

Fox, Geoffrey. *The Land and People of Venezuela.* New York: HarperCollins, 1991.

George, Uwe. "Venezuela's Islands in Time." *National Geographic,* May 1989, 526–562.

Haggerty, Richard A., ed. *Venezuela: A Country Study.* 4th ed. Washington, D.C.: Library of Congress, 1993.

Morrison, M. *Venezuela.* Chicago: Children's Press, 1989.

Nagel, Rob, and Anne Commire. "Simon Bolivar." In *World Leaders, People Who Shaped the World.* Volume III: North and South America. Detroit: U*X*L, 1994.

Venezuela in Pictures. Minneapolis: Lerner, 1987.

Waddell, D. A. G. *Venezuela.* Oxford, England, and Santa Barbara, Calif.: Clio Press, 1990.

VIET NAM

Socialist Republic of Viet Nam
Cong Hoa Xa Hoi Chu Nghia VietNam

CAPITAL: Hanoi.

FLAG: The flag is red with a five-pointed gold star in the center.

ANTHEM: *Tien Quan Ça (Forward, Soldiers!).*

MONETARY UNIT: The dong (D) is a paper currency of 10 hao and 100 xu. There are coins of 1, 2, and 5 xu, and notes of 5 xu, 1, 2, and 5 hao, and 1, 2, 5, and 10 dong. D1 = $0.0027 (or $1 = D368).

WEIGHTS AND MEASURES: The metric system is the legal standard, but some traditional measures are still used.

HOLIDAYS: Liberation of Saigon, 30 April; May Day, 1 May; Independence Day, 2 September. Movable holidays include the Vietnamese New Year (Tet).

TIME: 7 PM = noon GMT.

1 LOCATION AND SIZE

Situated on the eastern coast of mainland Southeast Asia, the Socialist Republic of Viet Nam (SRV) has an area of 329,560 square kilometers (127,244 square miles), slightly larger than the state of New Mexico, and a total boundary length of 7,262 kilometers (4,512 miles).

Viet Nam's capital city, Hanoi, is located in the northern part of the country.

2 TOPOGRAPHY

A single mountain chain, the Annam Cordillera (in Vietnamese, Truong Son), extends along Viet Nam's western border from north to south, connecting two "rice baskets," which are formed by the densely populated Red River Delta of the Tonkin region in the north and the rich Mekong River Delta in the south. The two low-lying delta regions are both composed of rich soils brought down from the mountainous regions of southern China and mainland Southeast Asia. The highest mountain peak is Fan Si Pan (3,143 meters/10,312 feet).

3 CLIMATE

Mean annual rainfall in the north varies from 172 centimeters (68 inches) for the city of Hanoi to over 406 centimeters (160 inches) in the mountains. Daily temperatures in the Red River Delta region can fluctuate from as low as 5°C (41°F) in the dry season to about 30°C (86°F) during the rainy season.

The south is more tropical; temperatures in Ho Chi Minh City vary only between 18° (64°F) and 33°C (91°F)

Photo credit: Corel Corporation.

A group of Vietnamese children eye the photographer with curiosity and excitement.

throughout the year. Temperatures in the Central Highlands range from a mean of about 17°C (63°F) in winter to 20°C (68°F) in summer. Annual rainfall averages about 200 centimeters (79 inches) in lowland regions. The typhoon season lasts from July through November, with the most severe storms occurring along the central coast.

4 PLANTS AND ANIMALS

The mountainous regions in the north, as well as the Annam Cordillera, are characterized by tropical rainforest broken by large areas of monsoon forest. In the higher altitudes of the far northwest there are pine forests. Tropical grasses are widespread, and there are mangrove forests fringing parts of the Red River Delta and in the Ca Mau peninsula, which juts into the Gulf of Thailand. Tropical evergreen forests predominate in the south.

Deer and wild oxen are found in the more mountainous areas. There are many species of tropical birds and insects.

5 ENVIRONMENT

During the Viet Nam War in the 1960s and 1970s, massive bombing raids and defoliation campaigns caused severe destruction of the natural foliage, especially in the Central Highlands of the south. Over 50% of the nation's forests have been eliminated, and dioxin, a toxic residue of the herbicide known as Agent Orange, had leached into the country's water supply.

Environmental damage has also been caused by slash-and-burn agriculture, practiced by nomadic tribal peoples in the Central Highlands and in the mountainous regions in the north. Air and water pollution result from the uncontrolled dumping of industrial and domestic contaminants. The nation has 90.2 cubic miles of water; 78% is used for farming activity and 9% is used for industrial purposes. Excessive use of pesticides and fertilizers has also damaged the nation's soils.

In 1994, 28 of Viet Nam's mammal species and 34 bird species were endangered. In addition, 338 types of plants were endangered.

6 POPULATION

Rapid population growth is a serious problem in Viet Nam. According to the 1989 census, the total population was 64,411,668. In 1995, the population was estimated at 73,811,000, making Viet Nam the thirteenth most populous nation in the world. Population density is estimated at 210 persons per square kilometer (544 per square mile).

The annual population growth rate averages 2.3%; the government is attempting to reduce it to 1.7% through family planning measures, including late marriages and small families, in order to stabilize the population at 75 to 80 million by the end of the twentieth century. The United Nations projection for the year 2000 is 81,516,000.

The three largest cities in 1989 were Ho Chi Minh City (3,924,435), Hanoi (3,056,146), and Haiphong (1,447,523).

7 MIGRATION

The Viet Nam War caused severe disruption of living patterns in both the north and the south. At the end of the war in 1975, many inhabitants were living in refugee camps on the edges of major cities. After seizing control of the south in 1975, the Hanoi regime (communists) moved nearly 1.5 million Vietnamese to New Economic Zones in the Central Highlands or along the Cambodian border as part of their plan for development of an advanced Socialist economy. Since 1981 another 2.1 million have been resettled.

In addition to this migration within the country, since the war there has been a

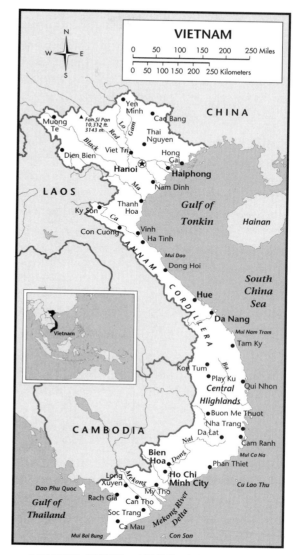

LOCATION: 102°10′ to 109°30′E; 8°30′ to 23°22′N.
BOUNDARY LENGTHS: China, 1,281 kilometers (796 miles); Cambodia, 982 kilometers (610 miles); Laos, 1,555 kilometers (966 miles). **COASTLINE:** 3,444 kilometers (2,140 miles). **TERRITORIAL SEA LIMIT:** 12 miles.

heavy outflow of Vietnamese fleeing to other countries. About 150,000 were evacuated from the south in the final weeks of the war with many eventually settling in the United States. During 1978–87, an estimated one million Vietnamese fled by sea to other countries in Southeast Asia or overland to China. Many, known as "boat people," emigrated illegally.

In 1979 the government instituted the Orderly Departure Program (ODP) allowing legal emigration to the United States. From 1979–84, 59,730 persons emigrated legally through this program, which was suspended by the Vietnamese government in 1986 but later resumed, with 57,000 emigrating to the United States in 1993 alone. In 1984, the United States started a program that offered asylum to Vietnamese political prisoners and all Amerasian children (children of Asian mothers and American fathers).

The major refugee community is in China, which was harboring 285,500 Vietnamese of Chinese ancestry at the end of 1992. There were 593,213 people of Vietnamese ancestry in the United States in 1990.

8 ETHNIC GROUPS

About 87% of the population of Viet Nam (SRV) is composed of ethnic Vietnamese. In addition to the ethnic Vietnamese, there are 53 other ethnic groups living in Viet Nam. Many are nomadic tribal peoples living in mountainous areas. The Vietnamese Chinese (Hoa) are descendants of peoples who migrated into the area in recent centuries. The Cham and the Khmer are remnants of past civilizations that controlled the southern parts of the country.

Until recently, the largest ethnic minority in the country was the Chinese, numbering more than two million. Many have fled the country for economic or political reasons in recent years, however, and the total number remaining in the mid-1980s was estimated at just over one million. Other sizable minority groups, with approximate populations, are the Tay (2 million), Montagnards (1 million), Khmer (600,000), Muong (750,000), Thai (650,000), and Nung (450,000).

9 LANGUAGES

The national language is Vietnamese (*Quoc ngu*). It bears similarities to Khmer, Thai, and Chinese, and at least one-third of the vocabulary is derived from Chinese. Formerly, Vietnamese was written in Chinese characters, but under French rule a romanized alphabet originally developed by Roman Catholic missionaries in the seventeenth century was adopted as the standard written form of the language. Most of the minority groups have their own spoken languages, and some have their own writing systems, but all Vietnamese children today receive instruction in the national language.

10 RELIGIONS

It was under Chinese rule that the three major religions and philosophical systems of traditional Viet Nam—Mahayana Buddhism, Taoism, and Confucianism—all entered the country.

Under French rule, Christianity prospered, and when Viet Nam restored its independence in 1954 there were more than two million Catholics in the country,

A seaside village located along the Vietnamese coast.

a population that increased to 4.6 million in 1989. Most of the remainder of the population is Buddhist, although two unorthodox religious sects, the Cao Dai and the Hoa Hao, became popular among peasants and townspeople in the Mekong Delta. In 1976, the Hoa Hao sect claimed 1.5 million members, but no recent statistics are available.

Since reunification of North and South Viet Nam in 1975, religious activities have been restricted, although freedom of religion is formally guaranteed in the 1980 constitution. In 1989, approximately 56% of the population was Buddhist.

11 TRANSPORTATION

The Viet Nam War wreaked massive damage on Viet Nam's transportation network, especially its railways, roads, and bridges. Most goods move by small barges or sampans along the countless waterways. Major ports such as Haiphong in the north and Da Nang in the south, are frequently clogged with goods because many dockworkers—often Vietnamese Chinese—have fled abroad.

In 1991, Viet Nam had 73 oceangoing freighters totaling 444,000 gross registered tons, and another 8 carriers and tankers, totaling 33,000 gross registered tons.

The railroads had 3,059 kilometers (1,900 miles) of track in 1991. There are 50 airports with permanent-surface runways. The nation's air fleet remains primitive, as the national airline (Hang Khong Viet Nam) uses Soviet passenger planes built in the 1950s. There are 85,000 kilometers (52,800 miles) of roads in the country.

12 HISTORY

During the first millennium (thousand years) BC, the Lac peoples, the ancestors of the modern-day Vietnamese, formed a Bronze Age civilization in the vicinity of the Red River Delta in northern Viet Nam. In the third century BC, the Red River Delta was incorporated into a kingdom in southern China. A century later, Viet Nam was integrated into the expanding Chinese empire. During 1,000 years of Chinese rule, Vietnamese society changed significantly as it was introduced to Chinese political and social institutions; Chinese architecture, art, and literature; and the Chinese written language. In AD 939, during a period of anarchy in China, Vietnamese rebels restored national independence.

During the next several hundred years, the Vietnamese Empire, then known as Dai Viet (Great Viet), gradually developed its own institutions and expanded steadily to the south. The entire Mekong River Delta came under Vietnamese rule during the seventeenth century, but the ruling Le dynasty slipped into civil war between two princely families, and the country was divided between the Trinh in the north and the Nguyen in the south.

The division of Viet Nam into two separate political entities came at a time when European adventurers were beginning to expand their commercial and missionary activities into East and Southeast Asia. The country was briefly reunited under a new Nguyen Dynasty (1802–1845), but when a new emperor refused to continue the commercial and missionary privileges granted by his predecessor to the French, French forces attacked near Saigon in 1858. In 1884, France completed its conquest of the country, establishing a protectorate over central and northern Viet Nam. In 1895, the three sections of Viet Nam were included with the protectorates of Laos and Cambodia in a French-ruled Indochinese Union.

Western-style nationalist movements began to form after World War I, and an Indochinese Communist Party, under the leadership of the veteran revolutionary Ho Chi Minh, was formed in 1930. After the collapse of France in World War II, Japan occupied Indochina. Shortly after Japan surrendered to Allied forces (the United States, United Kingdom, and the USSR) in August 1945, Viet-Minh forces, led by the Indochinese Communist Party, launched the nationwide August Revolution to restore Vietnamese independence.

On 2 September, President Ho Chi Minh declared the formation of an independent Democratic Republic of Viet Nam (DRV) in Hanoi. Under the Potsdam agreements, Nationalist Chinese troops occupied all of Indochina north of the sixteenth parallel, while British troops occupied the remainder of the old Indochinese Union. Chinese commanders permitted the

Viet-Minh to remain in political control of the north, and the British helped the French to restore their authority in the south.

During the summer of 1946, French and Vietnamese negotiators attempted to complete an agreement on the future of Viet Nam, but military clashes between Vietnamese and French troops in the north led to the outbreak of war in December 1946. The Franco–Viet-Minh war lasted nearly eight years, ending in July 1954 after a successful series of attacks on the French at Dien Bien Phu (Dien Bien) by Viet-Minh forces.

Viet Nam was temporarily partitioned along the seventeenth parallel, pending general elections to bring about national reunification. North of the parallel, the Vietnamese began to build a Socialist society, while in the south, an anti-Communist government under the Roman Catholic politician Ngo Dinh Diem attempted with American aid to build a viable and independent state.

On 26 October 1955, Diem proclaimed the Republic of Viet Nam (RVN), with its capital at Saigon. Vietnamese guerrillas, supported by the Democratic Republic of Viet Nam (DRV), initiated low-level political and military activities to weaken the Saigon regime. In 1960, revolutionary forces in the south formed a National Liberation Front (NLF) to coordinate political activities against the Diem regime.

Despite increasing economic and military assistance from the United States, the Diem regime continued to decline, and in November 1963, Diem was overthrown by a military coup. A Military Revolutionary Council, led by the popular southern general Duong Van (Big) Minh, was formed in Saigon but replaced early in 1964 by another military government. During the next 15 months, a number of governments succeeded each other, while the influence of the NLF steadily increased in the countryside. By early 1965, American intelligence was warning that without American intervention, South Viet Nam could collapse within six months.

Beginning in February 1965, American combat troops were introduced in growing numbers into the south, while a campaign of heavy bombing raids was launched on military and industrial targets in the north. In Saigon, a new military regime seized power in 1967 led by Nguyen Van Thieu and Nguyen Cao Ky, and General Thieu was elected president of the country. By 1967, American troop strength in South Viet Nam had reached over 500,000, while American air strikes over DRV territory were averaging about 100 sorties (missions) a day.

On 30 January 1968, Hanoi launched the Tet Offensive, a massive effort to seize towns and villages throughout the south. The attempt to force the collapse of the Saigon regime failed, but the secondary aim of undermining support for the war in the United States succeeded. President Lyndon B. Johnson agreed to pursue a political settlement. A complete bombing halt was ordered on 1 November, just before the presidential election in the United States that brought Richard M. Nixon to office as the new Republican president.

President Nixon announced a policy of "Vietnamization," according to which American forces would be gradually withdrawn and the bulk of the fighting in the south would be taken over by RVN forces. Following the divisive 1970 American invasion of neutral Cambodia to destroy enemy sanctuaries, and the DRV's 1972 "Easter Offensive" across the seventeenth parallel, both sides were willing to compromise to bring the war to an end.

The Paris Agreement was formally signed on 27 January 1973. However, clashes between revolutionary forces and South Vietnamese units continued in the south, while provisions for a political settlement quickly collapsed. In January 1975, North Vietnamese forces in the south launched a major military offensive, and by 30 April they had occupied the capital of the RVN, Saigon.

During the next 15 months, the DRV moved to complete national reunification of north and south. Nationwide elections for a new National Assembly were held on 25 April 1976. On 2 July the Socialist Republic of Viet Nam (SRV) was established, with its capital remaining at Hanoi.

Economic reconstruction proved more difficult than reunification. When the regime attempted to destroy the remnants of capitalism and private farming in the south in 1978, thousands fled, and the economy entered a period of severe crisis. Its problems were magnified by the outbreak of war with China over Vietnamese military intervention in Cambodia that had toppled the pro-Chinese Pol Pot government. After a short but bitter battle that caused severe casualties on both sides, the Chinese forces withdrew across the border, but China continued to support guerrilla operations against the current pro-Vietnamese government in Cambodia.

In January 1989 the first direct talks between Viet Nam and China since 1979 resulted in Viet Nam's agreement to withdraw its troops from Cambodia by the end of September 1989 and China's agreement to end aid to the Khmer Rouge guerrillas once the Vietnamese withdrawal had been achieved. On 23 October 1991 a Cambodian peace agreement was signed.

Viet Nam has also stepped up its efforts to attract foreign capital from the West and regularize relations with the world financial system. Issues that affect these processes are the status and treatment of Vietnamese refugees; border and troop withdrawal disputes with Cambodia, Thailand, and the People's Republic of China; conflicts over the Spratly and Paracel islands in the South China Sea; and conflicts with the United States over the recovery of the remains of American soldiers missing-in-action (MIA).

On 3 February 1994 President Bill Clinton lifted the American trade embargo against Viet Nam. After the dissolution of the Soviet Union, the government of the newly independent Russia assured the Vietnamese government that close economic relations would be maintained.

In 1994, a possible solution to the contested claims over the Spratly and Paracel archipelagos (island chains) off the coast of Viet Nam was proposed. It would create a Spratly Development Authority with

China and Taiwan sharing 51% of shares and the remainder divided among Brunei, Viet Nam, Malaysia, and the Philippines.

13 GOVERNMENT

Under the constitution of December 1980, the Socialist Republic of Viet Nam (SRV) is a "proletarian dictatorship" led by the Communist Party. The highest state authority is the National Assembly. Members are elected for five-year terms by universal adult suffrage at age 18. The Assembly appoints the Council of Ministers (a cabinet of 33 ministers), the chairman of which ranks as premier. The Council of State (12 members in 1987) formerly served as the collective presidency of Viet Nam, elected by the National Assembly from among its own members and accountable to it.

Under a new constitution adopted in 1992, the newly created position of president replaced the Council of State; the president has the right to appoint a prime minister subject to the approval of the National Assembly. The National Assembly, with a maximum of 400 members, retained legislative power.

Viet Nam is divided into 36 provinces, 1 special zone (*Vung Tau-Con Dao*), and 3 municipalities (Hanoi, Haiphong, and Ho Chi Minh City), all administered by the national government.

14 POLITICAL PARTIES

The government of the SRV is a one-party state ruled by the Vietnamese Communist Party (VCP). In theory, two other political parties, the Democratic Party and the Socialist Party, are granted legal existence.

15 JUDICIAL SYSTEM

The highest court in Viet Nam is the Supreme People's Court, whose members are appointed for five-year terms by the National Assembly. In addition, there are local people's courts at each administrative level; military courts; and "special courts" established by the National Assembly in certain cases.

16 ARMED FORCES

Since reunification in 1975, Viet Nam has emerged as one of the world's leading military powers. As of mid-1993, the People's Army of Viet Nam was estimated at 857,000 with 65 divisions and 25–40 brigades. Of that figure, the regular army had about 700,000 personnel, the air force 15,000, the air defense force 100,000, and the navy 42,000. Reserves numbered between 500,000 and 2 million. Military service is compulsory for two or three years.

Military expenditures were estimated to be $2.3 million of a national income of $15 billion (1990).

17 ECONOMY

Wet-rice agriculture is an important segment of the Vietnamese economy, and approximately 73% of the population was engaged in agriculture in 1986. The most diversified area in Southeast Asia in terms of mineral resources, Viet Nam is well endowed with coal, tin, tungsten, gold, iron, manganese, chromium, and anti-

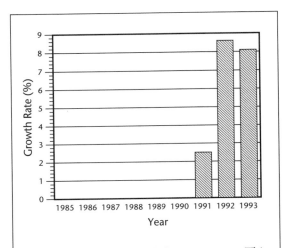

Yearly growth rate of the economy. This economic indicator tells by what percent the economy has increased or decreased when compared with the previous year.

Massive improvements to transport and communications networks, combined with industrial development and expansion of exports, are needed. Party leadership, moreover, is concerned about growing unemployment (estimated to be over 25%), the widening gap between rich and poor, bankruptcy, and corruption. However, the labor force, with its low wage base, good skill levels, and high motivation, is an excellent resource for growth in manufacturing.

18 INCOME

In 1992 the gross domestic product (GDP) was $16 billion in current US dollars. It is estimated that agriculture, hunting, forestry, and fishing contributed 41% to gross domestic product; manufacturing, 20%; construction, 3%; wholesale and retail trade, 12%; transport, storage, and communication, 4%; finance, insurance, real estate, and business services, 11%; community, social, and personal services, 9%; and other sources, 1%.

19 INDUSTRY

Like most countries in Southeast Asia, Viet Nam has a small and relatively primitive industrial sector. Most heavy and medium industry is concentrated in the north, including the state-owned coal, tin, chrome, and other mining enterprises; an engineering works at Hanoi; power stations; and modern tobacco, tea, and canning factories.

mony. Cement, textiles, silk, matches, and paper are the main industrial products.

Viet Nam's attempts to change from a state-controlled economy to a free-market economy have been slowed by the government's fear of changes that promote increased democracy. Policy changes have been introduced cautiously. Between 1988 and 1993, per person gross national product (GNP) was estimated at $170, which is low by world standards. Nevertheless, in 1994 Viet Nam enjoyed benefits from its decontrolled prices, currency control, and increased private business activity. The results have been growth, low inflation, and increased foreign investment. On 3 February 1994 American President Bill Clinton lifted the thirty-year-old trade embargo against Viet Nam.

The south typically has light industry and consumer goods industries, including pharmaceuticals, textiles, and food processing, although there are some large utilities and cement works. Much of the industrial sector in the north was badly damaged by American bombing raids during the war.

The regime now permits the existence of a small amount of private business, mainly in the area of consumer goods and other light industry. The results have been generally favorable; industrial production in the 1980s has increased at an average annual rate of 9.5%.

Production for the following major industries in 1991 (in metric tons) was: cement, 3,127,100; paper, 108,800; finished cloth, 280,400,000; chemical fertilizers, 450,300; and steel, 141,000.

In the 1990s industrial production was still burdened by uncompetitive state-owned enterprises, as well as inefficiency and low productivity due to obsolete plants and machinery and shortages of capital, raw materials, energy and transport. In 1992, the growth rate for industrial production was 15%, largely due to increases in the output of oil. Viet Nam's assets include low wages, good skill levels, and a motivated work force.

20 LABOR

The total employed labor force in Viet Nam was estimated at about 28.7 million persons by 1990. Of this total, 71% worked in agriculture, about 13% in industry and construction, 9% in trade, transportation, and communications, and 7% in services.

Unemployment has recently become a problem and is worsened by the army's planned demobilization of over 500,000

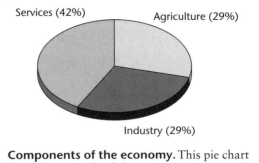

Components of the economy. This pie chart shows how much of the country's economy is devoted to agriculture (includes forestry, hunting, and fishing), industry, or services.

troops in the near future. However, a more prominent role given to private enterprise has the potential to lead to more job opportunities. Unemployment estimates as of 1991 ranged from 5% to 20%, with the number of unemployed rising.

As of 1992, Vietnamese workers were not free to form or join unions. The government-controlled Confederation of Vietnamese Workers is the sole labor organization, and all workers automatically become members of the union of their workplace. Strikes and collective bargaining are prohibited, and citizens allegedly are required by law to give 15 days of work per year to the state or pay a fee.

21 AGRICULTURE

Over 70% of the total population derives its livelihood from agriculture. Agriculture in the north is concentrated in the lowland areas of the Red River Delta and along the central coast to the south. The Mekong Delta, among the great rice-producing regions of the world, is the dominant agricultural region of the south. Excess grain from the area is shipped to the northern parts of the country. Annual food-grain production averaged 20 million tons in the early 1990s, reaching 22.1 million tons in 1992.

Rice, the main staple of the Vietnamese diet, accounted for 44% of agricultural exports and 17% of total exports in 1992. In 1990, 19.2 million tons of paddy rice were produced. Other crops include corn, sorghum, cassava, sweet potatoes, beans, fruits, and vegetables. In 1992, estimated production (in thousands of tons) was: sugarcane, 5,900; corn, 660; groundnuts in shell, 215; and soybeans, 87.

Rubber production was given high priority by the Hanoi regime and increased from 40,000 tons in 1975 to 65,000 tons in 1992. Other industrial and export crops produced in Viet Nam include coffee, tea, tobacco, pepper, and jute. In 1992, 65,000 tons of coffee, 35,000 tons of tea, 30,000 tons of jute, 28,000 tons of tobacco, and 11,200 tons of pepper were harvested.

The regime announced in mid-1986 that collectivization at a low level had been "basically completed" in the south, with 86.4% of the rural population enrolled in some form of collective organization. As of 1985, there were more than 15,600 agricultural cooperatives nationwide.

22 DOMESTICATED ANIMALS

The most important aspect of animal farming remains the raising of pack animals, mainly water buffalo. Lack of feed, shelter, and technical guidance and an inability to control disease, combined with war damage, hinder growth in this area. Increasing the livestock population is now a major priority of the Hanoi regime. The sizes of herds in 1992 (with 1975 figures in parentheses) was as follows: hogs, 12,140,000 (8,800,700); buffalo, 3,135,000 (2,193,000); and cattle 2,867,000 (1,485,000).

23 FISHING

Fresh and dried fish and fish sauce (known as nuoc mam) are major ingredients of the Vietnamese diet, and fishing is an important occupation. Shrimp, lobster, and more than 50 commercial species of fish are found in Vietnamese waters. Ha Long Bay, the major fishing area of the north, is particularly rich in shrimp and crayfish. Fish also abound in Viet Nam's rivers and canals.

The fishing industry was severely depleted after the Viet Nam War, when many fishermen (often ethnic Chinese) fled the country. In 1991, ocean production was estimated at 610,000 tons, and inland production was estimated at 267,000 tons.

24 FORESTRY

In 1991, forests covered 29% of the total land area of Viet Nam. Important forestry products include bamboo, resins, lacquer, quinine, turpentine, and pitch. Depletion of forests, however, has been serious, not only through American use of chemicals leading to defoliation in the south during the war, but also because of native farming and grazing practices.

According to scientists who have visited Viet Nam in recent years, the damaged areas are recovering faster than anticipated, although reforestation has been slow and some regions are faced with sterility and erosion. Official policy currently emphasizes the replacement of natural forests with export crops such as cinnamon, aniseed, rubber, coffee, and bamboo. Roundwood production was estimated at 29,525,000 cubic meters in 1991.

25 MINING

Viet Nam has some important mineral resources. The principal reserves, located mainly in the north, are anthracite coal, antimony, tin, chrome, apatite, phosphate, manganese, titanium, bauxite, copper, zinc, lead, nickel, graphite, mica, and some gold. Iron reserves are estimated at 250 million tons and apatite reserves at more than 1.7 billion tons.

Coal production dominates the country's mining. In 1991, estimated exports amounted to 783,000 tons of coal, or 25% of domestic production. Coal output has been seriously hindered by technical difficulties and the exodus of trained workers; according to official sources, coal production declined from 5.2 million tons in 1975 to 4 million tons in 1991. Output of chromium ore declined from 10,400 to 3,500 tons during the same period.

26 FOREIGN TRADE

Since reunification, Viet Nam has attempted with little success to address the chronic trade imbalance between imports and exports.

In 1992, Singapore was Viet Nam's largest trading partner. Other major trading partners were Japan, Thailand, Hong Kong, and Taiwan. Export commodities in 1992 were agricultural and handicraft products, coal, minerals, crude oil, ores, and seafood. Major exports were rice and crude oil, accounting for about half of 1992 exports. Import commodities in 1992 were petroleum and steel products, railroad equipment, chemicals, medicines, raw cotton, fertilizer, and grain.

27 ENERGY AND POWER

Lack of energy is one of Viet Nam's major obstacles to economic development. While coal output is substantial, most of it has been reserved for export. Hydroelectric power accounts for about one-sixth of the annual electrical output. In 1991, 8,550 million kilowatt hours of electricity were generated.

Proven oil reserves as of 1 January 1993 totaled 500 million barrels; production in 1992 amounted to 110,000 barrels per day. In 1992, exports of petroleum accounted for 33% of total exports. Natural gas is believed to exist throughout much of northern Viet Nam; reserves are estimated at 14 billion cubic meters (500 billion cubic feet).

28 SOCIAL DEVELOPMENT

Since the end of the war in 1975, Viet Nam has been attempting to lay the foundations of an advanced socialist society. However, attempts to improve social ser-

Selected Social Indicators

These statistics are estimates for the period 1988 to 1993. For comparison purposes, data for the United States and averages for low-income countries and high-income countries are also given.

Indicator	Vietnam	Low-income countries	High-income countries	United States
Per capita gross national product†	$170	$380	$23,680	$24,740
Population growth rate	2.3%	1.9%	0.6%	1.0%
Population growth rate in urban areas	3.2%	3.9%	0.8%	1.3%
Population per square kilometer of land	210	78	25	26
Life expectancy in years	65	62	77	76
Number of people per physician	2,298	>3,300	453	419
Number of pupils per teacher (primary school)	34	39	<18	20
Illiteracy rate (15 years and older)	12%	41%	<5%	<3%
Energy consumed per capita (kg of oil equivalent)	77	364	5,203	7,918

† The gross national product (GNP) is the total dollar value of all goods and services produced by a country in a year. The per capita GNP is calculated by dividing a country's GNP by its population. The World Bank defines low-income countries as those with a per capita GNP of $695 or less. High-income countries have a per capita GNP of $8,626 or more. Less than 14% of the world's 5.5 billion people live in high-income countries, while almost 60% live in low-income countries.

> = greater than   < = less than

Sources: World Bank, Social Indicators of Development 1995, Baltimore: Johns Hopkins University Press, 1995. Central Intelligence Agency, World Fact Book, Washington, D.C.: Government Printing Office, 1994.

vices have been hampered by the poor performance of the economy. During the late 1970s, severe food shortages put per capita caloric intake below the subsistence level. Housing and health services were seriously inadequate, and individual freedom was severely restricted. By 1987, equality for women had been largely achieved, but religious freedom was severely restricted, and potential dissidents were jailed without trial. Censorship was routinely practiced.

According to the US state department, Viet Nam had not completely improved its human rights situation as of 1992, and restrictions on freedom of the press, speech, and assembly continued. However, travel restrictions were eased, artistic and literary expression were tolerated, and there was an increasing separation between the Communist Party and the state.

29 HEALTH

Wars in Viet Nam since 1946 have undermined much of the progress made in the health field. Especially severe was the damage to urban hospitals in the north. The three decades of intermittent war also had a devastating effect on health conditions in the south. At the war's end in 1975, many infectious diseases were observed to be on the increase.

The World Health Organization (WHO) reported in 1976 that malaria had been both widespread and increasing in the south in 1975. During 1965–74, 5,000 cases of bubonic plague were occurring annually, with a mortality rate of 5%. Saigon was said to have had a tuberculosis rate two-to-three times that of neighboring countries, while leprosy (involving an estimated 80,000–160,000 cases) was increasing. Venereal diseases were said to have afflicted one million persons in the south (about 5% of the total population) and, WHO claimed, 80% of RVN soldiers. Opiate addiction, it was said, affected about 500,000 persons.

Since reunification in 1975, some progress in health care has been made. Tuberculosis has been largely controlled, and the incidence of many contagious diseases has been reduced. In 1991, 24% of the population had access to safe water, and 17% had adequate sanitation. Life expectancy is 65 years.

There are an estimated 2,298 people per physician. In 1990, there were 3.3 hospital beds per 1,000 inhabitants. About 91% of the population had access to health care services in 1992.

30 HOUSING

Housing is a serious problem in Viet Nam, particularly in urban areas of the north where war damage caused problems of overcrowding. By 1986, housing had become a critical problem in Hanoi, par-

ticularly in the central sections of the city, where per person living space was reduced to four square meters. Large flats are gradually being erected in the suburbs to ease the problem. In the meantime, many families live in temporary quarters built directly on the sidewalk or attached to other buildings.

Housing is less a problem in the countryside, where many farm families have begun to take advantage of a rising standard of living to build new houses of brick and stone. Similarly, in the rural south, housing is available to meet the requirements of the population because building construction continued at a relatively high level during the war years. In 1989, the majority of housing units were semi-permanent (structures with brick walls and tile roofs lasting about 20 years).

31 EDUCATION

By 1990, the adult literacy rate for the reunified country was 88% (males, 92.0% and females, 83.6%). After 1975, the educational system in the south was restructured to conform to the socialist guidelines that had been used in the north. The 12-year school cycle was reduced to 10 years, and the more than 20,000 teachers in the south were among those subjected to "reeducation." Today, education is free at all levels, and five years of primary education is compulsory.

In 1990, primary schools had 252,413 teachers and 8,862,292 students. The same year, general secondary schools had 179,493 teachers and 3,235,992 students. There are 90 colleges and three universities. The major university is in Hanoi.

Photo credit: AP/Wide World Photos.

Vietnamese school children are seen heaped onto cyclos as they are peddled to a school early one Monday morning. The cyclo is a cheap mode of transportation still used in Vietnam.

32 MEDIA

There were 115,000 telephones in 1991. Hanoi has a strong central broadcasting station, the Voice of Viet Nam, boosted by local relay transmitters. Since 1975, almost the entire country has been blanketed by a wired loudspeaker system. Radio programs beamed abroad include broadcasts in Chinese, English, French, Japanese, Spanish, Thai, Bahasa Indonesia, Russian, Khmer, and Lao, and there are special broadcasts to mountain tribes.

Television was introduced into Viet Nam in 1966, and an extensive service, reaching some 80% of the population, was in operation by the early 1970s.

Many of the major cities now have television stations. In 1991, there were 7,050,000 radios and 2,800,000 television sets.

All press is strictly controlled by the Ministry of Culture and Information. Principal Vietnamese dailies (with their estimated 1991 circulations) are *Nhan Dan* (160,000); *Quan Doi Nhan Dan* (55,000); *Hanoi Moi* (32,000); and *Gai Phong* (100,000).

33 TOURISM AND RECREATION

Viet Nam possesses a number of historic and scenic areas of interest to tourists. In the north, the beauty of Ha Long Bay, with its countless grottoes and rock spits jutting vertically into the sea, is well known. Hanoi itself, with its historical monuments, its lakes and pagodas, and its extensive French colonial architecture, is extremely picturesque, but hotel facilities are both inadequate and expensive.

The tourism industry is growing rapidly: there were 170,000 visitors in 1990, 250,000 in 1991; 325,000 in 1992; and 650,000 in 1993. In Hanoi, the increased presence of a foreign community is spurring the availability of western-style restaurants and bars, hotel and airport renovation and upgrading, accessible public telephones, and advertising of consumer goods.

34 FAMOUS VIETNAMESE

Important figures in Vietnamese history include the sisters Trung Trac and Trung Nhi, national heroines who led a revolt (AD 40–43) against China when that nation was imperial master of Tonkin and North Annam; Ngo Quyen, who regained Vietnamese independence from China in 938; Tran Hung Dao, who defeated the forces of Kublai Khan in 1288; Emperor Le Loi, national hero and brilliant administrator, in whose reign the Vietnamese legal code was promulgated in 1407; and Emperor Gia Long (d.1820), who reunified Viet Nam in the early 19th century.

The 13th-century writer Nguyen Si Co is regarded as one of the first truly Vietnamese authors; he is best known for his collection titled *Chieu Quan Cong Ho*. Other leading literary figures are two 15th-century poets, Ho Huyen Qui and Nguyen Binh Khien, whose collection,

Bach Van Thi Tap, is a classic of Vietnamese literature. Nguyen Du (1765–1820) wrote a famous novel in verse, *Kim Van Kieu*. Hoang Ngoc Phach, who wrote the romantic novel *To Tam* (1925), is credited with the introduction of Western literary standards into Vietnamese literature.

Phan Boi Chau (1875–1940) was Viet Nam's first modern nationalist and, like China's Sun Yat-sen, is claimed by Vietnamese Communists and nationalists alike as their spiritual leader. Ho Chi Minh ("The Enlightener") was born Nguyen That Thanh (1890–1969). Often referred to as "Uncle Ho," he was president of the DRV from 1945 until his death. General Vo Nguyen Giap (b.1912), a professor of history turned strategist, organized the first anti-French guerrilla groups in 1944, led the Viet-Minh in its eight-year struggle against France, and defeated the French at Dien Bien Phu.

Le Duan (1907–86), first secretary of the Communist Party, presided over Viet Nam's reunification and the formation of the SRV. Le Duc Tho (b.1911), a member of the Communist Party Politburo but with no post in the government, was the DRV's chief negotiator in talks that led to the 1973 Paris Peace Agreement; for his role, Le shared with United States Secretary of State Henry Kissinger the 1973 Nobel Peace Prize.

Prominent political figures in the formation of the RVN included Bao Dai (Nguyen Vinh Thuy; b.France, 1913), who had served as nominal emperor of Annam under the Japanese and had attempted to form a unified national government after the war, and Ngo Dinh Diem (1901–63), who served as president of the RVN from its founding on 26 October 1955 until his overthrow and death in November 1963. Nguyen Cao Ky (b.1930), an RVN air force commander, took control of the government in the coup of June 1965.

General Nguyen Van Thieu (b.1923) was elected president of the RVN in the elections of September 1967 (with Ky as his vice-presidential running mate), an office he retained until the RVN's defeat in 1975. Both Thieu and Ky left the country in 1975, Thieu taking up residence in Taiwan and Ky in the US. Pham Hung became premier of the SRV in 1987, and Vo Chi Cong (b.1913?) became president of the Council of State. Nguyen Van Linh (b.1913) became general secretary of the Communist Party in December 1986.

35 BIBLIOGRAPHY

Buttinger, Joseph. *A Dragon Defiant: A Short History of Vietnam.* New York: Praeger, 1972.

Cima, Ronald J., ed. *Vietnam: A Country.* Washington, D.C.: Library of Congress, 1989.

Dahlby, Tracy. "The New Saigon." *National Geographic,* April 1995, 60–87.

Fall, Bernard B., ed. *Ho Chi Minh on Revolution: Selected Writings, 1920–66.* New York: Praeger, 1967.

Kolko, Gabriel. *Anatomy of a War: Vietnam, the United States, and the Modern Historical Experience.* New York: Pantheon, 1985.

Marr, David G., and Kristine Alilunas-Rodgers. *Vietnam.* Santa Barbara, Calif.: Clio Press, 1992.

Nagel, Rob, and Anne Commire. "Ho Chi Minh." In *World Leaders, People Who Shaped the World.* Volume I: Africa and Asia. Detroit: U*X*L, 1994.

Olson, James Stuart. *Where the Domino Fell: America and Vietnam, 1945 to 1990.* New York: St. Martin's, 1991.

Pimlott, John. *Vietnam, the Decisive Battles.* New York: Macmillan, 1990.

Short, Anthony. *The Origins of the Vietnam War.* New York: Longman, 1989.

Truong Nhu Tang. *Vietcong Memoir.* San Diego: Harcourt Brace Jovanovich, 1986.

White, Peter T. "Hanoi: The Capital Today." *National Geographic,* November 1989, 561–594.

Williams, Michael C. *Vietnam at the Crossroads.* New York: Council on Foreign Relations Press, 1992.

Wright, D. *Vietnam.* Chicago: Children's Press, 1989.

WESTERN SAMOA

Independent State of Western Samoa
Malo Sa'oloto Tuto'atasi o Samoa i Sisifo

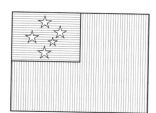

CAPITAL: Apia.

FLAG: The upper left quarter of the flag is blue and bears five white, five-rayed stars representing the Southern Cross; the remainder of the flag is red.

ANTHEM: *The Flag of Freedom.*

MONETARY UNIT: The Western Samoa tala (WS$) is a paper currency of 100 sene. There are coins of 1, 2, 5, 10, 20, and 50 sene and 1 tala, and notes of 2, 5, 10, 20, and 100 talas. WS$1 = US$0.3858 (or US$1 = WS$2.5920).

WEIGHTS AND MEASURES: British weights and measures are used.

HOLIDAYS: New Year's, 1–2 January; Independence Holidays (first three workdays of June), Anzac Day, 25 April; Christmas Day, 25 December; Boxing Day, 26 December. Movable religious holidays are Good Friday, Easter Monday, and Whitmonday.

TIME: 1 AM = noon GMT.

1 LOCATION AND SIZE

Western Samoa consists of the islands of Savai'i and Upolu and several smaller islands, of which only two are inhabited. The group, situated in the Pacific Ocean among the South Sea islands, has a total land area of 2,860 square kilometers (1,104 square miles), slightly smaller than the state of Rhode Island. Its total boundary length is 371 kilometers (231 miles).

2 TOPOGRAPHY

The islands are volcanic, with coral reefs surrounding most of them. Rugged ranges rise to 1,100 meters (3,609 feet) on Upolu and 1,858 meters (6,096 feet) on Savai'i.

3 CLIMATE

The mean daily temperature is about 27°C (81°F). Rainfall averages 287 centimeters (113 inches) annually, and the average yearly relative humidity is 83%.

4 PLANTS AND ANIMALS

Along the coast there are mangrove forests, pandanus, hibiscus, and beach vegetation. Inland, the rainforests contain many kinds of trees. The higher elevations of Savai'i contain moss forest and mountain scrub (low-growing shrubs).

The 16 native species of birds include small doves, parrots, pigeons, and wild ducks. The only mammals native to Western Samoa are the rat and the flying fox.

Photo credit: Susan D. Rock.

One of Apia's 72 churches.

5 ENVIRONMENT

According to United Nation's sources, the forests are eliminated at a rate of 4,000–8,000 hectares (9,800–21,600 acres) per year due to the expansion of farmland. A lack of adequate sewage disposal and other forms of pollution are a threat to both the reefs and the marine life which inhabit them.

6 POPULATION

The population of Western Samoa in 1991 was 159,862. The population density in 1991 was 56 persons per square kilometer (145 per square mile). Upolu had a population of 112,228 in 1986; the population of Savai'i was 44,930.

7 MIGRATION

Emigration (estimated at 5,278 in 1988) consists mainly of students going to New Zealand to continue their education and Samoans seeking work there. In addition, several thousand Western Samoans live in American Samoa and other parts of the United States. The total number of Western Samoans living abroad in these countries and Australia was estimated at 76,200 in 1989.

8 ETHNIC GROUPS

Samoans comprise more than 90% of the total population. The Samoans are the second-largest branch of the Polynesians, a people occupying the scattered islands of the Pacific from Hawaii to New Zealand and from eastern Fiji to Easter Island. Most of the remaining Western Samoans are of mixed Samoan and European or Asian descent. Europeans, other Pacific islanders, and Asians make up less than 1% of the total.

9 LANGUAGES

Samoan is the universal language, but both Samoan and English are official. Some Chinese is also spoken. Most of the part-Samoans and many others speak English, and it is taught in the schools.

10 RELIGIONS

Over 99% of Samoans profess some form of Christianity. The Congregational Christian Church of Western Samoa is the largest religious body in the country, with members comprising some 47% of the population in 1986. The Roman Catholic (36,700) and Methodist (36,000) churches had large followings in 1993. Mormon and Seventh-Day Adventist churches, the Baha'is, and a number of other denominations have smaller congregations.

11 TRANSPORTATION

The road system in 1991 totaled 2,042 kilometers (1,269 miles). In 1992 there were 10,830 passenger cars and 1,204 commercial vehicles. Diesel-powered launches carry passengers and freight around the islands, and small motor vessels maintain services between Apia and Pago Pago in American Samoa.

Apia is the principal port. Polynesian Airlines provides daily air connections with Pago Pago and regularly scheduled

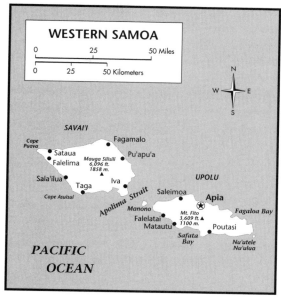

LOCATION: 13° to 15°s; 171° to 173°w. **BOUNDARY LENGTHS:** Savai'i 188 kilometers (117 miles); Upolu coastline, 183 kilometers (114 miles). **TERRITORIAL SEA LIMIT:** 12 miles.

flights to other Pacific destinations. Faleolo Airport, 35 kilometers (22 miles) west of Apia, is the principal air terminal.

12 HISTORY

The western world knew little about Samoa until after the arrival of the missionary John Williams in 1830. Representatives of Great Britain and the United States were soon stationed in Apia. Between 1847 and 1861, the United States appointed a commercial agent, and Britain and the city of Hamburg appointed consuls.

British, American, and German consular agents aligned themselves with various feuding tribal chiefs until the resulting tension and intrigues led to civil war in 1889.

Britain, the United States, and Germany set up a neutral government under King Malietoa Laupepea, but after the king's death in 1898 the three powers intervened once again and abolished the kingship. In 1900, Western Samoa became a German protectorate. With the outbreak of World War I (1914–18), New Zealand military forces occupied Western Samoa, and from 1919 to 1946, New Zealand administered the islands under a mandate of the League of Nations.

Between 1927 and 1936, a nationalistic organization known as the Mau embarked on a program of civil disobedience. In 1946, the Untied Nations General Assembly and New Zealand began a process leading toward ultimate self-government of Samoa. On 1 January 1962, Western Samoa became an independent nation. Upon independence, Fiame Faumuina Mataafa was Western Samoa's first prime minister (1962–70) and served again in that post from 1973 until his death in 1975.

During the late 1970s and early 1980s, Western Samoa suffered from a worsening economy and growing political and social unrest. A divisive public-sector strike from 6 April to 2 July 1981 cut many essential services to a critical level. Controversy erupted in 1982 over the signing by the HRPP (Human Rights Protection Party) government in August of a protocol with New Zealand that reduced the right of Western Samoans to New Zealand citizenship. Va'ai Kolone became prime minister in January 1986 as head of a new coalition government.

13 GOVERNMENT

The powers and functions of the head of state are far-reaching. All legislation must have his assent before it becomes law. He also has power to grant pardons and reprieves and to suspend or commute any sentence by any court. The parliament consists of the head of state and the Fono, which is made up of one elected member from each of 45 Samoan constituencies. Local government is carried out by the village *fono*, or council.

14 POLITICAL PARTIES

Political parties are becoming increasingly important. In a general election held in April 1991, the ruling HRPP (Human Rights Protection Party) won 28 of 47 seats in the Parliament (*Fono*).

15 JUDICIAL SYSTEM

The Supreme Court has full civil and criminal jurisdiction for the administration of justice in Western Samoa. The Court of Appeal consists of three judges who may be judges of the Supreme Court. Magistrates' courts are subordinate courts with varying degrees of authority.

The Land and Titles Court has jurisdiction in disputes over Samoan land and succession to Samoan titles. Some civil and criminal matters are handled by village traditional courts which apply a very different procedure than that used in the official western-style courts.

16 ARMED FORCES

Western Samoa has no armed forces.

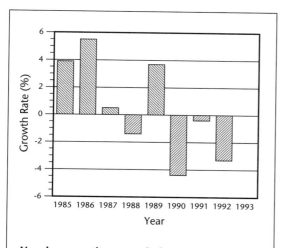

Yearly growth rate of the economy. This economic indicator tells by what percent the economy has increased or decreased when compared with the previous year.

17 ECONOMY

The economy is based largely on agriculture. Tourist revenues and earnings by overseas workers are important sources of foreign exchange. Economic performance has suffered since 1990 due to the devastation to crops and tourism caused by two cyclones, Ofa and Val. Western Samoa has the highest unemployment rate and the lowest wages in Oceania, the south Pacific region.

18 INCOME

In 1992, Western Samoa's gross national product (GNP) was US$153 million at current prices, or US$940 per person. For the period 1985–92, the average inflation rate was 10.6%, resulting in a real growth rate in per person GNP of –0.1%.

19 INDUSTRY

Industries include food- and timber-processing facilities, a brewery, cigarette and match factories, and small individual enterprises for processing coffee and for manufacturing curios, soap, carbonated drinks, light metal products, garments, footwear, and other consumer products.

20 LABOR

No Samoan is entirely dependent on wages for sustenance; all share in the products of their family lands and can always return to them. Agriculture, forestry and fishing account for half of wage employment. Over the years, thousands of skilled and semiskilled Samoans have left the islands, mainly drawn away by better economic opportunities in New Zealand, Australia, and the United States.

21 AGRICULTURE

Most Samoans grow food crops for home consumption and cash crops for export. In 1992, coconut production was 95,000 tons, and taro (coco yam) production amounted to 32,000 tons. Exports of cocoa have fallen in recent years, thereby discouraging production. In 1992, no production over 1,000 tons was reported. Exports of food products in 1990 amounted to US$5 million, or about 46% of total exports.

22 DOMESTICATED ANIMALS

Pigs and cattle form the bulk of the livestock. In 1992, pigs, which are common in the villages, were estimated to number 270,000 and cattle, 31,000.

23 FISHING

The local fish catch has steadily fallen from 4,020 tons in 1982 to 565 tons in 1991.

24 FORESTRY

The nation's forest area is estimated at 134,600 hectares (331,000 acres). Timber exports were estimated at US$11,000 in 1992.

25 MINING

No minerals of commercial value are known to exist in Western Samoa.

26 FOREIGN TRADE

Imports consist chiefly of food, fuels and chemicals, machinery, transportation equipment, and other manufactured articles. The principal exports are taro, coconut cream, and automotive seat belts. Also exported are coconut oil, coconuts, copra (dried coconut meat), cocoa, timber, and clothing. Western Samoa imports more than it exports. Western Samoa's leading trade partners are Australia, New Zealand, Germany, the United States, Japan, and other Pacific islands.

27 ENERGY AND POWER

Western Samoa has depended heavily on imported energy, but hydroelectric power accounted for 43% of electrical generation in 1991. Electricity production totaled 47 million kilowatt hours in 1991.

28 SOCIAL DEVELOPMENT

A social security system provides for employee retirement pensions, disability

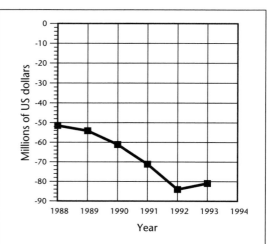

Yearly balance of trade measured in millions of US dollars. The balance of trade is the difference between what a country sells to other countries (its exports) and what it buys (its imports). If a country imports more than it exports, it has a negative balance of trade (a trade deficit). If exports exceed imports there is a positive balance of trade (a trade surplus).

benefits, and death benefits. Workers' compensation is compulsory.

In Western Samoan society, obligations to the *aiga*, or extended family, are often given precedence over individual rights. While there is some discrimination against women, they can play an important role in society, especially female *matai*, or heads of families.

29 HEALTH

In 1990, there were 50 physicians in Western Samoa. District nurses are stationed at strategic points throughout the islands. Child health clinics are a regular feature of their work. Life expectancy was 66 years.

30 HOUSING

Most Samoans live in traditional houses called fales. A fale is usually round or oval, with pebble floors and a thatch roof. It has no walls, being supported on the sides by posts. Coconut-leaf blinds can be lowered to keep out wind and rain. A popular Samoan-European type of dwelling is an oblong concrete house with some walls, often with separate rooms in each corner; like the fale it is open at the sides.

31 EDUCATION

The adult literacy rate is estimated to be over 97%. In 1991 there were 30 primary schools with 7,884 pupils and 524 teachers. At the secondary level, there were 3,643 pupils and 266 teachers.

The University of the South Pacific School of Agriculture maintains a campus at Alafua. Enrollment at all higher level institutions was 909 in 1988. The University of Samoa offers courses in both arts and sciences.

32 MEDIA

In 1992 there were 7,500 telephones in use. The Western Samoan Broadcasting Service transmits radio programs on two stations in Samoan and English and provides direct broadcasts from the Fono. In 1991 there were an estimated 75,000 radios in use. There is no domestic television service.

There are several bilingual weeklies, including the *Samoa Weekly* (1991 circulation 4,500), *Samoa Observer* (3,500), *Samoa Times* (3,000), and *South Sea Star* (3,000).

Photo credit: Susan D. Rock

Vendors selling their goods at a new market in Apia.

33 TOURISM AND RECREATION

Since 1966, the government has encouraged tourism. The major tourist attractions are the beaches and traditional villages.

The head of state lives on the island of Apia, which was also once the home of author Robert Louis Stevenson; Stevenson's grave is there. Pastimes include swimming, water skiing, and fishing. Soccer and cricket are popular local sports.

34 FAMOUS WESTERN SAMOANS

The Scottish author Robert Louis Stevenson (1850–94) lived principally on one of the tiny islands of Western Samoa, and on Apia, from 1889 until his death. Western Samoans famous since independence include Malietoa Tanumafili II (b.1913), who was named head of state in 1962, and Fiame Faumuina Mataafa (d.1975), who served as prime minister from 1962 to 1970 and again from 1973 until his death. Tofilau Eti (b. American Samoa, 1925?) was prime minister from December 1982 to December 1985, when he resigned and was succeeded by Va'ai Kolone.

35 BIBLIOGRAPHY

Henderson, Faye. *Western Samoa*, a country profile. 2d ed. Washington, D.C.: Library of Congress, 1980.

Mead, Margaret. *Coming of Age in Samoa.* London: Penguin, 1961 (orig. 1928).

YEMEN

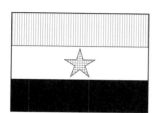

Republic of Yemen
Al-Jumhuriyah al-Yamaniyah

CAPITAL: Sana (Ṣanʻā).

FLAG: The national flag is a tricolor of red, white, and black horizontal stripes, with a green star on the white stripe.

ANTHEM: *Al-Watani (Peace to the Land).*

MONETARY UNIT: The Yemeni riyal (YR) is a paper currency of 100 fils. There are coins of 1, 5, 10, 25, and 50 fils and notes of 1, 5, 10, 20, 50, and 100 riyals. YR1 = $0.1013 (or $1 = YR9.875).

WEIGHTS AND MEASURES: The metric system is being introduced, but local measures remain in common use.

HOLIDAYS: International Women's Day, 8 March; Corrective Movement Day, 13 June; National Day, 14 October. Movable Muslim holidays include Laylat al-Miraj, 'Id al-Fitr, 'Id al-'Adha', Milad an-Nabi, and 1st of Muharram.

TIME: 3 PM = noon GMT.

1 LOCATION AND SIZE

Yemen, located in the southern part of the Arabian Peninsula, is slightly larger than twice the size of the state of Wyoming with a total area of 527,970 square kilometers (203,850 square miles). Yemen has a total boundary length of 3,652 kilometers (2,269 miles).

Sana, the capital, is in the western part of the country.

2 TOPOGRAPHY

The topography of Yemen features a narrow coastal plain backed by flat-topped hills and rugged mountains. The interior of the country is desert. The highest known point rises 3,760 meters (12,336 feet) above the Red Sea coast. The western part of the country contains fertile soil on highland plateaus.

3 CLIMATE

Extreme humidity combines with high temperatures—as high as 54°C (129°F) in the shade—to produce a stiflingly hot climate in parts of the country. The climate of the highlands is generally considered the best in Arabia, with temperatures between 22°C (72°F) in June, the hottest month, to 14°C (57°F) in January. Rainfall in the highlands ranges from 41 centimeters (16 inches) to 81 centimeters (32 inches).

4 PLANTS AND ANIMALS

Vegetation is scarce along the coast, but in the highlands and stream beds it is plentiful. Acacia, date palm, and many fruit trees are common. Many varieties of grapes are cultivated.

Wild mammals include the baboon, gazelle, leopard, and mountain hare. Many varieties of birds are found, as well as over 27,000 varieties of insects and over 600 species of flowering plants.

5 ENVIRONMENT

Yemen's main environmental problems have long been scarcity of water, soil erosion, and expansion of the desert. Water pollution is a problem due to contaminants from the oil industry and untreated sewage. The nation uses 93.4% of its available water for farming activity and 2% for industrial purposes. Natural forests in mountainous areas have been destroyed by agricultural clearing and livestock overgrazing. As of 1987, endangered species included the northern bald ibis, the South Arabian leopard, and two species of turtle.

6 POPULATION

The population of Yemen was officially estimated at 11,279,470 in 1990. The United Nations estimated the 1995 population to be 13,897,00 and projected a population of 16,424,00 for the year 2000. Recent estimates place the population density at 24 persons per square kilometer (62 per square mile). Aden, the chief port and capital of the former People's Democratic Republic of Yemen (PDRY or South Yemen), had a population of 417,366 in 1987.

7 MIGRATION

There were 1,168,199 citizens of Yemen working abroad in 1986, mostly in Sa'udi Arabia and other Gulf states. Yemen took Iraq's side in the Persian Gulf War, which followed Iraq's 1990 annexation of Kuwait. As a result, Sa'udi Arabia expelled an estimated 800,000–1,000,000 Yemeni workers by revoking their work privileges.

In 1969, following the establishment of a leftist regime in the People's Democratic Republic of Yemen (PDRY or South Yemen) in 1969, more than 300,000 people fled to the north to the Yemen Arab Republic (YAR), and virtually all minority groups left the country.

In 1992 more than 60,000 Yemenis returned from the Horn of Africa (region of Africa south of Yemen), chiefly because of turmoil in Somalia. Yemen was harboring 56,200 Somali refugees at the end of 1992.

8 ETHNIC GROUPS

Since independence, the population has been almost entirely Arab. Many ethnologists contend that the purest "Arab" stock is to be found in Yemen. There is a small minority of Akhdam.

9 LANGUAGES

Arabic, the national language, is spoken in a variety of dialects. Mahri, a rare and relatively unstudied language of unknown origins, is spoken in the east. English is widely understood.

10 RELIGIONS

The Republic of Yemen is a Muslim country. Almost all of the inhabitants are Sunni Muslims of the Shafi'i school. Most of those remaining are Shi'ite Muslims of the

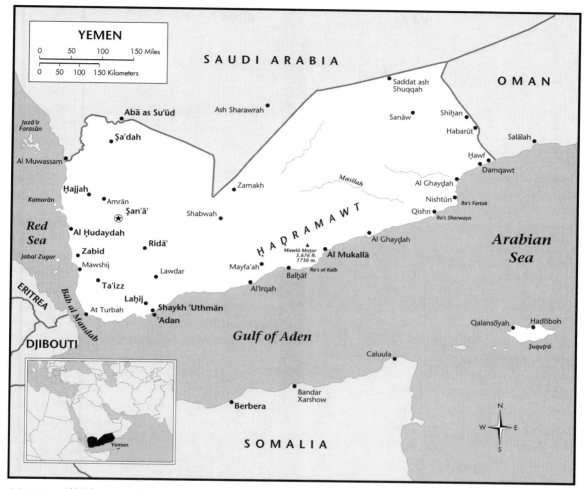

LOCATION 12°41′ to 17°32′N; 42°32′ to 53°5′E. **BOUNDARY LENGTHS:** Oman, 288 kilometers (179 miles); Saʻudi Arabia, 1,458 kilometers (907 miles); coastline, 1,906 kilometers, (1,183 miles).

Zaydi sect. In addition, there is a small minority of Isma'ilis, members of another Shi'ite Muslim sect. Of the 45,000 Jews who lived in the country in 1949, about 1,100 remained in 1990. In remote areas there is still evidence of shamanism, spirit worship, and other native forms of religion.

11 TRANSPORTATION

In 1991, Yemen had about 15,000 kilometers (9,630 miles) of roadway. Passenger cars numbered only 165,438 in 1991, and there were 237,957 commercial vehicles. The main port is Al-Hudaydah. Yemen Airways (Yemenia), the national airline, operates services between San'a, Ta'izz, and Al-Hudaydah and also schedules flights to Egypt, Ethiopia, Kuwait, Sa'udi Arabia, and the United Arab Emirates (UAE). The airline carried 99,500 passengers during six months of operation in 1991. The principal airfield is Ar-Rahba International Airport, north of Sana.

12 HISTORY

In mid-1994, the future of the Republic of Yemen was in doubt. North (the Yemen Arab Republic, or YAR) and South Yemen (the People's Democratic Republic of Yemen, or PDRY) had united in 1990 but, four years later, they fought a bitter civil war and it was not clear whether the union would survive.

For thousands of years before the Christian era, present-day Yemen was the site of a series of wealthy kingdoms that dominated world trade. The kingdom of Sheba (tenth to second centuries BC) is the best known of these. Ethiopian Christians invaded in AD 525, followed by Persians fifty years later. Islam was accepted in the next century, and Yemen became the battleground of Muslim religious factions.

In the ninth century, a Zaydi ruler, Yahya al-Hadi ila'l Haqq, founded a line of imams (leaders) that survived until the second half of the twentieth century. The Ottoman Turks overran the country in 1517 and maintained varying degrees of control over it for the next 400 years. By the twentieth century they controlled only the northwestern part, which they evacuated at the close of World War I (1918–18), leaving the current Zaydi imam in power. This area, although only part of present-day Yemen, was called Yemen at the time.

British Influence

Meanwhile, the British had established a presence in the southern part of the region in the nineteenth century, first occupying Aden in 1839. The port was used as a refueling station on the route to India and then became a major trading center after the opening of the Suez Canal in 1869.

To protect its foothold in Aden, the United Kingdom had signed agreements with rulers of the surrounding tribes and states, grouping them into two separate protectorates. In 1959, the United Kingdom formed the six states of the western protectorate into the Federation of Arab Emirates of the South. In 1963, Aden was merged into the federation, which later became known as the Federation of South Arabia. The dispute over the future form and direction of this new political unit, as well as over which other states would join it, resulted in several years of violence, as various political parties and other groups struggled for power.

On 30 November 1967, all the states of the protectorates were combined, the last British soldiers withdrew, and the National Liberation Front (NLF) took control, declaring the independence of the People's Republic of South Yemen. On 22 June 1969, the head of the NLF was ousted by a group of young leftists within the organization. The new regime, headed by a five-man council, renamed the country the People's Democratic Republic of Yemen (PDRY), developed close ties with the Soviet Union, and secured economic aid from it and China.

Meanwhile, in the north, Yemen (the formerly Turkish-controlled area) joined the League of Arab States in 1945, and, in 1958, formed a federation with the newly established United Arab Republic (UAR), comprised of Egypt and Syria. In December 1961, however, this union was dissolved.

Period of Civil Strife

In September 1962, Yemen's royal government was overthrown by revolutionary forces that established the Yemen Arab Republic (YAR). A civil war between the royalists (defenders of the imamate) and the republican government lasted until 1970, and drew intervention by other Arab states in the area. Sa'udi Arabia supported the royalist cause, and Egypt came to the assistance of the republic, dispatching up to 70,000 troops to the YAR. The republican government remained in control.

Following its formation in 1969, the PDRY in the north was involved in conflicts with all three of its neighbors. A separatist movement was supported in Oman; there were border skirmishes with Sa'udi forces in 1969 and 1973; and the PDRY fought a brief war with the YAR in February–March 1979. The war with YAR ended with a truce, mediated by the Arab League, and an agreement in principle to seek unification of the two Yemens.

Movement toward unification proceeded, although with numerous delays, throughout the 1980s. It was slowed by

Photo credit: Paty Lam Kim, Gif sur Yvette, France.

The mosque is decorated in Persian style, Jibla.

internal problems in each country, including a 1986 civil war in the PDRY that set back relations between the two countries, especially since 50,000 refugees fled the YAR. Both governments later confirmed their commitment to unity.

Unification

On 22 May 1990, the unified Republic of Yemen was proclaimed. A 30-month transition period was set for unifying the different political and economic systems. The army, police, and civil service were never integrated as planned, however. Meanwhile, the economy was hard hit by the consequences of Yemen's support for Iraq after that country invaded Kuwait. It is estimated that Sa'udi Arabia expelled between 800,000 and 1,000,000 Yemeni workers, thus depriving Yemen of some $3 billion in foreign exchange. In addition, Sa'udi Arabia and the other Persian Gulf states ended $2 billion in foreign aid. Unemployment in Yemen reached 30%.

Free and fair parliamentary elections were held in April 1992 with President Saleh's General People's Congress just missing a majority victory. A three-party coalition was formed, but started to come apart in late 1993. Although the quarrel appeared to be patched up with an agreement in February 1994, fighting broke out in May of that year.

In a few months, thousands of casualties had been suffered; tribes, clans, and militias were engaged in seeking their own conflicting goals, and the city of Aden was under siege. Some observers attributed the civil conflict to the recent discovery of massive oil reserves in the south and to Sa'udi Arabia's interest in weakening Yemen by promoting the breakup of the union. The future was bleak, despite efforts of the United Nations and some Arab states to promote peace.

13 GOVERNMENT

The 1990 unity constitution established a political system based on free, multiparty elections. During the transitional period a presidential council was created with five members, three from the North and two from the South, to oversee executive operations. The council appointed a prime minister who picked a 38-member cabinet. A 301-member parliament was also formed, with 159 members chosen from the North, 111 from the South, and 31 at large.

The unified government established 17 governorates, subdivided into districts.

In the May 1990 election, 121 seats were won by the northern General People's Congress, 62 by Islaah (an Islamist and tribalist party), 56 by the southern Yemeni Socialist Party, 47 by independents, and 15 by five other parties.

14 POLITICAL PARTIES

The Yemen Social Party (YSP)—originally the National Liberation Front—was the PDRY's only political party, and survived to represent southern interests in the unified Yemen. Before unification, political parties played no role in North Yemen. Tribal allegiances were more important political factors.

After unity, the northern leader, General Saleh, formed the General People's Congress which became the country's largest party. The second largest bloc in the parliament is held by the Islaah Party, a fusion of tribal and Islamic interests which opposed the unity constitution because it did not sufficiently adhere to Islamic principles. At least five smaller parties have been active in the politics of unified Yemen.

15 JUDICIAL SYSTEM

Under a 1991 decree, the separate judicial systems of the former YAR and the former PDRY have been unified at the Supreme

Court level. The separate lower courts systems continue to function in their respective halves of the country.

16 ARMED FORCES

In 1990, the consolidated armed forces numbered 63,500, based on two years of required service. The army of 60,000 has all 45,000 draftees. The navy of 1,500 mans 16 patrol and coast combatants and 17 other ships. The air force, with 2,000 members, has 101 combat aircraft. Reserve forces number 40,000. Yemen spends $1 billion a year for defense.

17 ECONOMY

The unification in 1990 of North and South Yemen posed the immediate challenge of merging two different economies. When Yemen aligned itself with Iraq during the Persian Gulf War, Sa'udi Arabia and the Gulf states, Yemen's main aid donors and hosts to large numbers of Yemeni workers and their families, ended the Yemenis' privileged status. The economic impact of lost payments is estimated at about $1 billion per year.

After the Gulf crisis, Yemen was confronted with high unemployment (perhaps as high as 25–30%), lost income, halving of US military aid, a sharp cutback in US foreign aid programs, and other canceled foreign assistance. Yemen also faced the cost of food imports and social services for the returnees totaling about $500 million. In addition, the civil conflict in 1994 between the north and south has increased the need for external aid.

18 INCOME

In 1992, Yemen's gross national product (GNP) was reported to be $6.7 billion at current prices, or $520 per person. In 1992 the inflation rate for consumer prices was 100%.

19 INDUSTRY

The governments of both North and South Yemen had invested extensively in manufacturing, but their industries had required continued government assistance. In North Yemen about 50% of industry has been based on food processing. Building materials, textiles, leather wear, jewelry, and glass making are other industries.

The largest industry in South Yemen was the British Petroleum refinery at Little Aden (capacity 176,000 barrels per day). Local manufactured goods included clothing, processed food, metal products, soap, and perfumes.

Fertilizer plants, another refinery, and a lubricant plant are projects under consideration. The top priority project, however, is the modernization of the Aden refinery, which is expected to cost several hundred million dollars.

20 LABOR

In 1992, Yemen's work force was estimated at 2.8 million. According to 1992 estimates, 64% of the labor force is employed in agriculture and fishing, 25% in services, and 11% in commerce and industry.

As of 1992, the labor codes of the former YAR and PDRY remained in

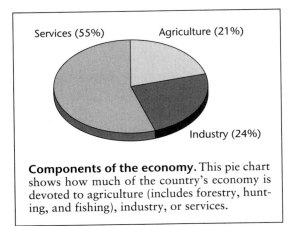

Services (55%) Agriculture (21%)

Industry (24%)

Components of the economy. This pie chart shows how much of the country's economy is devoted to agriculture (includes forestry, hunting, and fishing), industry, or services.

effect. The labor federations of the two countries merged in 1990, creating the Yemeni Confederation of Labor Unions.

21 AGRICULTURE

As of July 1993, Yemen imported 70% of its food requirements, including 1.8 million tons of wheat annually. Traditionally, Yemen was famous for its coffee, shipped from the port of Mukallā, from which the English word *mocha* derives. The main cash crop is qat, a mild stimulant chewed by many Yemenis on a daily basis.

Agricultural output in 1992 (in 1,000 tons) included sorghum, 459; tomatoes, 172; wheat, 152; grapes, 145; bananas, 55; seed cotton, 21; sesame seed, 12; coffee, 8; and cotton, 7.

22 DOMESTICATED ANIMALS

Animal farming is an important part of the economy. In 1992, the livestock population was estimated at 3,850,000 sheep, 3,470,000 goats, 1,190,000 head of cattle, 690,000 donkeys, and 185,000 camels.

There were approximately 24 million chickens in 1992.

23 FISHING

The annual fish catch in 1991 was about 85,261 tons. Principal species included Indian and Spanish mackerel, cuttlefish, lobster, and scavengers. Exports of fish and fish products were valued at $13.6 million in 1991.

24 FORESTRY

Grazing by goats and the cutting of timber for fuel and construction have almost completely eliminated Yemen's forests. Roundwood production totaled 324,000 cubic meters in 1991; much lumber is imported.

25 MINING

Until the recent discovery of petroleum, the mineral industry had been limited to the production of cement, dimension stone, gypsum, and salt. In 1991, production of cement amounted to 850,000 tons; dimension stone, 410,000 cubic meters; gypsum, 75,000 tons; and salt, 225,000 tons.

26 FOREIGN TRADE

In 1990, over half of the unified Yemen's oil exports went to the United States, which is one of Yemen's main suppliers of agricultural commodities. In 1991, oil accounted for over 70% ($454.3 million) of Yemen's total export earnings. Other than oil, Yemen exports little. In 1990, fisheries products, the second largest export, earned only $15.6 million, or

Selected Social Indicators

These statistics are estimates for the period 1988 to 1993. For comparison purposes, data for the United States and averages for low-income countries and high-income countries are also given.

Indicator	Yemen	Low-income countries	High-income countries	United States
Per capita gross national product†	**$520**	$380	$23,680	$24,740
Population growth rate	**5.5%**	1.9%	0.6%	1.0%
Population growth rate in urban areas	**8.5%**	3.9%	0.8%	1.3%
Population per square kilometer of land	**24**	78	25	26
Life expectancy in years	**51**	62	77	76
Number of people per physician	**5,561**	>3,300	453	419
Number of pupils per teacher (primary school)	**n.a.**	39	<18	20
Illiteracy rate (15 years and older)	**62%**	41%	<5%	<3%
Energy consumed per capita (kg of oil equivalent)	**285**	364	5,203	7,918

† The gross national product (GNP) is the total dollar value of all goods and services produced by a country in a year. The per capita GNP is calculated by dividing a country's GNP by its population. The World Bank defines low-income countries as those with a per capita GNP of $695 or less. High-income countries have a per capita GNP of $8,626 or more. Less than 14% of the world's 5.5 billion people live in high-income countries, while almost 60% live in low-income countries.

n.a. = data not available   > = greater than   < = less than

Sources: World Bank, *Social Indicators of Development 1995,* Baltimore: Johns Hopkins University Press, 1995. Central Intelligence Agency, *World Fact Book,* Washington, D.C.: Government Printing Office, 1994.

2.5% of the total for exports, far behind oil's $515 million.

27 ENERGY AND POWER

As of 1993, Yemen had two operating refineries. In April 1993, oil production amounted to 200,000 barrels per day. Proven oil reserves as of 1 January 1993 were four billion barrels. Total electricity production was 1,750 million kilowatt hours in 1991.

28 SOCIAL DEVELOPMENT

While the government has expanded its role in providing assistance, traditional means still prevail. Families and tribes care for their sick, handicapped, unemployed, and widows and orphans. Those without family or tribal ties beg or have recourse to Islamic pious foundations (*waqfs*).

The state operates orphanages and finances other welfare measures. Effective in 1988, a provident fund system provides old age, disability, survivor, and workers' compensation benefits. The Yemen Family Planning Association provides contraceptives and advisory services through local clinics and health centers.

29 HEALTH

Malaria, typhus, tuberculosis, dysentery, whooping cough, measles, hepatitis, schistosomiasis, and typhoid fever are widespread, and inadequate sewage disposal is a general health hazard. Life expectancy is 51 years.

From 1988 to 1993, Yemen averaged 1 doctor per 5,561 people. Only about 38% of the population had access to health care services as of 1992.

30 HOUSING

About one-fourth of urban housing units are huts, tents, or other makeshift structures. In the hot coastal region, most dwellings are straw huts. In the highlands, the poorer people live in huts of stone or baked brick. Wealthier Yemenis live in large houses whose upper parts, which may rise from two to eight stories, are usually of baked brick with windows outlined in decorative designs.

31 EDUCATION

In the unified Republic of Yemen, the literacy rate was estimated to be over 38%. The country has over 5,000 schools including over 100 secondary schools. Prior to unification in 1990, the PDRY (South Yemen) had 13,240 primary teachers and 379,905 pupils. The YAR (North Yemen) had 35,350 teachers and 1,291,372 pupils the same year.

At the secondary level in 1990, PDRY had 34,179 pupils in general secondary schools; YAR had 394,578 pupils in general secondary schools. There are two universities: San'a University and the University of Aden. Total university enrollment now exceeds 27,800.

32 MEDIA

There were about 65,000 telephones in 1991. The government operates several radio stations and two television networks, one of them partly commercial. There were about 325,000 radios and 330,000 television sets in 1991. In the same year there were four daily newspapers includind *Al-Thawrah* with a circulation of 40,000.

33 TOURISM AND RECREATION

Tourists can visit historic and religious sites (such as the Ghumdau Palace and the Great Mosque in Sana) and exotic markets, and enjoy scenic areas including the Red Sea coast. In 1991, there were 43,656 tourist arrivals in hotels and other establishments, 49% from Europe and 24% from the Middle East.

34 FAMOUS YEMENIS

Imam Yahya ibn Muhammad Hamid ad-Din (1869?–1948) ruled during the period when Yemen established its independence. 'Ali 'Abdallah Salih (b.1942) became president of the YAR in 1978, ending a period of upheaval in which his two immediate predecessors were assassinated.

35 BIBLIOGRAPHY

Crouch, Michael. *An Element of Luck: To South Arabia and Beyond.* New York: Radcliffe Press, 1993.

Dresch, Paul. *Tribes, Government, and History in Yemen.* New York: Oxford University Press, 1989.

Wenner, Manfred W. *The Yemen Arab Republic: Development and Change in an Ancient Land.* Boulder, Colo.: Westview Press, 1991.

ZAIRE

Republic of Zaire
République du Zaïre

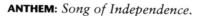

CAPITAL: Kinshasa.

FLAG: The flag adopted on 27 October 1971 is green with a yellow circle in the center; inside the circle is a forearm and hand clasping a red lighted torch.

ANTHEM: *Song of Independence.*

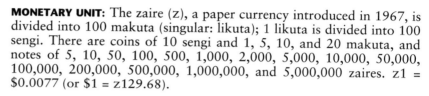

MONETARY UNIT: The zaire (z), a paper currency introduced in 1967, is divided into 100 makuta (singular: likuta); 1 likuta is divided into 100 sengi. There are coins of 10 sengi and 1, 5, 10, and 20 makuta, and notes of 5, 10, 50, 100, 500, 1,000, 2,000, 5,000, 10,000, 50,000, 100,000, 200,000, 500,000, 1,000,000, and 5,000,000 zaires. z1 = $0.0077 (or $1 = z129.68).

WEIGHTS AND MEASURES: The metric system is the legal standard.

HOLIDAYS: New Year's Day, 1 January; Commemoration of Martyrs of Independence, 4 January; Labor Day, 1 May; Anniversary of the Popular Movement of the Revolution, 20 May; Promulgation of the 1967 Constitution, 24 June; Independence Day, 30 June; Parents' Day, 1 August; Youth Day and Birthday of President Mobutu, 14 October; Anniversary of Zaire, 27 October; Army Day, 17 November; the Anniversary of the Regime, 24 November; and Christmas Day, 25 December.

TIME: In Kinshasa, 1 PM = noon GMT; in Lubumbashi, 2 PM = noon GMT.

1 LOCATION AND SIZE

Zaire is crossed by the equator in its north-central region. The third-largest country in Africa, it covers an area of 2,345,410 square kilometers (905,568 square miles), or slightly more than one-quarter the size of the United States. It has a total boundary length of 10,308 kilometers (6,405 miles). Zaire's capital city, Kinshasa, is located in the western part of the country.

2 TOPOGRAPHY

The principal river is the Zaire (formerly Congo). Plateaus rise around a densely forested central section known as the cuvette, which covers nearly half the area of the country. Margherita Peak, on the border with Uganda, is third highest in Africa. All major rivers are tributaries of the Zaire, including the Lomami, the Aruwimi or Ituri, the Ubangi, the Uélé, and the Kasai. The largest lakes include

Tanganyika, Albert, and Edward, all on the eastern border.

3 CLIMATE

The climate is tropically hot and humid in the lower western and central regions. In the cuvette, temperatures average 24°C (75°F), with high humidity and almost no seasonal variation. Annual rainfall is between 130 centimeters and 200 centimeters (51–79 inches). In the northern and southern plateaus there are wet and dry seasons and annual rainfall of 100–160 centimeters (39–63 inches). The eastern highlands have temperatures averaging 18°C (64°F) and 24°C (75°F), depending on the season. Rainfall averages 120–180 centimeters (47–71 inches).

4 PLANTS AND ANIMALS

The plants and animals of Zaire include some 95% of all the varieties found in Africa. Among the many species of trees are the red cedar, mahogany, oak, walnut, the silk-cotton tree, and various palms. Orchids, lilies, lobelias, and gladioli are some of the flowers found. Larger species of mammals include the lion, elephant, buffalo, rhinoceros, zebra, leopard, cheetah, and gorilla. Hippopotamuses and crocodiles are found in the rivers. Lizards and chameleons are among the numerous small reptiles.

Birds are mainly of species common to much of Africa, including the eagle, vulture, owl, goose, duck, parrot, pigeon, sunbird, and cuckoo. The rivers and lakes have many kinds of fish, among them catfish, tigerfish, and electric eels. Insects include various dragonflies, bees, wasps, beetles, mosquitoes, and the tsetse fly, as well as scorpions, spiders, centipedes, ants, and termites.

5 ENVIRONMENT

In 1986 there were nine national parks, and the total protected area covered 8,827,000 hectares (21,812,000 acres). Forest land has been reduced by increased farming activity and the nation's dependency on wood for fuel. By 1985, 1,429 square miles of forestland had been lost. The main environmental problems are poor water and sanitation systems, which result in the spread of insect- and rodent-borne diseases. The nation has 244.5 cubic miles of water with 17% used for farming activities and 25% used for industrial purposes. Roughly one-third of the nation's city dwellers and 76% of the people living in rural areas do not have pure water. In 1994, 31 of Zaire's mammal species and 27 of its bird species were endangered, as were 3 types of plants.

6 POPULATION

A US Census Bureau estimate put the population at 41,691,200 in mid-1994. A population of 50,970,000 was projected for the year 2000. Density is approximately 17 persons per square kilometer (44 per square mile). Kinshasa, the capital, had an estimated population of 3,455,000 in 1990.

7 MIGRATION

Political tensions and crises in neighboring African countries have resulted in large-scale migration to Zaire. At the end of

ZAIRE

LOCATION: 5°28′N to 13°27′S; 12°12′ to 31°18′E. **BOUNDARY LENGTHS:** Central African Republic, 1,577 kilometers (980 miles); Sudan, 628 kilometers (390 miles); Uganda, 765 kilometers (475 miles); Rwanda, 217 kilometers (135 miles); Burundi, 233 kilometers (145 miles); Zambia; 1,930 kilometers (1,206 miles); Angola, 2,511 kilometers (1,565 miles); Atlantic coastline, 37 kilometers (23 miles); Congo, 2,410 kilometers (1,486 miles). **TERRITORIAL SEA LIMIT:** 12 miles.

1992 there were 391,100 refugees registered with the United Nations High Commissioner for Refugees (UNHCR) in Zaire, including 198,000 from Angola, 21,100 from Uganda, 50,900 from Rwanda, and 9,500 from Burundi. There were 60,200 officially registered Zairians living in neighboring countries at the end of 1992, including 25,800 in Burundi, 16,000 in Tanzania, 15,600 in Uganda, and 2,300 in Sudan.

8 ETHNIC GROUPS

Bantu-speaking peoples form about 80% of the population. Most of the rest are Sudanic-speaking groups. In the cuvette, (densely forested center of the country) are about 80,000–100,000 Pygmies. Among the Bantu-speaking peoples, major groups include the Kongo, or Bakongo; the Luba, or Baluba; the Mongo and related groups; and the Lunda and Chokwe. Non-Africans, estimated around 200,000 in the early 1990s, include Belgians, Greeks, Lebanese, and Asian Indians.

9 LANGUAGES

As many as 700 languages and dialects are spoken in Zaire. Serving as regional common languages are four African languages: Lingala, Swahili, Kikongo, and Tshiluba. Lomongo is widely spoken in the cuvette. French is the official language and is widely used in government and commerce.

10 RELIGIONS

In 1990, it was estimated that 50.6% of the population was Roman Catholic. About 28% was Protestant in 1989. Officially recognized denominations are the Roman Catholic Church; the Church of Christ in Zaire; and the Kimbangist Church, which claims to be the largest independent African church on the continent. There is a Muslim minority in the northeast, numbering approximately 450,000. The rest follow mostly traditional African beliefs.

11 TRANSPORTATION

No single railroad runs the full length of the country, and paved highways are few and short. Inland waterways—rivers and lakes—are the main channels of transportation. A total of 16,037 kilometers (9,965 miles) of river and lake waterways are in service. The chief seaport and only deepwater port is Matadi on the Zaire River, 148 kilometers (92 miles) from the Atlantic Ocean. Zaire had one merchant vessel at the end of 1991, totaling 13,000 gross registered tons. Of 49,000 kilometers (30,400 miles) of true road in 1985, only 2,800 kilometers (1,740 miles) were paved. Motor vehicles in 1991 included 100,000 passenger cars and 90,000 commercial vehicles.

There were 5,254 kilometers (3,265 miles) of railway in 1991. The southeastern network connects with the Angolan and Zambian railroad systems. Air transport has become an important factor in the country's economy. Zaire has five international airports—N'Djili (Kinshasa), Luano (Lubumbashi), Bukavu, Goma, and Kisangani—which can accommodate long-distance jet aircraft.

12 HISTORY

Bantu-speaking peoples (from central and southern Africa) entered the area now called Zaire from the west by AD 150, while non-Bantu-speakers penetrated what is now northern Zaire from the north. These peoples brought with them agriculture and developed iron tools. In 1482, the Portuguese navigator Diogo Cão visited the mouth of the Zaire (Congo) River, marking the first known European contact with the region.

In 1789, a Portuguese explorer, José Lacerdu e Almeida, explored the cuvette, the nation's central area, where he learned of the rich copper mines. A thriving Arab trade in slaves and ivory reached the region from the east in the late 1850s or early 1860s.

In 1876–77, King Leopold II of Belgium commissioned Welsh-American explorer Henry M. Stanley to undertake explorations and make treaties with the tribal chiefs. The Berlin Conference of 1884–85 recognized the Independent State of the Congo, set up by Leopold under his personal rule. The new country's boundaries were established by treaties with other colonial powers. In 1908 the territory was transferred to Belgium as a colony called the Belgian Congo, and the Colonial Charter set up its basic structure of government.

The rise of nationalism in the various African territories following World War II (after 1945) seemed to have bypassed the colony, which remained without self-government (except for a few large cities) until 1959. Then Congolese demanded independence and rioted, first in Léopoldville (now Kinshasa) and then elsewhere. At first, the Belgian government proposed gradual progress toward self-rule in the colony, but as the independence movement persisted and grew, Belgium agreed to grant the Congo its independence in mid-1960 and to continue economic and other aid after independence.

Independence Brings Problems

The newly independent Republic of the Congo was inaugurated on 30 June 1960, with Joseph Kasavubu as its first head of state and Patrice Lumumba its first premier. It was immediately confronted by massive economic, political, and social problems. A week after independence the armed forces mutinied (rebelled), as separatist movements and intertribal conflict threatened to split the country.

A major blow to the new republic was the secession of the mineral-rich southwest province, announced on 11 July 1960 by Moïse Tshombe, head of the provincial government. The central government was crippled by the loss of revenues from its richest province and by the departure of Belgian civil servants, doctors, teachers, and technicians. Faced with the threatened collapse of a new nation, the United Nations responded with what grew into a program of massive assistance—financial, military, administrative, and technical.

In September 1960, Kasavubu and Lumumba each attempted to remove the other from the government. Finally, Kasavubu, with the help of army chief of staff Colonel Joseph-Désiré Mobutu, took

Lumumba prisoner and turned him over to the authorities in the province that had seceded. They put Lumumba to death early in 1961.

In September 1961, UN Secretary-General Dag Hammarskjöld flew to the Congo, where he boarded a plane for Northern Rhodesia (now Zambia) to meet with Moise Tshombe, head of the government of Katanga, the seceded province. The plane crashed, killing him and all others on board. United Nations troops eventually resorted to broad-scale military operations to disarm the Katanga forces throughout the province. Tshombe capitulated (gave in), and the secession of Katanga was ended on 14 January 1963.

A new series of rebellions soon began. However, United Nations troops were withdrawn on 30 June 1964. The self-exiled Tshombe was recalled and offered the position of prime minister. Rebel-held Stanleyville (now Kisangani) was recaptured in November 1964.

Mobutu Assumes Power

On 13 October 1965 Tshombe was removed from office by Kasavubu, who attempted to replace him with Evariste Kimba, also from Katanga. When Kimba was not endorsed by the parliament, General Mobutu, commander-in-chief of the Congolese National Army, seized power in a coup d'état (takeover of the government) on 24 November 1965 and assumed the presidency. Tshombe's hopes for a comeback were dashed when he was kidnapped in June 1967 and imprisoned in Algeria, where he died two years later.

The country was officially transformed into a one-party state in 1970. In 1971, the name of the country was changed from Congo to Zaire. Mobutu was elected without opposition to a new seven-year term as president in 1977, but he continued to face opposition, both external and internal. In 1982, Mobutu resumed diplomatic ties with Israel, which had been broken in 1974; five Arab nations quickly cut ties with Zaire, and $350 million in promised Arab aid to Zaire was blocked. In 1983, Zaire sent 2,700 troops to Chad to aid the government against Libyan-backed rebels; they were withdrawn in 1984. Mobutu was reelected "unopposed" to a new seven-year presidential term in July 1984.

For their support of Western (United States) positions through the Cold War (tension between the United States [and its allies] and the USSR [and its allies]), Zaire, and in particular Mobutu, were handsomely rewarded. Mobutu is now said to be the wealthiest person in Africa. However, widely publicized human rights violations in the late 1980s put Mobutu on the defensive.

In September 1991 he was forced to call a National Conference of some 2,800 delegates to draft a new constitution. It often failed to arrive at a consensus, and when it did, Mobutu thwarted its decisions. In November 1991, Mobutu split the coalition known as the Sacred Union by naming Nguza Karl-I-Bond of the Union of Federalists and Independent Republicans (UFERI) as prime minister. Nguza closed the National Conference in February 1992. On 14 August 1992, the Conference elected Etienne Tshisekedi of

Children wait outside the general hospital of Kikwit, Zaire, 370 miles southeast of Kinshasa, where a deadly Ebola virus broke out killing dozens. These two children were waiting for the body of their relative who was reportedly killed by the internal hemorrhagic disease and covered their faces in a misguided effort to protect themselves from the virus.

the Union for Democracy and Social Progress (UDPS) as prime minister of a transitional government.

Mobutu, who countered by forming a new government under his control and dismissing Tshisekedi in December 1992, controlled the army, the central bank, and the police. The High Council of the Republic, the interim legislature, continued to recognize Tshisekedi as did Zaire's principal economic partners abroad.

Two parallel governments attempt to rule Zaire. One controls the country's wealth and the media, the other has a pop-ular following and professed support from Western governments.

In 1993, Mobutu's Bank of Zaire introduced new currency on three occasions, but it soon became worthless. Merchants would not accept it and riots broke out when soldiers could not spend their pay. Anarchy, corruption, uncontrolled violence, and poverty now prevail. Government authority has dissolved, leaving the country to pillaging soldiers and roaming gangs. The situation has led one journalist to call Zaire "a stateless country." The southwest province of Shaba (formerly Katanga) has declared its autonomy. AIDS is rampant. The struggle of two rival claimants to power continues. Neither can mount much overt support, yet the stalemate continues.

13 GOVERNMENT

After his takeover in November 1965, General Mobutu combined the office of prime minister with the presidency. In June 1967, a new constitution provided for a highly centralized form of presidential government. In 1970 a single-party system was established, with the Popular Movement of the Revolution (MPR), as the republic's sole party. Instead of directly electing the president of the republic, voters confirmed the choice made by the MPR for its chairman, who automatically became the head of state and head of the government. The MPR governed through an 80-member Central Committee; the 16-member Political Bureau; the Party Congress, which was supposed to meet every five years; the National Executive Council (or cabinet); and the National Legislative Council, a single-chamber body with 310 members. However, most government functions were directly controlled by President Mobutu.

Mobuto is now challenged by a rival government. A rival legislature, the 435-member High Council of the Republic (HCR), was established by the National Conference in December 1992, and a government set up by the HCR and headed by Prime Minister Tshisekedi claims to rule. Yet the army has evicted his officers from government facilities. Mobutu has repeatedly tried to remove Tshisekedi from office. Mobutu has de facto (actual) control of the administration but it is unable to act effectively. As a result of this stalemate, the government has virtually collapsed.

14 POLITICAL PARTIES

In 1970, General Mobuto established a single-party system, with the sole legal party the ruling MPR (Popular Movement of the Revolution). The chairman of the MPR automatically holds the office of head of state; party and state are effectively one, and every citizen is automatically a member of the MPR.

The constitution was amended to permit party activity in April 1990. The most important among the new parties combined to form a coalition known as the Sacred Union. These include the Union for Democracy and Social Progress (UDPS), the Union of Federalists and Independent Republicans (UFERI), the Unified Lumumbist Party (PALU), and the Social Democratic Christian Party (PDSC).

15 JUDICIAL SYSTEM

The courts include courts of first hearing, appeals courts, a Supreme Court, and the Court of State Security. Many disputes are settled at the local level by administrative officials or traditional authorities.

16 ARMED FORCES

There was an army of 26,000 in 1993, composed of 2 divisions and 5 brigades. The navy of 1,300 had about 24 patrol craft. There was an air force of 1,800 personnel, with 28 combat aircraft. Paramilitary forces numbered about 25,000, and

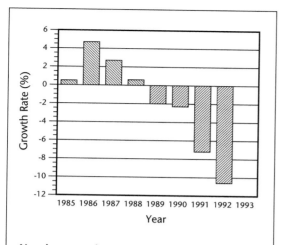

Yearly growth rate of the economy. This economic indicator tells by what percent the economy has increased or decreased when compared with the previous year.

there was a civil guard of 10,000. In 1988 Zaire spent $49 million on defense.

17 ECONOMY

Zaire has a wealth of natural resources that should provide the foundation for a stable economy. However, in September 1991 mutinous military troops looted all major urban centers, practically bringing the economy to a standstill. A large government deficit, primarily to pay salaries for the military and civil servants, was financed by printing currency. Severe inflation and economic collapse followed. Many multinational businesses have left the country. Although Zaire possesses large amounts of unused agricultural land, its urban population is dependent on imported food due to the lack of a transportation network.

18 INCOME

In 1992 Zaire's gross national product (GNP) was $235 per person. For the period 1985–92 the average inflation rate was 35.0%.

19 INDUSTRY

Much of Zaire's industry involves the processing of agricultural products (sugar, flour) and mineral-bearing ore (copper, zinc, petroleum, cement). The production of consumer goods (beer, soft drinks, textiles) plays a leading role in the sector as well.

20 LABOR

Unemployment and underemployment have remained serious problems for Zaire. In 1991 there was an estimated labor force of 20,000,000; perhaps fewer than 20% were wage and salary workers. Agriculture employs about 80% of the population. The official workweek is six days (48 hours). Unionization stands at about 20%.

21 AGRICULTURE

Agriculture supports about four-fifths of the people. The principal crops are cassava, yams, plantains, rice, and maize. In 1992, food-crop production included manioc, 18,300,000 tons; sugarcane, 1,150,000 tons; corn, 920,000 tons; peanuts, 440,000 tons; and rice, 365,000 tons. In 1992, plantains totaled 1,830,000 tons; sweet potatoes, 380,000 tons; bananas, 405,000 tons; yams, 310,000 tons; and pineapples, 145,000 tons.

Coffee is Zaire's third most important export (after copper and crude oil) and is the leading agricultural export. An estimated 98,000 tons were produced in 1992. Rubber is the second most important export cash crop. In 1992, production amounted to 11,000 tons. Palm oil production is concentrated in three large operations, two of them foreign-owned. Production in 1992 totaled 183,000 tons. The production of cotton engages about 250,000 farmers, who annually produce 22–26,000 tons. Other cash crops produced in 1992 were 4,000 tons of tobacco, 3,000 tons of tea, and 4,000 tons of cocoa.

22 DOMESTICATED ANIMALS

In 1992, local meat production was an estimated 212,000 tons. The number of head of cattle in 1992 was estimated at 1,650,000, located in the higher eastern regions above the range of the tsetse fly. The number of goats in 1992 was estimated at 3,080,000; hogs totaled 840,000; and sheep, 920,000.

23 FISHING

Fish are the single most important source of animal protein in Zaire. Total production of marine, river, and lake fisheries in 1991 was estimated at 160,000 tons, all but 2,000 tons from inland waters.

24 FORESTRY

Forest and woodland covers over three-quarters of the total land area of Zaire. Zaire possesses 61 million hectares (150 million acres) of exploitable wooded area. Roundwood removals were estimated at

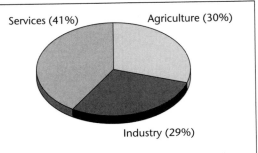

Components of the economy. This pie chart shows how much of the country's economy is devoted to agriculture (includes forestry, hunting, and fishing), industry, or services.

40,079,000 cubic meters in 1991, about 93% for fuel. Some 14 species are presently being harvested.

25 MINING

Zaire is a leading producer of cobalt and the world's second largest producer of diamonds. Other minerals include zinc, tin, manganese, gold, silver, cadmium, tantalum, and tungsten. Uranium for the first American atomic bomb was mined in Zaire.

Copper output (recoverable copper content of ores and concentrates) in 1991 was 8,620,000 tons. Until 1986, Zaire was the world's leading producer of industrial diamonds. Société Minière de Bakwanga (MIBA), 80% government owned, produced 19.0 million carats in 1991. Other production figures for 1991 were: cobalt from mined ore, 20,900 tons; zinc metal production 81,400 tons; cassiterite (tin ore), 1,635 tons; low-grade coal, 60,000 tons; tantalum, 16 tons; columbium, 15 tons; silver, 80,000 kilograms;

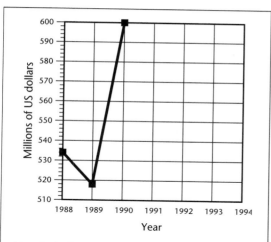

Yearly balance of trade measured in millions of US dollars. The balance of trade is the difference between what a country sells to other countries (its exports) and what it buys (its imports). If a country imports more than it exports, it has a negative balance of trade (a trade deficit). If exports exceed imports there is a positive balance of trade (a trade surplus).

wolfram (tungsten), 15,000 kilograms; and gold, 8,800 kilograms. Small-scale diamond and gold mining was legalized in October 1982 in an effort to get the proceeds recorded and into the banks. Many peasants, teachers, and students left their previous pursuits to go prospecting.

26 FOREIGN TRADE

Zaire is highly sensitive to changes in the world market prices for copper and cobalt, two of its principal exports. Other principal exports in 1985 were crude oil and diamonds. Principal imports in the same year were machinery and transport equipment; food, drink, and tobacco; and mineral oils. Belgium is Zaire's most

important trade partner, accounting for about 32% of total exports and about 22% of total imports in 1985. European Community (EC) countries together accounted for about 61% of total trade.

27 ENERGY AND POWER

In 1992, eight Atlantic Ocean and Zaire River oil fields were in operation, and production totaled 9.9 million barrels. Proven reserves amount to 127.7 million barrels, with offshore reserves accounting for only 20%. Zaire has vast resources for the development of hydroelectric power: its potential is thought to exceed 100 million kilowatts. In 1991, production was 6,168 million kilowatt hours, of which more than half was used for mining and metallurgy in the southwest province of Shaba, and 198 million kilowatt hours was exported. Only about 2% of the population has access to electricity.

28 SOCIAL DEVELOPMENT

Social security is handled by the National Social Security Institute. In addition to pension funds, the institute administers compensation for accidents and illness; old age, disability, and death benefits; and family allowances. The Department of Social Affairs administers a number of welfare agencies. They offer vocational training for unemployed youths, adult education programs, and a number of activities for women. However, the Roman Catholic Church still provides most of the nation's welfare and social programs.

Selected Social Indicators

These statistics are estimates for the period 1988 to 1993. For comparison purposes, data for the United States and averages for low-income countries and high-income countries are also given.

Indicator	Zaire	Low-income countries	High-income countries	United States
Per capita gross national product†	**$235**	$380	$23,680	$24,740
Population growth rate	**3.3%**	1.9%	0.6%	1.0%
Population growth rate in urban areas	**4.0%**	3.9%	0.8%	1.3%
Population per square kilometer of land	**17**	78	25	26
Life expectancy in years	**52**	62	77	76
Number of people per physician	**n.a.**	>3,300	453	419
Number of pupils per teacher (primary school)	**42**	39	<18	20
Illiteracy rate (15 years and older)	**28%**	41%	<5%	<3%
Energy consumed per capita (kg of oil equivalent)	**48**	364	5,203	7,918

† The gross national product (GNP) is the total dollar value of all goods and services produced by a country in a year. The per capita GNP is calculated by dividing a country's GNP by its population. The World Bank defines low-income countries as those with a per capita GNP of $695 or less. High-income countries have a per capita GNP of $8,626 or more. Less than 14% of the world's 5.5 billion people live in high-income countries, while almost 60% live in low-income countries.

n.a. = data not available   > = greater than   < = less than

Sources: World Bank, *Social Indicators of Development 1995*, Baltimore: Johns Hopkins University Press, 1995. Central Intelligence Agency, *World Fact Book*, Washington, D.C.: Government Printing Office, 1994.

29 HEALTH

Medical personnel in 1990 included 2,469 physicians. Total health care expenditures were $179 million in 1990. In 1992, only 26% of the population had access to health care services.

Diseases include malaria, trypanosomiasis, onchocerciasis, schistosomiasis, tuberculosis, measles, leprosy, dysentery, typhoid, and hookworm; acquired immune deficiency syndrome (AIDS) has also been recognized and, in 1987, tests indicated that 9% of babies were born with the virus. Malnutrition is a serious health problem, especially among children. Average life expectancy was 52 years.

30 HOUSING

The massive migration to the cities that began after independence led to a fourfold increase in the population of Kinshasa, creating a massive housing problem that is still far from solved. Tens of thousands of squatters are crowded into squalid shantytowns on the outskirts of the capital. Unable to come up with adequate alternatives, the government began extending basic utilities to the new settlements. As of 1984, 52% of housing units were traditional one-room adobe, straw, or mud structures, and 45% were modern houses of durable or semi-durable material containing one or more rooms.

31 EDUCATION

Education is compulsory between ages 6 and 12. Primary-school enrollment rose to 4,356,516 in 1987. The development of secondary education has also been dramatic: the number of secondary-school students rose from 38,000 in 1960–61 to 1,066,350 in 1987. In 1990 adult illiteracy was 28% (males: 16.4%, and females: 39%).

The National University of Zaire is organized into three separate campuses located in Kinshasa, Lubumbashi, and Kisangani. The three campuses were reorganized as separate universities in 1981. In 1988 all higher level institutions had 3,873 teaching staff and 61,422 pupils. Zaire also has numerous university institutes, including ones specializing in agriculture, applied technology, business, and the arts.

32 MEDIA

The postal, telephone, and telegraph services are owned and operated by the government. Telephones in 1991 numbered 32,116. Radio and television broadcasts are in French and in African languages. In 1991 there were some 3.7 million radios and 41,000 television sets.

Journalists must be members of the state-controlled union to practice their profession. The largest dailies, with 1992 circulations, are *La Dépêche* in Lubumbashi, 20,000; *Courrier d'Afrique* in Kinshasa, 15,000; and *L'Essor du Zaïre* in Lubumbashi, 10,000. Other dailies are *Centre-Afrique* (Bukavu), *Le Stanleyvillois* (Kisangani), *Taifa* (Lubumbashi), *Mjumbe* (Lubumbashi), and *Salongo* (Kinshasa).

33 TOURISM AND RECREATION

Virunga National Park in the Virunga Mountains around Lake Edward is one of the best game preserves in Africa and is particularly noted for lions, elephants, and hippopotamuses. Kahuzi-Biega Park, west of Lake Kivu, is one of the last refuges of the endangered mountain gorilla. Kinshasa has two zoos and a presidential garden. In 1989 there were 51,000 tourist arrivals, and tourist receipts came to $6 million. There were 21,824 hotel rooms and 27,262 beds.

34 FAMOUS ZAIRIANS

In the period of the transition to independence, two Zairian political leaders emerged as national figures: Joseph Kasavubu (1917–69) became the first chief of state; Patrice Emery Lumumba (1926–61) became the new nation's first premier, and his subsequent murder made him a revolutionary martyr in Communist and many third-world countries.

In 1960, Moïse Kapenda Tshombe (1919–69), who headed the government of Katanga Province, became prominent when he declared Katanga an independent state with himself as its president and maintained the secession until early 1963. General Mobutu Sese Seko (Joseph-Désiré Mobutu, b.1930), commander-in-chief of the Congolese National Army from 1961 to 1965, assumed the presidency after he deposed President Kasavubu on 25 November 1965. The MPR party congress promoted Mobutu to the rank of field marshal in December 1982.

35 BIBLIOGRAPHY

American University. *Zaire: A Country Study.* Washington, D.C.: Government Printing Office. 3d ed., 1979.

Bailey, Robert C. "The Efe: Archers of the Rain Forest." *National Geographic,* November 1989, 664–686.

Bobb, F. Scott. *Historical Dictionary of Zaire.* Metuchen, N.J.: Scarecrow Press, 1988.

Caputo, Robert. "Lifeline for a Nation—Zaire River." *National Geographic,* November 1991, 5–35.

Harms, Robert W. *River of Wealth, River of Sorrow: The Central Zaire Basin in the Era of the Slave and Ivory Trade, 1500 to 1891.* New Haven, Conn.: Yale University Press, 1981.

Heinz, G., and H. Donnay. *Lumumba: The Last Fifty Days.* New York: Grove, 1969.

Hyland, Paul. *The Black Heart: A Voyage into Central Africa.* London: Gollancz, 1988.

Turnbull, Colin M. *Lonely African.* New York: Touchstone Books, 1968.

Zaire in Pictures. Minneapolis: Lerner, 1992.

ZAMBIA

Republic of Zambia

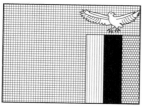

CAPITAL: Lusaka.

FLAG: The flag is green, with a tricolor of dark red, black, and orange vertical stripes at the lower corner of the fly, topped by a golden flying eagle.

ANTHEM: *Stand and Sing for Zambia.*

MONETARY UNIT: The kwacha (κ) of 100 ngwee replaced the Zambian pound (z£) on 15 January 1968. There are coins of 1, 2, 5, 10, 20, and 50 ngwee, and notes of 1, 2, 5, 10, 20, 50, 100, and 500 kwacha. κ1 = $0.1202 (or $1 = κ8.3216).

WEIGHTS AND MEASURES: The metric system is used.

HOLIDAYS: New Year's Day, 1 January; Youth Day, 11 March; Labor Day, 1 May; African Freedom Day, 24 May; Heroes' Day, 1st Monday after 1st weekend in July; Unity Day, Tuesday after Heroes' Day; Farmers' Day, 5 August; Independence Day, 24 October; Christmas, 25 December. Movable religious holidays include Good Friday and Easter Monday.

TIME: 2 PM = noon GMT.

1 LOCATION AND SIZE

A landlocked country in southcentral Africa, Zambia has an area of 752,610 square kilometers (290,584 square miles), slightly larger than the state of Texas, with a total boundary length of 5,664 kilometers (3,519 miles). Zambia's capital city, Lusaka, is located in the southcentral part of the country.

2 TOPOGRAPHY

Most of the landmass in Zambia is a high plateau. In the northeast, the Muchinga Mountains exceed 1,800 meters (5,900 feet) in height. Lower elevations are encountered in the valleys of the major river systems. The Luangwa and Kafue rivers are both tributaries of the upper Zambezi. There are three large natural lakes (Bangweulu, Mweru, and Tangany-ika) and one of the world's largest man-made lakes, Lake Kariba.

3 CLIMATE

Although Zambia lies within the tropics, much of it has a pleasant climate because of the altitude. There are wide seasonal variations in temperature and rainfall. The northern and northwestern provinces have an annual rainfall of about 125 centimeters (50 inches), while areas in the far south have as little as 75 centimeters (30 inches). Daytime temperatures may range from 23° to 31°C (73–88°F), dropping at night to as low as 5°C (41°F) in June and July.

4 PLANTS AND ANIMALS

Most of the territory is plateau, and the prevailing type of vegetation is open woodland. Acacia and baobab trees, thorn trees and bushes, and tall perennial grasses are widespread, becoming coarser and sparser in the drier areas to the south. To the north and east grows a thin forest. The southwest has forests of Zambian teak.

The national parks and game reserves, such as the Kafue National Park, conserve the wildlife threatened by settlement. In the Luangwa River valley can be found giraffe, zebra, rhinoceros, elephant, baboon, monkey, hyena, wolf, and lion. Zambia has a wealth of bird life, including the eagle, gull, kingfisher, lark, babbler, sunbird, stork, and bee-eater. There are more than 150 recorded species of reptiles, including 78 species of snakes and 66 of lizards. The range of species of fish is also wide.

5 ENVIRONMENT

Both traditional and modern farming methods in Zambia involve clearing large areas of forest. As of 1985, the nation had lost 700 square kilometers (270 square miles) of forestland, mainly to slash-and-burn agriculture but also to firewood gathering and charcoal production. Water pollution is a problem due to contamination by sewage and toxic industrial chemicals. The nation uses 26% of its available water supply for farming and 11% for industry. Roughly one-fourth of Zambia's city dwellers and 57% of the people living in rural areas do not have pure water. Air pollution is created by the use of oil products for cars and coal in industrial activity.

Wildlife is endangered in some areas by hunting; the National Parks and Wildlife Act (1982) requires automatic imprison-

ment for trading illicitly (illegally) in elephant tusks and rhinoceros horns. In 1994, 10 of the nation's mammal species, including the black rhinoceros, and 10 bird species were threatened, as well as 1 type of plant.

6 POPULATION

In 1990, the population was 7,818,447, and in 1994, it was estimated at 9,371,621. The projected population for the year 2000 was 10,672,000. Lusaka, the capital, had 979,000 inhabitants in 1990. Overall, population density is 11 persons per square kilometer (28 per square mile).

7 MIGRATION

At the end of 1992, there were an estimated 142,100 refugees in Zambia, including 101,800 Angolans and 26,300 Mozambicans.

8 ETHNIC GROUPS

The African community, more than 99% of Zambia's total population, belongs to various Bantu groups, including the Bemba (37% of Zambia's African population), Tonga (19%), Lunda (12%), and Nyanja (11%). In all, there are at least 73 different African societal classifications. Counting Asians, mainly migrants from the Indian subcontinent, and people of mixed race, there were about 60,000 non-Africans in 1986. The Europeans, numbering about 17,000 in 1984, are mainly of British stock.

ZAMBIA

ZAMBIA

0   50   100   150   200 Miles

0   50   100   150   200 Kilometers

LOCATION: 9° to 18°s; 23° to 34°E. **BOUNDARY LENGTHS:** Tanzania, 338 kilometers (210 miles); Malawi, 837 kilometers (523 miles); Mozambique, 419 kilometers (260 miles); Zimbabwe, 797 kilometers (498 miles); Namibia, 233 kilometers (145 miles); Angola, 1,110 kilometers (690 miles); Zaire, 1,930 kilometers (1,193 miles).

9 LANGUAGES

Some 80 different languages have been identified, most of them of the Bantu family (of south and central Africa). For educational and administrative purposes, seven main languages are recognized: Bemba, Lozi, Lunda, Kaonde, Luvale, Tonga, and Nyanja. English is the official language.

10 RELIGIONS

An estimated 70% of the population follows African tribal religions, while 20% profess some form of Christianity, more than one-third being Roman Catholics.

11 TRANSPORTATION

The Zambia Railways system consists of 1,266 kilometers (787 miles) of track. Zambia had 36,370 kilometers (22,600 miles) of roadway in 1991, of which 18% was paved. In 1991, there were 170,000 registered motor vehicles, including 100,000 passenger cars. Zambia Airways provides international service from Lusaka to several African and European countries, as well as domestic service to 17 Zambian centers. It carried 246,000 passengers in 1992. Mpulungu on Lake Tanganyika is Zambia's only port.

12 HISTORY

Iron working and agriculture were practiced in some parts of Zambia by about AD 100. By AD 900, mining and trading were present in southern Zambia. Between the fifteenth and the eighteenth centuries, various groups of Bantu migrants from the southern Congo (now Zaire) settled in Zambia. By the beginning of the nineteenth century, three large-scale political units existed in Zambia: the Bemba system of chieftainships; the Lunda kingdom of Kazembe; and the kingdom of the Lozi. Zambia was affected by two "invasions" in the mid-nineteenth century. There were a series of migrations, commonly referred to as the mfecane, by groups fleeing across the Zambezi River to avoid raids by Shaka's Zulu empire in South Africa. The other invasion came in the form of traders from the north—Nyamwezi, Arabs, and Swahili—drawing Zambia into long-distance trading systems.

The first significant European contact was through Christian missionaries. In 1884, François Coillard, a French Protestant missionary, settled in Barotseland (now the Western Province). In the 1890s, Cecil Rhodes's British South Africa Company extended its charter north of the Zambezi River. From 1891 to the end of 1923, the territory of Zambia—then known as Northern Rhodesia—was ruled by this private company. In the 1920s, new methods of exploiting the extensive mineral deposits in the "copperbelt" region transformed the economic life of the territory. Northern Rhodesia now was seen for the first time as a source of wealth, and European settlements multiplied rapidly.

In 1953, Northern Rhodesia became a member of the Federation of Rhodesia and Nyasaland, an arrangement opposed by an overwhelming majority of Africans in the territory. However, the Federation continued through the 1950s. In 1960, despite clear economic benefits, the majority of Africans in both Northern Rhodesia and Nyasaland opposed the continuance of the federation in its present form.

The Republic of Zambia is Born

On 31 December 1963, the Federation of Rhodesia and Nyasaland was formally dissolved. On 24 October 1964, Northern Rhodesia became an independent republic, and its name was changed to Zambia. Kenneth Kaunda, the leader of the ruling United National Independence Party (UNIP), became the nation's first president. Kaunda was reelected in 1969, 1973, 1978, and 1983, surviving a series of coup (overthrow) attempts during 1980–81. During the 1970s, Zambia played a key

Photo credit: Edson P. Tembo of the Zambia National Tourist Board.

Kayila Lodge under the shade of a baobab tree in the lower Zambezi National Park.

role in the movement toward black majority rule in Rhodesia, providing a base from which Patriotic Front guerrillas infiltrated Rhodesia. A drastic decline of world copper prices in the early 1980s, coupled with a severe drought, left Zambia in a perilous economic position. The continuing civil war in Angola also had repercussions in Zambia, bringing disruption of Zambian trade routes and casualties among Zambians along the border.

By 1990, a growing opposition to UNIP's monopoly of power had coalesced in the Movement for Multiparty Democracy (MMD). In December 1990, after a tumultuous year that included riots in Lusaka and a coup attempt, Kaunda signed legislation ending UNIP's legal monopoly of power. After difficult negotiations between the government and opposition groups, Zambia enacted a new constitution in August 1991. It enlarged the National Assembly, established an electoral commission, and allowed for more than one presidential candidate. Candidates no longer are required to be UNIP members.

In September, Kaunda announced the date for Zambia's first multiparty parliamentary and presidential elections in 19 years. Frederick J. T. Chiluba (MMD) defeated Kaunda, 81% to 15%. Once in power, Chiluba's MMD became tyrannical and corrupt. The press began to criticize Chiluba's government and Chiluba lashed back. On 4 March 1993, government declared a three-month state of emergency and detained 26 UNIP members, including three of Kaunda's sons. Chiluba lifted the state of emergency on May 25 and released all but eight of the detainees, whom he charged with offenses from treason to possession of seditious documents.

13 GOVERNMENT

In August 1991, a new constitution was adopted. The president is now elected directly by universal suffrage and may serve a maximum of two five-year terms. The National Assembly has 150 directly elected members and up to eight appointed by the president, also for five-year terms. Candidates for office no longer are required to be members of the ruling party (UNIP).

14 POLITICAL PARTIES

With the proclamation of a one-party state in December 1972, Kenneth Kaunda's United National Independence Party (UNIP) became the only legal party in Zambia. With growing unrest in the late 1980s, a Movement for Multiparty Democracy (MMD) was formed. Finally, in December 1990, Kaunda signed into law a bill legalizing opposition political parties.

Multiparty presidential and parliamentary elections on 31 October and 1 November 1991, the first in 19 years. The MMD's leader, Frederick Chiluba, easily won the presidency, 81% to 15% for Kaunda. The MMD got 125 seats to 15

for UNIP in the National Assembly. Since then, new opposition parties have been formed: the Multi-Racial Party (MRP), the National Democratic Alliance (NADA), the United Democratic Party, and the United Democratic Congress Party.

15 JUDICIAL SYSTEM

The law is administered by a High Court consisting of a chief justice and 16 puisne judges. Resident magistrate courts are also established at various centers. The local courts deal mainly with customary law, especially cases relating to marriage, property, and inheritance. Under the constitution of 1973, the Supreme Court is the highest court in Zambia and serves as the final court of appeal. The chief justice and other judges are appointed by the president.

16 ARMED FORCES

As of 1993, the strength of the armed forces was 24,000; paramilitary forces, consisting of two police battalions, totaled 1,400. The army numbered 20,000; the air force had 4,000 members and 67 combat aircraft. Military service is voluntary. Defense spending is estimated at around $200 million a year.

17 ECONOMY

As of 1994, the Zambian economy is in an unstable state. High inflation, severe drought, declining export prices, and failed economic policies have all taken their toll. In 1992, Zambia was classified as a least developed country by the United Nations. The impact of inflation on the poor, the middle class, and business has eroded public support for the government's reform policies, and the expected recovery of the early 1990s has been slow to appear.

18 INCOME

In 1992, Zambia's gross national product (GNP) was $2,580 million at current prices, or about $380 per person. For the period 1985–92, the average inflation rate was 69.1%.

19 INDUSTRY

In 1990 the food, beverage, and tobacco industry accounted for 37% of industrial output, textiles and clothing for 12%, and chemicals for 11%. Apart from copper refining, the most important industries are those connected with the manufacture of sulfuric acid, fertilizer, glass, batteries, cigarettes, textiles, yarn, vehicle and tractor assembling, sawmilling, tire retreading, processing of food and drink, and the manufacture of cement and cement products.

20 LABOR

In 1992, recorded employment in Zambia totaled 300,000 persons, of whom 15% were engaged in mining, about 31% in services, 6% in construction, 7% each in commerce, finance, and transportation/communication, 14% in manufacturing, and 13% in other sectors. The majority of Zambian laborers work not as wage earners but in agriculture. Unemployment is estimated at more than one-third of the potential labor force.

About 60% of wage earners are unionized. There were at least 19 labor unions

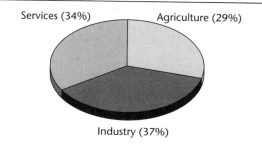

Components of the economy. This pie chart shows how much of the country's economy is devoted to agriculture (includes forestry, hunting, and fishing), industry, or services.

in 1992, most of them affiliated with the Zambia Congress of Trade Unions (ZCTU). Strikes were common in 1992 as salaries and working conditions suffered from harsh economic conditions and large cost of living increases.

21 AGRICULTURE

The majority of Zambia's population engages in farming. The principal crops for domestic consumption are corn, sorghum, and cassava, while the main export crops are tobacco, corn, sugarcane, peanuts, and cotton. Production of tobacco, the most important export crop, was estimated at 10,000 tons in 1993, the largest on record and double the 1992 harvest. Marketed corn production in 1992 was 464,000 tons (down from 1,096,000 tons in 1991). Cotton production reached 10,000 tons of fiber. Also marketed in 1992 were 1,150,000 tons of sugarcane, 6,000 tons of sunflowers, 21,000 tons of peanuts, and 62,000 tons of wheat.

22 DOMESTICATED ANIMALS

The estimated livestock population in 1992 included 3,095,000 head of cattle, 623,000 sheep and goats, and 290,000 hogs. Cattle production in certain regions is limited by sleeping sickness, carried by the tsetse fly. During 1992, cattle slaughterings totaled 254,000 head.

23 FISHING

The fishing industry plays an important part in the rural economy. Large quantities of fish are transported by rail to processing centers, where they are frozen or dried. The catch in 1991 was 65,945 tons.

24 FORESTRY

About 40% of Zambia was covered by woodland in the early 1990s. Roundwood production was about 13,719,000 cubic meters in 1991, 94% of it for fuel needs.

25 MINING

Mining is central to Zambia's economy; the nation was the world's fourth largest producer of copper and second leading producer of cobalt in 1991. In 1991, copper content of concentrates mined amounted to 345,519 tons, down from 403,450 tons in 1987.

Production figures for the following minerals in 1991 were: coal, 345,000 tons; zinc, 19,825 tons; lead, 9,084 tons; and cobalt from mined concentrates, 6,991 tons. Minor quantities of silver, gold, selenium, iron ore, feldspar, and tin are produced. Gemstones, in the form of amethysts and emeralds, are also mined.

26 FOREIGN TRADE

Copper is by far the leading export item, accounting for 84.9% in 1987. Other leading export commodities were cobalt, zinc, and lead. Of Zambia's total imports in 1985, oil accounted for 30.6%; other major imports include machinery and transport equipment and basic manufactured goods.

Zambia's leading export partner in 1985 was Japan (23.1%), followed by the United Kingdom (7.4%) and China (6.8%). Imports arrived from South Africa (18.7%), the United Kingdom (15.3%), the United States (9.3%), and Japan (5.3%).

27 ENERGY AND POWER

As of 1984, the mining industry was the largest consumer of energy, accounting for more than 48% of the total commercial energy demand. The main source of electricity was hydropower (70%), followed by petroleum products (20%), and coal (10%). A total of 7,775 million kilowatt hours of electricity was produced in 1991. Crude oil is imported by means of a leaking pipeline from Tanzania, which, as of 1993, was to be repaired with World Bank assistance.

28 SOCIAL DEVELOPMENT

Social welfare services are provided by the government in association with local authorities and voluntary agencies. Statutory and remedial welfare services include emergency relief, care for the aged, protection of children, adoption, and probation. Employers and employees are required to make contributions toward a worker's retirement at age 55. The Zambia Youth Service operates specially constructed camps that provide vocational training for unemployed and unskilled youth.

29 HEALTH

As of 1992, government records indicate nine hospitals and a few small outpatient clinics. Medical personnel in 1990 included 713 doctors and 1,503 nurses. For the years 1988 to 1993 there was an average of 1 doctor per 11,431 people. In 1992, an estimated 75% of the population had access to health care services and, in 1990, Zambia spent only $117 million on health care.

Malaria and tuberculosis are major health problems, and hookworm and schistosomiasis afflict a large proportion of the population. In 1991, only 53% of the population had access to safe water, and a mere 37% had adequate sanitation. Average life expectancy is estimated at 48 years. In mid-1986, blood surveys indicated that 15% of the population was carrying the AIDS virus.

30 HOUSING

Widespread instances of overcrowding and slum growth have for many years focused government attention on urban housing problems. Mining companies have constructed townships for the families of African workers. About 67% of the population had access to safe water in the mid-1980s.

31 EDUCATION

Primary education lasts for seven years and is compulsory. Secondary education is for five years. In 1990, 1,461,206 pupils were in 3,587 primary schools and in 1988, 170,299 students attended secondary schools. Adult literacy is estimated at 73%. The University of Zambia was established in 1965. Other institutions of higher learning include technical colleges and a two-year college of agriculture. All higher level institutions had 15,343 pupils in 1990.

32 MEDIA

The central government is responsible for postal and telecommunication services. About 95,281 telephones were in use in 1991. The Zambia Broadcasting Service, which provides radio programs in English and seven local languages, and Zambian Television are government owned and operated. In 1991 there were 680,000 radio receivers and 217,000 television receivers.

Zambia has two daily newspapers: owned by the United National Independence Party (UNIP) is *Times of Zambia,* founded in 1943, with an estimated 1991 circulation of 45,000; and the government-owned *Zambia Daily Mail,* published in Lusaka, with a circulation of 25,000.

33 TOURISM AND RECREATION

One of the most impressive tourist attractions in Zambia is Victoria Falls on the border with Zimbabwe. In 1972, a new national park system created 17 parks covering 8% of the entire country. The Kafue National Park, one of the largest in Africa, with 22,500 square kilometers

Selected Social Indicators

These statistics are estimates for the period 1988 to 1993. For comparison purposes, data for the United States and averages for low-income countries and high-income countries are also given.

Indicator	Zambia	Low-income countries	High-income countries	United States
Per capita gross national product†	**$380**	$380	$23,680	$24,740
Population growth rate	**3.3%**	1.9%	0.6%	1.0%
Population growth rate in urban areas	**3.3%**	3.9%	0.8%	1.3%
Population per square kilometer of land	**11**	78	25	26
Life expectancy in years	**48**	62	77	76
Number of people per physician	**11,431**	>3,300	453	419
Number of pupils per teacher (primary school)	**44**	39	<18	20
Illiteracy rate (15 years and older)	**27%**	41%	<5%	<3%
Energy consumed per capita (kg of oil equivalent)	**146**	364	5,203	7,918

† The gross national product (GNP) is the total dollar value of all goods and services produced by a country in a year. The per capita GNP is calculated by dividing a country's GNP by its population. The World Bank defines low-income countries as those with a per capita GNP of $695 or less. High-income countries have a per capita GNP of $8,626 or more. Less than 14% of the world's 5.5 billion people live in high-income countries, while almost 60% live in low-income countries.

> = greater than   < = less than

Sources: World Bank, *Social Indicators of Development 1995,* Baltimore: Johns Hopkins University Press, 1995. Central Intelligence Agency, *World Fact Book,* Washington, D.C.: Government Printing Office, 1994.

(8,700 square miles) of bush, forest, and plain, is well-served with tourist facilities. South Luangwa National Park is another outstanding wildlife area. In 1990, Zambia received 141,004 foreign visitors, 74% from Africa and 16% from Europe. In 1991, there were 3,962 hotel rooms with 6,889 beds and a 54% occupancy rate.

34 FAMOUS ZAMBIANS

Kenneth David Kaunda (b.1924) has been Zambia's president since independence. Nalumino Mundia (b.1927), long prominent in Zambian political affairs, was prime minister 1981–85, when he became ambassador to the United States.

35 BIBLIOGRAPHY

Burdette, Marcia M. *Zambia: Between Two Worlds.* Boulder, Colo.: Westview Press, 1988.

Grotpeter, John J. *Historical Dictionary of Zambia.* Metuchen, N.J.: Scarecrow, 1979.

Hansen, Karen Tranberg. *Distant Companions: Servants and Employers in Zambia, 1900–1985.* Ithaca: Cornell University Press, 1989.

Lauré. J. *Zambia.* Chicago: Children's Press, 1989.

Rotberg, Robert I. *The Rise of Nationalism in Central Africa: The Making of Malawi and Zambia, 1873–1964.* Cambridge, Mass.: Harvard University Press, 1965.

ZIMBABWE

Republic of Zimbabwe

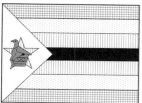

CAPITAL: Harare.

FLAG: The flag has seven equal horizontal stripes of green, yellow, red, black, red, yellow, and green. At the hoist is a white triangle, which contains a representation in yellow of the bird of Zimbabwe superimposed on a red star.

ANTHEM: *God Bless Africa.*

MONETARY UNIT: The Zimbabwe dollar (z$) is a paper currency of 100 cents. There are coins of 1, 5, 10, 20, and 50 cents and 1 dollar, and notes of 2, 5, 10, and 20 dollars. z$1 = US$0.0057 (or US$1 = z$175.00).

WEIGHTS AND MEASURES: The metric system is used.

HOLIDAYS: New Year's Day, 1 January; Independence Day, 18 April; Workers' Day, 1 May; Africa Day, 25 May; Heroes' Days, 11–13 August; Christmas Day, 25 December; Boxing Day, 26 December. Movable holidays are Good Friday, Holy Saturday, Easter Monday, and Whitmonday.

TIME: 2 PM = noon GMT.

1 LOCATION AND SIZE

A landlocked country of southcentral Africa, Zimbabwe (formerly Rhodesia) lies between the Zambezi River on the north and the Limpopo River on the south. It has an area of 390,580 square kilometers (150,804 square miles), slightly larger than the state of Montana. Zimbabwe's total boundary length is 3,066 kilometers (1,905 miles). The capital city, Harare, is located in the northeast part of the country.

2 TOPOGRAPHY

Most of Zimbabwe is rolling plateau. The highveld (or high plateau) stretches southwest to northeast, ending in the Inyanga mountains. On either side of the highveld is the middleveld. The lowveld is made up of wide, grassy plains in the basins of the Zambezi and the Limpopo rivers. Streams flow southeast from the watershed of the highveld to the Limpopo and Sabi rivers and northwest into the Zambezi.

3 CLIMATE

Temperatures on the highveld vary from 12–13°C (54–55°F) in winter to 24°C (75°F) in summer. On the lowveld the temperatures are usually 6°C (11°F) higher, and summer temperatures in the Zambezi and Limpopo valleys average between 32° and 38°C (90–100°F).

Rainfall decreases from east to west. The eastern mountains receive more than 100 centimeters (40 inches) annually, while Harare has 81 centimeters (32 inches) and Bulawayo 61 centimeters (24

Elephant crossing, Hwange National Park.

inches). The south and southwest receive little rainfall.

4 PLANTS AND ANIMALS

The country is mostly grassland, although the moist and mountainous east supports tropical evergreen and hardwood forests. Trees include teak and mahogany, knob-thorn, msasa, and baobab. Among the numerous flowers and shrubs are hibiscus, spider lily, leonotus, cassia, tree wisteria, and dombeya.

Mammals include elephant, lion, buffalo, hippopotamus, rhinoceros, gorilla, chimpanzee, baboon, giraffe, eland, gemsbok, waterbuck, zebra, warthog, lynx, aardvark, porcupine, fox, badger, otter, hare, bat, shrew, and scaly anteater. Snakes and lizards abound. About 500 species of birds include the ant-thrush, bee-eater, bishop bird, bush-warbler, emerald cuckoo, grouse, and pheasant.

5 ENVIRONMENT

Among the most serious of Zimbabwe's environmental problems is erosion of its agricultural lands and expansion of the desert. Air and water pollution result from the combined effects of transportation vehicles, mining, fertilizers, and the cement industry. Zimbabwe's cities produce 500,000 tons of solid waste per year. In 1994, nine of the nation's mammal species and six bird species were endangered,

ZIMBABWE

| 0 | 25 | 50 | 75 | 100 | 125 | 150 Miles |
| 0 | 25 | 50 | 75 | 100 | 125 | 150 Kilometers |

LOCATION: 15°37′ to 22°25′s; 25°14′ to 33°4′e. **BOUNDARY LENGTHS:** Mozambique, 1,231 kilometers (762 miles); South Africa, 225 kilometers (140 miles); Botswana, 813 kilometers (505 miles); Zambia, 797 kilometers (498 miles).

as well as 96 types of plants. Zimbabwe has about half of the world's population of black rhinoceroses, an endangered species.

6 POPULATION

The population was estimated at 11,669,803 in 1994 and projected to be 13,194,000 in the year 2000. Population density is about 27 persons per square kilometer (69 per square mile). At the time of the 1992 census, Harare, the capital, had a population of 1,478,810.

7 MIGRATION

By early 1987, 110,000 whites were estimated to have remained in Zimbabwe, about half the number on independence in 1980. There were also about 25,000 of mixed race and 10,000 Asians. By the end of 1992, famine and civil war in Mozambique had driven an estimated 136,600 Mozambicans into Zimbabwe. In 1991 there were 24,442 Zimbabwe-born whites and 13,568 blacks living in South Africa.

8 ETHNIC GROUPS

Africans in Zimbabwe are mainly related to the two major Bantu-speaking groups, the Shona (about 77% of the population) and the Ndebele (about 18%). Europeans are almost entirely either immigrants from the United Kingdom or South Africa or their descendants.

9 LANGUAGES

Six major dialects of the same Bantu language, Shona, are spoken. The Ndebele speak modified versions of Ndebele (or Sindebele). English, the official language, is spoken by most Europeans and by an increasing number of Africans.

10 RELIGIONS

About 55% of the total population was Christian as of 1993. Traditional religious practices are still followed by at least 40% of the population. Of professing Christians, Protestants constitute some 17%, followers of African native churches, 14%, and Roman Catholics, 8.7%. There are small populations of Jews and Muslims, as well as some Baha'is and Hindus.

11 TRANSPORTATION

In 1991, the National Railways of Zimbabwe, a public corporation, operated 4,304 kilometers (2,675 miles) of rail lines. In the same year, there were 85,237 kilometers (52,966 miles) of road, traveled by 265,000 motor vehicles, including 200,000 passenger cars. Harare and Bulawayo are the principal airports.

12 HISTORY

The remains of ironworking cultures that date back to AD 300 have been discovered in what is now Zimbabwe. Bantu-speaking Shona arrived from the north between the tenth and eleventh centuries AD. They gradually developed gold and ivory trade with the coast, and by the mid-fifteenth century had established a strong empire, with its capital at the ancient city of Zimbabwe.

By the time the British began arriving in the mid-nineteenth century, the Shona people had long been subjected to slave raids and their empire destroyed by the Ndebele, fleeing the Zulus in South Africa. David Livingstone, a Scottish missionary and explorer, was chiefly responsible for opening Central Africa to the Europeans.

To prevent Portuguese and Boer (Dutch) expansion into the area, both the British government and Cecil Rhodes actively sought to acquire territory. In 1888, Lobengula, king of the Ndebele, accepted a treaty with Great Britain and granted Rhodes exclusive mineral rights to the lands he controlled. Rhodes was then able to obtain a royal charter for his British South Africa Company (BSAC) in 1889. The BSAC sent a group of settlers into Mashonaland, where they founded the town of Salisbury (now Harare). With the defeat of the Ndebele and the Shona between 1893 and 1897, Europeans were guaranteed unlimited settlement. The name Rhodesia was commonly used by 1895.

In 1923, Southern Rhodesia was annexed to the British government; its African inhabitants thereby became British subjects, and the colony received its basic constitution. In 1953, the Central African Federation was formed, consisting of the three British territories of Northern Rhodesia (now Zambia), Nyasaland (now Malawi), and Southern Rhodesia, with each territory retaining its original constitution. In 1962, Nyasaland and Northern Rhodesia withdrew from the federation, which disbanded in 1963, and Southern Rhodesia sought independence under the name of Rhodesia.

The white-settler government demanded independence under the existing political framework. The African nationalists also demanded independence, but under conditions of universal franchise and African majority rule. Negotiations repeatedly broke down, and on 11 November 1965, the government of Rhodesian Prime Minister Ian Smith issued a unilateral declaration of independence (since known as UDI). In December, the United Nations Security Council passed a resolution calling for selective mandatory sanctions against Rhodesia. Further attempts at a negotiated settlement ended in failure. In a referendum held on 20 June 1969, Rhodesia's voters—92% white—approved the establishment of a republic.

Rhodesia declared itself a republic on 2 March 1970. The United Kingdom called the declaration illegal, and 11 countries closed their consulates in Rhodesia. The United Nations Security Council called on member states not to recognize any acts by the illegal regime and condemned Portugal and South Africa for maintaining relations with Rhodesia. Problems in Rhodesia deepened after UDI, largely as a result of regional and international political pressure, African nationalist demands, and African guerrilla activities. A meeting took place in Geneva in October 1976 between the British and Smith governments and four African nationalist groups. On 3 March 1978, the Smith regime signed an internal agreement with Bishop Abel Muzorewa, Ndabaningi Sithole, and other leaders, providing for qualified majority rule and universal suffrage. Bishop Muzorewa, whose party won a majority in the elections of April 1979, became the first black prime minister of the country (now renamed Zimbabwe-Rhodesia).

However, fighting between the different factions continued, and further negotiations in England later that year resulted in an agreement, by 21 December, on a new, democratic constitution, democratic elections, and independence. Following elections held in February, Robert Mugabe became prime minister and formed a coalition government that included Joshua Nkomo. The independent nation of Zimbabwe was proclaimed on 18 April 1980, and the new parliament opened on 14 May 1980.

Independence and Factionalism

Following independence, Zimbabwe initially made significant economic and social progress, but internal dissent was a growing problem. A long-simmering rivalry erupted between Mugabe's dominant Zimbabwe African National Union (ZANU)-Patriotic Front Party, which represented the

Photo credit: Barbara K. Deans, Montreal, Canada

Life in the countryside.

majority Shona tribes, and Nkomo's Zimbabwe African People's Union (ZAPU), which had the support of the minority Ndebele. Mugabe ousted Nkomo from the cabinet in February 1982. On 8 March 1983, Nkomo went into exile, but returned to Parliament in August.

Armed rebels continued to operate in Matabeleland until 1987, when the two largest political parties, ZANU and ZAPU, agreed to merge. By this point, however, the political instability of Zimbabwe's neighbors to the south and east was threatening the country. In 1986, South African forces raided the premises of the South African black-liberation African National Congress in Harare, and

10,000 Zimbabwean troops were deployed in Mozambique. They were seeking to keep antigovernment forces in that country from severing Zimbabwe's rail, road, and oil-pipeline links with the port of Beira in Mozambique.

In the meantime dissatisfaction with the economic situation at home led to growing opposition to Mugabe. In January 1992, Sithole returned from seven years of self-imposed exile in the United States. In July, Ian Smith chaired a meeting of Rhodesian-era parties seeking to form a coalition in opposition to Mugabe. In May 1992 a new pressure group, the Forum for Democratic Reform, was launched in preparation for the 1995 elections. It evolved into the

Forum Party, which advocates free enterprise, clean government, respect for human rights, and a drastic reduction of state control of the economy.

In the March 1990 elections, Mugabe was reelected with 78.3% of the vote. There was a sharp drop in voter participation, and the election was marred by restrictions on opposition activity and open intimidation of opposition voters. With a slumping economy, worsened by an extensive drought in 1991 and 1992, the Mugabe government lost support. It responded by restricting human and political rights, placing checks on the formerly independent judiciary, and tampering with the election process.

13 GOVERNMENT

Under the constitution that took effect on 18 April 1980, independent Zimbabwe has a two-chamber Parliament. The lower house, the House of Assembly, had 100 members, and the upper house, or Senate, had 40 members. In August 1987, as soon as the constitution allowed, the separate representation for whites in Parliament was abolished. The two houses of Parliament were merged after the 1990 elections into a chamber of 150 members. Another constitutional change created an executive presidency and abolished the office of prime minister. The president is directly elected for a 6-year term and may be reelected. There is universal suffrage (voting) beginning at age 18.

14 POLITICAL PARTIES

The principal black parties in Zimbabwean politics originated in the struggle for independence on a tribal basis. The Zimbabwe African People's Union (ZAPU) was formed in December 1961 and led by Joshua Nkomo. It was split in July 1963 by the creation of the Zimbabwe African National Union (ZANU), led by the Reverend Ndabaningi Sithole, and later by Robert Mugabe. Both ZAPU and ZANU took up arms against the government and in 1976 allied themselves in the Patriotic Front (PF).

After much hostility and bitterness during most of the 1980s, ZAPU and ZANU finally agreed in late 1987 to merge under the name of ZANU. New parties began to emerge in the late 1980s and early 1990s in preparation for the expected elections in 1995, including Tekere's Zimbabwe Unity Movement (ZUM). In January, long-time Mugabe rival Sithole returned from exile and created his own party, also using the ZANU name as ZANU-Ndonga or sometimes ZANU-Sithole.

15 JUDICIAL SYSTEM

A four-member Supreme Court, headed by the chief justice, hears cases involving violations of fundamental rights guaranteed in the constitution and hears appeals of other cases. There is a High Court consisting of general and appeals divisions. Below the High Court are regional courts with civil jurisdiction and courts with both civil and criminal jurisdiction.

16 ARMED FORCES

Regular armed forces numbered 48,500 in 1993. The army had 6,000 troops organized into 26 infantry battalions, 1 artillery regiment, 1 armored regiment, 1 engineer

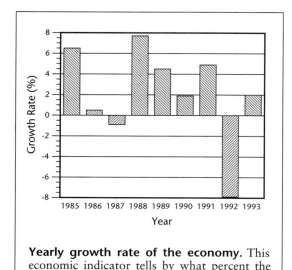

Yearly growth rate of the economy. This economic indicator tells by what percent the economy has increased or decreased when compared with the previous year.

18 INCOME

In 1992, Zimbabwe's gross national product (GNP) was US$5,896 million at current prices, or US$520 per person. For the period 1985–92 the average inflation rate was 17.6%, resulting in a real growth rate in per person GNP of –0.6%.

19 INDUSTRY

Zimbabwe has a substantial cotton and textile industry and a sizeable metal and engineering sector. Other leading industries are food processing, sugar refining, tobacco, clothing, chemicals, beverages, industrial coke, cement, pig iron and crude steel, nitrogenous and phosphate fertilizers, unwrought nickel and tin, wood pulp, and furniture.

20 LABOR

In 1991, there were 1,187,300 employed civilians in Zimbabwe: 681,400 in services, 266,500 in industry, and 239,400 in agriculture. The total labor force is estimated at 2.75 million, or 27% of the total population. Average monthly nonagricultural earnings in 1992 were US$5.31. Average monthly wages were lowest in agriculture (US$1.15 in 1991). The unemployment rate in 1991 was believed to be at least 17–31% or higher.

21 AGRICULTURE

In 1992, drought severely affected the output of every crop except tobacco. Tobacco production in 1992 exceeded 200,000 tons. Corn production in 1992 totaled only 362,000 tons, down from 1,586,000 tons in 1991 because of the drought. In 1992, cotton production totaled 27,000

regiment, and supporting units. The air force had 2,500 personnel and 36 combat aircraft. The national militia came to 4,000. Estimated defense expenditures for 1991 were US$412 million.

17 ECONOMY

Zimbabwe has developed one of the most varied economies in Africa. It has abundant agricultural and mineral resources and well-developed industry. However, problems abound. Although Zimbabwe began to recover from the effects of the devastating 1991–92 drought, the unemployment rate is almost 45% and thousands remain chronically dependent on food support. Together with the International Monetary Fund (IMF), Zimbabwe drew up a 1991–95 economic reform plan.

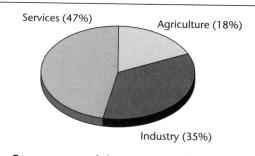

Components of the economy. This pie chart shows how much of the country's economy is devoted to agriculture (includes forestry, hunting, and fishing), industry, or services.

tons. Marketed production figures for other crops in 1992 were wheat, 81 tons; sorghum, 29 tons; soybeans, 51 tons; peanuts, 34 tons; coffee, 4 tons; and sugarcane, 300 tons. Rice, potatoes, tea, and pyrethrum are also grown.

22 DOMESTICATED ANIMALS

In 1992, some 4,700,000 head of cattle, 580,000 sheep, 290,000 hogs, and 2,570,000 goats were held. Chickens numbered about 13 million. In 1992, cattle slaughterings totaled 440,000 head; sheep, 38,000 head; pigs, 203,000 head. Fresh milk production from cows totaled 415,000 tons.

23 FISHING

There is some commercial fishing on Lake Kariba. The total catch in 1991 was estimated at 22,155 tons.

24 FORESTRY

About 100,000 tons of teak, mahogany, and mukwa (*kiaat*) are cut annually.

Roundwood production totaled 7.9 million cubic meters in 1991; sawn wood production was 190,000 cubic meters (in 1984).

25 MINING

Zimbabwe is a world leader in the production of lithium and asbestos, and has more than half of the world's known reserves of chromium. In order of value, the most important minerals in 1991 were gold, asbestos, nickel, coal, copper, chromite, tin, and silver. Mineral output in 1991 included coal, 5,616,000 tons; chromium ore, 563,634 tons; asbestos, 141,697 tons; copper, 14,420 tons; nickel, 12,371 tons; and gold, 17,820 kilograms.

26 FOREIGN TRADE

Gold was the export leader in 1991 (13.6%), followed by tobacco (12.7%), cotton, textiles, ferro-alloys, food and live animals, crude inedible non-food materials, nickel, asbestos, copper, sugar, and iron and steel bars, ingots, and billets. During 1990, Germany took 11.6% of Zimbabwe's exports; the United Kingdom, 10.8%; and South Africa, 8.9%. Imports came mainly from South Africa, 20.2%; the United Kingdom, 11.7%; and the United States, 10.6%.

27 ENERGY AND POWER

Zimbabwe relies heavily on hydroelectricity and coal for its energy needs. Wood is also still important. Petroleum accounts for only 9% of Zimbabwe's total energy consumption, but provides most motor fuels. Coal production in 1991 totaled 5.6 million tons, with much of that amount

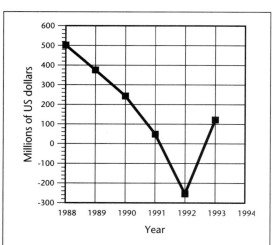

Yearly balance of trade measured in millions of US dollars. The balance of trade is the difference between what a country sells to other countries (its exports) and what it buys (its imports). If a country imports more than it exports, it has a negative balance of trade (a trade deficit). If exports exceed imports there is a positive balance of trade (a trade surplus).

going to the coal-fired Hwange plant for electricity production. In 1982, a plant producing ethanol from sugarcane opened and now produces some 20% of motor fuel requirements. The use of solar energy is increasing. In 1991, Zimbabwe produced 9,565 million kilowatt hours of electricity.

28 SOCIAL DEVELOPMENT

The Ministry of Labour, Manpower Planning, and Social Welfare deals with child welfare, delinquency, adoption, family problems, refugees, the aged, and public assistance. Voluntary welfare organizations providing facilities for the aged, the handicapped, and care of children receive some government assistance. Workers' compensation is provided to those Africans whose earnings fall below a set minimum yearly wage.

29 HEALTH

About 85% of the population had access to health care services in 1992. There were four levels of health care delivery in Zimbabwe as of 1992: (1) 56 rural hospitals and 927 health centers; (2) 55 district hospitals; (3) 8 provincial and 4 general hospitals; and (4) 5 central hospitals located in major cities. For the period 1988 to 1993, there was 1 doctor per 5,994 people.

Tuberculosis has been a major health problem. Local campaigns are underway to control schistosomiasis, which affects a large percentage of the African population. Average life expectancy is 53 years.

30 HOUSING

In rural areas, Africans live in villages and on farms in housing that is mainly of brick or mud and stick construction with thatch or metal roofs. Urban housing is generally of brick.

31 EDUCATION

The adult literacy rate is 67%: 73.7% for men and 60.3% for women. In 1992 there were 2,301,642 students in 4,567 primary schools with 60,834 teachers. The same year, general secondary schools had 657,344 students. In 1991, students in secondary schools numbered 710,619 with 25,225 teachers. The University of Zimbabwe provides higher education on a multiracial basis; there were 9 colleges in 1987.

Selected Social Indicators

These statistics are estimates for the period 1988 to 1993. For comparison purposes, data for the United States and averages for low-income countries and high-income countries are also given.

Indicator	Zimbabwe	Low-income countries	High-income countries	United States
Per capita gross national product†	**$520**	$380	$23,680	$24,740
Population growth rate	**3.0%**	1.9%	0.6%	1.0%
Population growth rate in urban areas	**5.3%**	3.9%	0.8%	1.3%
Population per square kilometer of land	**27**	78	25	26
Life expectancy in years	**53**	62	77	76
Number of people per physician	**5,994**	>3,300	453	419
Number of pupils per teacher (primary school)	**38**	39	<18	20
Illiteracy rate (15 years and older)	**33%**	41%	<5%	<3%
Energy consumed per capita (kg of oil equivalent)	**471**	364	5,203	7,918

† The gross national product (GNP) is the total dollar value of all goods and services produced by a country in a year. The per capita GNP is calculated by dividing a country's GNP by its population. The World Bank defines low-income countries as those with a per capita GNP of $695 or less. High-income countries have a per capita GNP of $8,626 or more. Less than 14% of the world's 5.5 billion people live in high-income countries, while almost 60% live in low-income countries.

> = greater than   < = less than

Sources: World Bank, *Social Indicators of Development 1995*, Baltimore: Johns Hopkins University Press, 1995. Central Intelligence Agency, *World Fact Book*, Washington, D.C.: Government Printing Office, 1994.

In 1992, there were 3,076 teaching staff and 61,553 students in all higher level institutions.

32 MEDIA

In 1991 there were 286,600 telephones, about 3 per 100 people. Radio Zimbabwe broadcasts over two AM and three FM channels, and government-produced television programs are broadcast from Harare and Bulawayo. In 1991 there were 860,000 radios and 270,000 television sets. There are 2 daily papers and more than 40 periodicals published in Zimbabwe. The dailies, with their 1991 circulations, are the *Herald* (Harare), 110,000; and the *Chronicle* (Bulawayo), 41,000.

33 TOURISM AND RECREATION

Tourist attractions include Victoria Falls and the Kariba Dam on the Zambezi River; numerous wildlife sanctuaries and game reserves, including Hwange National Park; the eastern highlands; the Matobo Hills; and the Zimbabwe ruins near Masvingo. There are safari areas in the Zambezi Valley below the Kariba Dam.

Photo credit: Barbara K. Deans, Montreal, Canada

A local artist applies a coat of wax to his nearly finished piece, a wood carving of a giraffe.

In 1991, 513,580 tourists visited Zimbabwe, 39% from South Africa, 29% from Zambia, and 9% from Europe. There were 4,147 hotel rooms with a 50% occupancy rate.

34 FAMOUS ZIMBABWEANS

The country's former name, Rhodesia, was derived from Cecil John Rhodes (1853–1902), whose company administered the area during the late 19th and early 20th centuries. Lobengula (1833–94), king of the Ndebele, headed an unsuccessful rebellion of his people against the settlers in 1893.

Prominent African nationalist leaders are Joshua Nkomo (b.1917), leader of ZAPU; Bishop Abel Muzorewa (b.1925) of the United Methodist Church, who became the nation's first black prime minister in 1979; and ZANU leader Robert Gabriel Mugabe (b.1924), who became prime minister after independence. Ian Smith (b.1919) was prime minister from 1964 to 1979.

Many of the early works of the British novelist Doris Lessing (b.1919) are set in the Rhodesia where she grew up.

35 BIBLIOGRAPHY

Cheney, Patricia. *The Land and People of Zimbabwe.* New York: Lippincott, 1990.

Nkomo, Joshua. *The Story of My Life.* London: Mowbrays, 1984.

O'Toole, Thomas. *Zimbabwe in Pictures.* Minneapolis: Lerner Pub. Co., 1988.

GLOSSARY

aboriginal: The first known inhabitants of a country. A species of animals or plants which originated within a given area.

acid rain: Rain (or snow) that has become slightly acid by mixing with industrial air pollution.

adobe: A brick made from sun-dried heavy clay mixed with straw, used in building houses. A house made of adobe bricks.

adult literacy: The ability of adults to read and write.

afforestation: The act of turning arable land into forest or woodland.

agrarian economy: An economy where agriculture is the dominant form of economic activity. A society where agriculture dominates the day-to-day activities of the population is called an agrarian society.

air link: Refers to scheduled air service that allows people and goods to travel between two places on a regular basis.

airborne industrial pollutant: Pollution caused by industry that is supported or carried by the air.

allies: Groups or persons who are united in a common purpose. Typically used to describe nations that have joined together to fight a common enemy in war.

In World War I, the term Allies described the nations that fought against Germany and its allies. In World War II, Allies described the United Kingdom, United States, the USSR and their allies, who fought against the Axis Powers of Germany, Italy, and Japan.

aloe: A plant particularly abundant in the southern part of Africa, where leaves of some species are made into ropes, fishing lines, bow strings, and hammocks. It is also a symbolic plant in the Islamic world; anyone who returns from a pilgrimage to Mecca (Mekkah) hangs aloe over his door as a token that he has performed the journey.

Altaic language family: A family of languages spoken in portions of northern and eastern Europe, and nearly the whole of northern and central Asia, together with some other regions. The family is divided into five branches: the Ugrian or Finno-Hungarian, Smoyed, Turkish, Mongolian, and Tunguse.

althing: A legislative assembly.

amendment: A change or addition to a document.

Amerindian: A contraction of the two words, American Indian. It describes native peoples of North, South, or Central America.

amnesty: An act of forgiveness or pardon, usually taken by a government, toward persons for crimes they may have committed.

Anglican: Pertaining to or connected with the Church of England.

animism: The belief that natural objects and phenomena have souls or innate spiritual powers.

annual growth rate: The rate at which something grows over a period of 12 months.

annual inflation rate: The rate of inflation in prices over the course of a year.

anthracite coal: Also called hard coal, it is usually 90 to 95 percent carbon, and burns cleanly, almost without a flame.

anti-Semitism: Agitation, persecution, or discrimination (physical, emotional, economic, political, or otherwise) directed against the Jews.

apartheid: The past governmental policy in the Republic of South Africa of separating the races in society.

appeasement: To bring to a state of peace.

appellate: Refers to an appeal of a court decision to a high authority.

applied science: Scientific techniques employed to achieve results that solve practical problems.

aquaculture: The culture or "farming" of aquatic plants or other natural produce, as in the raising of catfish in "farms."

aquatic resources: Resources that come from, grow in, or live in water, including fish and plants.

aquifer: An underground layer of porous rock, sand, or gravel that holds water.

arable land: Land that can be cultivated by plowing and used for growing crops.

arbitration: A process whereby disputes are settled by a designated person, called the arbitrator, instead of by a court of law.

archipelago: Any body of water abounding with islands, or the islands themselves collectively.

archives: A place where records or a collection of important documents are kept.

arctic climate: Cold, frigid weather similar to that experienced at or near the north pole.

aristocracy: A small minority that controls the government of a nation, typically on the basis of inherited wealth.

armistice: An agreement or truce which ends military conflict in anticipation of a peace treaty.

artesian well: A type of well where the water rises to the surface and overflows.

ASEAN *see* Association of Southeast Asian Nations

Association of Southeast Asian Nations: ASEAN was established in 1967 to promote political, economic, and social cooperation among its six member countries: Indonesia, Malaysia, the Philippines, Singapore, Thailand, and Brunei. ASEAN headquarters are in Jakarta, Indonesia. In January 1992, ASEAN agreed to create the ASEAN Free Trade Area (AFTA).

atheist: A person who denies the existence of God or of a supreme intelligent being.

atoll: A coral island, consisting of a strip or ring of coral surrounding a central lagoon.

atomic weapons: Weapons whose extremely violent explosive power comes from the splitting of the nuclei of atoms (usually uranium or plutonium) by neutrons in a rapid chain reaction. These weapons may be referred to as atom bombs, hydrogen bombs, or H-bombs.

austerity measures: Steps taken by a government to conserve money or resources during an economically difficult time, such as cutting back on federally funded programs.

Australoid: Pertains to the type of aborigines, or earliest inhabitants, of Australia.

Austronesian language: A family of languages which includes practically all the languages of the Pacific Islands—Indonesian, Melanesian, Polynesian, and Micronesian sub-families. Does not include Australian or Papuan languages.

authoritarianism: A form of government in which a person or group attempts to rule with absolute authority without the representation of the citizens.

autonomous state: A country which is completely self-governing, as opposed to being a dependency or part of another country.

autonomy: The state of existing as a self-governing entity. For instance, when a country gains its independence from another country, it gains autonomy.

average inflation rate: The average rate at which the general prices of goods and services increase over the period of a year.

average life expectancy: In any given society, the average age attained by persons at the time of death.

Axis Powers: The countries aligned against the Allied Nations in World War II, originally applied to Nazi Germany and Fascist Italy (Rome-Berlin Axis), and later extended to include Japan.

bagasse: Plant residue left after a product, such as juice, has been extracted.

Baha'i: The follower of a religious sect founded by Mirza Husayn Ali in Iran in 1863.

Baltic states. The three formerly communist countries of Estonia, Latvia, and Lithuania that border on the Baltic Sea.

Bantu language group: A name applied to the languages spoken in central and south Africa.

banyan tree: An East Indian fig tree. Individual trees develop roots from the branches that descend to the ground and become trunks. These roots support and nourish the crown of the tree.

Baptist: A member of a Protestant denomination that practices adult baptism by complete immersion in water.

barren land: Unproductive land, partly or entirely treeless.

barter: Trade practice where merchandise is exchanged directly for other merchandise or services without use of money.

bedrock: Solid rock lying under loose earth.

bicameral legislature: A legislative body consisting of two chambers, such as the U.S. House of Representatives and the U.S. Senate.

bill of rights: A written statement containing the list of privileges and powers to be granted to a body of people, usually introduced when a government or other organization is forming.

bituminous coal: Soft coal; coal which burns with a bright-yellow flame.

black market: A system of trade where goods are sold illegally, often for excessively inflated prices. This type of trade usually develops to avoid paying taxes or tariffs levied by the government, or to get around import or export restrictions on products.

bloodless coup: The sudden takeover of a country's government by hostile means but without killing anyone in the process.

boat people: Used to describe individuals (refugees) who attempt to flee their country by boat.

bog: Wet, soft, and spongy ground where the soil is composed mainly of decayed or decaying vegetable matter.

Bolshevik Revolution. A revolution in 1917 in Russia when a wing of the Russian Social Democratic party seized power. The Bolsheviks advocated the violent overthrow of capitalism.

bonded labor: Workers bound to service without pay; slaves.

border dispute: A disagreement between two countries as to the exact location or length of the dividing line between them.

Brahman: A member (by heredity) of the highest caste among the Hindus, usually assigned to the priesthood.

broadleaf forest: A forest composed mainly of broadleaf (deciduous) trees.

Buddhism: A religious system common in India and eastern Asia. Founded by and based upon the teachings of Siddhartha Gautama, Buddhism asserts that suffering is an inescapable part of life. Deliverance can only be achieved through the practice of charity, temperance, justice, honesty, and truth.

buffer state: A small country that lies between two larger, possibly hostile countries, considered to be a neutralizing force between them.

bureaucracy: A system of government that is characterized by division into bureaus of administration with their own divisional heads. Also refers to the inflexible procedures of such a system that often result in delay.

Byzantine Empire: An empire centered in the city of Byzantium, now Istanbul in present-day Turkey.

CACM *see* Central American Common Market.

candlewood: A name given to several species of trees and shrubs found in the British West Indies, northern Mexico, and the southwestern United States. The plants are characterized by a very resinous wood.

canton: A territory or small division or state within a country.

capital punishment: The ultimate act of punishment for a crime, the death penalty.

capitalism: An economic system in which goods and services and the means to produce and sell them are privately owned, and prices and wages are determined by market forces.

Caribbean Community and Common Market (CARICOM): Founded in 1973 and with its headquarters in Georgetown, Guyana, CARICOM seeks the establishment of a common trade policy and increased cooperation in the Caribbean region. Includes 13 English-speaking Caribbean nations: Antigua and Barbuda, the Bahamas, Barbados, Belize, Dominica, Grenada, Guyana, Jamaica, Montserrat, Saint Kitts-Nevis, Saint Lucia, St. Vincent/Grenadines, and Trinidad and Tobago.

CARICOM *see* Caribbean Community and Common Market.

carnivore: Flesh-eating animal or plant.

carob: The common English name for a plant that is similar to and sometimes used as a substitute for chocolate.

cartel: An organization of independent producers formed to regulate the production, pricing, or marketing practices of its members in order to limit competition and maximize their market power.

cash crop: A crop that is grown to be sold rather than kept for private use.

cassation: The reversal or annulling of a final judgment by the supreme authority.

cassava: The name of several species of stout herbs, extensively cultivated for food.

caste system: One of the artificial divisions or social classes into which the Hindus are rigidly separated according to the religious law of Brahmanism. Membership in a caste is hereditary, and the privileges and disabilities of each caste are transmitted by inheritance.

Caucasian: The white race of human beings, as determined by genealogy and physical features.

Caucasoid: Belonging to the racial group characterized by light skin pigmentation. Commonly called the "white race."

cease-fire: An official declaration of the end to the use of military force or active hostilities, even if only temporary.

CEMA *see* Council for Mutual Economic Assistance.

censorship: The practice of withholding certain items of news that may cast a country in an unfavorable light or give away secrets to the enemy.

census: An official counting of the inhabitants of a state or country with details of sex and age, family, occupation, possessions, etc.

Central American Common Market (CACM): Established in 1962, a trade alliance of five Central American nations. Participating are Costa Rica, El Salvador, Guatemala, Honduras, and Nicaragua.

Central Powers: In World War I, Germany and Austria-Hungary, and their allies, Turkey and Bulgaria.

centrally planned economy: An economic system all aspects of which are supervised and regulated by the government.

centrist position: Refers to opinions held by members of a moderate political group; that is, views that are somewhere in the middle of popular thought between conservative and liberal.

cession: Withdrawal from or yielding to physical force.

chancellor: A high-ranking government official. In some countries it is the prime minister.

cholera: An acute infectious disease characterized by severe diarrhea, vomiting, and, often, death.

Christianity: The religion founded by Jesus Christ, based on the Bible as holy scripture.

Church of England: The national and established church in England. The Church of England claims continuity with the branch of the Catholic Church that existed in England before the Reformation. Under Henry VIII, the spiritual supremacy and jurisdiction of the Pope were abolished, and the sovereign (king or queen) was declared head of the church.

circuit court: A court that convenes in two or more locations within its appointed district.

CIS *see* Commonwealth of Independent States

city-state: An independent state consisting of a city and its surrounding territory.

civil court: A court whose proceedings include determinations of rights of individual citizens, in contrast to criminal proceedings regarding individuals or the public.

civil jurisdiction: The authority to enforce the laws in civil matters brought before the court.

civil law: The law developed by a nation or state for the conduct of daily life of its own people.

civil rights: The privileges of all individuals to be treated as equals under the laws of their country; specifically, the rights given by certain amendments to the U.S. Constitution.

civil unrest: The feeling of uneasiness due to an unstable political climate, or actions taken as a result of it.

civil war: A war between groups of citizens of the same country who have different opinions or agendas. The Civil War of the United States was the conflict between the states of the North and South from 1861 to 1865.

climatic belt: A region or zone where a particular type of climate prevails.

Club du Sahel: The Club du Sahel is an informal coalition which seeks to reverse the effects of drought and the desertification in the eight Sahelian zone countries: Burkina Faso, Chad, Gambia, Mali, Mauritania, Niger, Senegal, and the Cape Verde Islands. Headquarters are in Ouagadougou, Burkina Faso.

CMEA see Council for Mutual Economic Assistance.

coalition government: A government combining differing factions within a country, usually temporary.

coastal belt: A coastal plain area of lowlands and somewhat higher ridges that run parallel to the coast.

coastal plain: A fairly level area of land along the coast of a land mass.

coca: A shrub native to South America, the leaves of which produce organic compounds that are used in the production of cocaine.

coke: The solid product of the carbonization of coal, bearing the same relation to coal that charcoal does to wood.

cold war: Refers to conflict over ideological differences that is carried on by words and diplomatic actions, not by military action. The term is usually used to refer to the tension that existed between the United States and the USSR from the 1950s until the breakup of the USSR in 1991.

collective bargaining: The negotiations between workers who are members of a union and their employer for the purpose of deciding work rules and policies regarding wages, hours, etc.

collective farm: A large farm formed from many small farms and supervised by the government; usually found in communist countries.

collective farming: The system of farming on a collective where all workers share in the income of the farm.

colloquial: Belonging to ordinary, everyday speech: often especially applied to common words and phrases which are not used in formal speech.

colonial period: The period of time when a country forms colonies in and extends control over a foreign area.

colonist: Any member of a colony or one who helps settle a new colony.

colony: A group of people who settle in a new area far from their original country, but still under the jurisdiction of that country. Also refers to the newly settled area itself.

COMECON see Council for Mutual Economic Assistance.

commerce: The trading of goods (buying and selling), especially on a large scale, between cities, states, and countries.

commercial catch: The amount of marketable fish, usually measured in tons, caught in a particular period of time.

commercial crop: Any marketable agricultural crop.

commission: A group of people designated to collectively do a job, including a government agency with certain law-making powers. Also, the power given to an individual or group to perform certain duties.

commodity: Any items, such as goods or services, that are bought or sold, or agricultural products that are traded or marketed.

common law: A legal system based on custom and decisions and opinions of the law courts. The basic system of law of England and the United States.

common market: An economic union among countries that is formed to remove trade barriers (tariffs) among those countries, increasing economic cooperation. The European Community is a notable example of a common market.

commonwealth: A commonwealth is a free association of sovereign independent states that has no charter, treaty, or constitution. The association promotes cooperation, consultation, and mutual assistance among members.

Commonwealth of Independent States: The CIS was established in December 1991 as an association of 11 republics of the former Soviet Union. The members include: Russia, Ukraine, Belarus (formerly Byelorussia), Moldova (formerly Moldavia), Armenia, Azerbaijan, Uzbekistan, Turkmenistan, Tajikistan, Kazakhstan, and Kirgizstan (formerly Kirghiziya). The Baltic states—Estonia, Latvia, and Lithuania—did not join. Georgia maintained observer status before joining the CIS in November 1993.

Commonwealth of Nations: Voluntary association of the United Kingdom and its present dependencies and associated states, as well as certain former dependencies and their dependent territories. The term was first used officially in 1926 and is embodied in the Statute of Westminster (1931). Within the Commonwealth, whose secretariat (established in 1965) is located in London, England, are numerous subgroups devoted to economic and technical cooperation.

commune: An organization of people living together in a community who share the ownership and use of property. Also refers to a small governmental district of a country, especially in Europe.

communism: A form of government whose system requires common ownership of property for the use of all citizens. All profits are to be equally distributed and prices on goods and services are usually set by the state. Also, communism refers directly to the official doctrine of the former U.S.S.R.

compulsory: Required by law or other regulation.

compulsory education: The mandatory requirement for children to attend school until they have reached a certain age or grade level.

conciliation: A process of bringing together opposing sides of a disagreement for the purpose of compromise. Or, a way of settling an international dispute in which the disagreement is submitted to an independent committee that will examine the facts and advise the participants of a possible solution.

concordat: An agreement, compact, or convention, especially between church and state.

confederation: An alliance or league formed for the purpose of promoting the common interests of its members.

Confucianism: The system of ethics and politics taught by the Chinese philosopher Confucius.

coniferous forest: A forest consisting mainly of pine, fir, and cypress trees.

conifers: Cone-bearing plants. Mostly evergreen trees and shrubs which produce cones.

conscription: To be required to join the military by law. Also known as the draft. Service personnel who join the military because of the legal requirement are called conscripts or draftees.

conservative party: A political group whose philosophy tends to be based on established traditions and not supportive of rapid change.

constituency: The registered voters in a governmental district, or a group of people that supports a position or a candidate.

constituent assembly: A group of people that has the power to determine the election of a political representative or create a constitution.

constitution: The written laws and basic rights of citizens of a country or members of an organized group.

constitutional monarchy: A system of government in which the hereditary sovereign (king or queen, usually) rules according to a written constitution.

constitutional republic: A system of government with an elected chief of state and elected representation, with a written constitution containing its governing principles. The United States is a constitutional republic.

consumer goods: Items that are bought to satisfy personal needs or wants of individuals.

continental climate: The climate of a part of the continent; the characteristics and peculiarities of the climate are a result of the land itself and its location.

continental shelf: A plain extending from the continental coast and varying in width that typically ends in a steep slope to the ocean floor.

copra: The dried meat of the coconut; it is frequently used as an ingredient of curry, and to produce coconut oil. Also written *cobra, coprah,* and *copperah.*

Coptic Christians: Members of the Coptic Church of Egypt, formerly of Ethiopia.

cordillera: A continuous ridge, range, or chain of mountains.

corvette: A small warship that is often used as an escort ship because it is easier to maneuver than larger ships like destroyers.

Council for Mutual Economic Assistance (CMEA): Also known as Comecon, the alliance of socialist economies was established on 25 January 1949 and abolished 1 January 1991. It included Afghanistan*, Albania, Angola*, Bulgaria, Cuba, Czechoslovakia, Ethiopia*, East Germany, Hungary, Laos*, Mongolia, Mozambique*, Nicaragua*, Poland, Romania, USSR, Vietnam, Yemen*, and Yugoslavia. Nations marked with an asterisk were observers only.

counterinsurgency operations: Organized military activity designed to stop rebellion against an established government.

county: A territorial division or administrative unit within a state or country.

coup d'ètat or coup: A sudden, violent overthrow of a government or its leader.

court of appeal: An appellate court, having the power of review after a case has been decided in a lower court.

court of first appeal: The next highest court to the court which has decided a case, to which that case may be presented for review.

court of last appeal: The highest court, in which a decision is not subject to review by any higher court. In the United States, it could be the Supreme Court of an individual state or the U.S. Supreme Court.

cricket (sport): A game played by two teams with a ball and bat, with two wickets (staked target) being defended by a batsman. Common in the United Kingdom and Commonwealth of Nations countries.

criminal law: The branch of law that deals primarily with crimes and their punishments.

crown colony: A colony established by a commonwealth over which the monarch has some control, as in colonies established by the United Kingdom's Commonwealth of Nations.

Crusades: Military expeditions by European Christian armies in the eleventh, twelfth, and thirteenth centuries to win land controlled by the Muslims in the middle east.

cultivable land: Land that can be prepared for the production of crops.

Cultural Revolution: An extreme reform movement in China from 1966 to 1976; its goal was to combat liberalization by restoring the ideas of Mao Zedong.

Cushitic language group: A group of Hamitic languages that are spoken in Ethiopia and other areas of eastern Africa.

customs union: An agreement between two or more countries to remove trade barriers with each other and to establish common tariff and nontariff policies with respect to imports from countries outside of the agreement.

cyclone: Any atmospheric movement, general or local, in which the wind blows spirally around and in towards a center. In the northern hemisphere, the cyclonic movement is usually counter-clockwise, and in the southern hemisphere, it is clockwise.

Cyrillic alphabet: An alphabet adopted by the Slavic people and invented by Cyril and Methodius in the ninth century as an alphabet that was easier for the copyist to write. The Russian alphabet is a slight modification of it.

decentralization: The redistribution of power in a government from one large central authority to a wider range of smaller local authorities.

deciduous species: Any species that sheds or casts off a part of itself after a definite period of time. More commonly used in reference to plants that shed their leaves on a yearly basis as opposed to those (evergreens) that retain them.

declaration of independence: A formal written document stating the intent of a group of persons to become fully self-governing.

deficit: The amount of money that is in excess between spending and income.

deficit spending: The process in which a government spends money on goods and services in excess of its income.

deforestation: The removal or clearing of a forest.

deity: A being with the attributes, nature, and essence of a god; a divinity.

delta: Triangular-shaped deposits of soil formed at the mouths of large rivers.

demarcate: To mark off from adjoining land or territory; set the limits or boundaries of.

demilitarized zone (DMZ): An area surrounded by a combat zone that has had military troops and weapons removed.

demobilize: To disband or discharge military troops.

democracy: A form of government in which the power lies in the hands of the people, who can govern directly, or can be governed indirectly by representatives elected by its citizens.

denationalize: To remove from government ownership or control.

deportation: To carry away or remove from one country to another, or to a distant place.

depression: A hollow; a surface that has sunken or fallen in.

deregulation: The act of reversing controls and restrictions on prices of goods, bank interest, and the like.

desalinization plant: A facility that produces freshwater by removing the salt from saltwater.

desegregation: The act of removing restrictions on people of a particular race that keep them socially, economically, and, sometimes, physically, separate from other groups.

desertification: The process of becoming a desert as a result of climatic changes, land mismanagement, or both.

détente: The official lessening of tension between countries in conflict.

devaluation: The official lowering of the value of a country's currency in relation to the value of gold or the currencies of other countries.

developed countries: Countries which have a high standard of living and a well-developed industrial base.

development assistance: Government programs intended to finance and promote the growth of new industries.

dialect: One of a number of regional or related modes of speech regarded as descending from a common origin.

dictatorship: A form of government in which all the power is retained by an absolute leader or tyrant. There are no rights granted to the people to elect their own representatives.

diplomatic relations: The relationship between countries as conducted by representatives of each government.

direct election: The process of selecting a representative to the government by balloting of the voting public, in contrast to selection by an elected representative of the people.

disarmament: The reduction or depletion of the number of weapons or the size of armed forces.

dissident: A person whose political opinions differ from the majority to the point of rejection.

dogma: A principle, maxim, or tenet held as being firmly established.

domain: The area of land governed by a particular ruler or government, sometimes referring to the ultimate control of that territory.

domestic spending: Money spent by a country's government on goods used, investments, running of the government, and exports and imports.

dominion: A self-governing nation that recognizes the British monarch as chief of state.

dormant volcano: A volcano that has not exhibited any signs of activity for an extended period of time.

dowry: The sum of the property or money that a bride brings to her groom at their marriage.

draft constitution: The preliminary written plans for the new constitution of a country forming a new government.

Druze: A member of a Muslim sect based in Syria, living chiefly in the mountain regions of Lebanon.

dual nationality: The status of an individual who can claim citizenship in two or more countries.

duchy: Any territory under the rule of a duke or duchess.

due process: In law, the application of the legal process to which every citizen has a right, which cannot be denied.

durable goods: Goods or products which are expected to last and perform for several years, such as cars and washing machines.

duty: A tax imposed on imports by the customs authority of a country. Duties are generally based on the value of the goods (*ad valorem* duties), some other factors such as weight or quantity (specific duties), or a combination of value and other factors (compound duties).

dyewoods: Any wood from which dye is extracted.

dynasty: A family line of sovereigns who rule in succession, and the time during which they reign.

earned income: The money paid to an individual in wages or salary.

Eastern Orthodox: The outgrowth of the original Eastern Church of the Eastern Roman Empire, consisting of eastern Europe, western Asia, and Egypt.

EC *see* European Community

ecclesiastical: Pertaining or relating to the church.

echidna: A spiny, toothless anteater of Australia, Tasmania, and New Guinea.

ecological balance: The condition of a healthy, well-functioning ecosystem, which includes all the plants and animals in a natural community together with their environment.

ecology: The branch of science that studies organisms in relationship to other organisms and to their environment.

economic depression: A prolonged period in which there is high unemployment, low production, falling prices, and general business failure.

economically active population: That portion of the people who are employed for wages and are consumers of goods and services.

ecotourism: Broad term that encompasses nature, adventure, and ethnic tourism; responsible or wilderness-sensitive tourism; soft-path or small-scale tourism; low-impact tourism; and sustainable tourism. Scientific, educational, or academic tourism (such as biotourism, archetourism, and geotourism) are also forms of ecotourism.

elected assembly: The persons that comprise a legislative body of a government who received their positions by direct election.

electoral system: A system of choosing government officials by votes cast by qualified citizens.

electoral vote: The votes of the members of the electoral college.

electorate: The people who are qualified to vote in an election.

emancipation: The freeing of persons from any kind of bondage or slavery.

embargo: A legal restriction on commercial ships to enter a country's ports, or any legal restriction of trade.

emigration: Moving from one country or region to another for the purpose of residence.

empire: A group of territories ruled by one sovereign or supreme ruler. Also, the period of time under that rule.

enclave: A territory belonging to one nation that is surrounded by that of another nation.

encroachment: The act of intruding, trespassing, or entering on the rights or possessions of another.

endangered species: A plant or animal species whose existence as a whole is threatened with extinction.

endemic: Anything that is peculiar to and characteristic of a locality or region.

Enlightenment: An intellectual movement of the late seventeenth and eighteenth centuries in which scientific thinking gained a strong foothold and old beliefs were challenged. The idea of absolute monarchy was questioned and people were gradually given more individual rights.

enteric disease: An intestinal disease.

epidemic: As applied to disease, any disease that is temporarily prevalent among people in one place at the same time.

Episcopal: Belonging to or vested in bishops or prelates; characteristic of or pertaining to a bishop or bishops.

ethnolinguistic group: A classification of related languages based on common ethnic origin.

EU *see* European Union

European Community: A regional organization created in 1958. Its purpose is to eliminate customs duties and other trade barriers in Europe. It promotes a common external tariff against other countries, a Common Agricultural Policy (CAP), and guarantees of free movement of labor and capital. The original six members were Belgium, France, West Germany, Italy, Luxembourg, and the Netherlands. Denmark, Ireland, and the United Kingdom became members in 1973; Greece joined in 1981; Spain and Portugal in 1986. Other nations continue to join.

European Union: The EU is an umbrella reference to the European Community (EC) and to two European integration efforts introduced by the Maastricht Treaty: Common Foreign and Security Policy (including defense) and Justice and Home Affairs (principally cooperation between police and other authorities on crime, terrorism, and immigration issues).

exports: Goods sold to foreign buyers.

external migration: The movement of people from their native country to another country, as opposed to internal migration, which is the movement of people from one area of a country to another in the same country.

fallout: The precipitation of particles from the atmosphere, often the result of a ground disturbance by volcanic activity or a nuclear explosion.

family planning: The use of birth control to determine the number of children a married couple will have.

Fascism: A political philosophy that holds the good of the nation as more important than the needs of the individual. Fascism also stands for a dictatorial leader and strong oppression of opposition or dissent.

federal: Pertaining to a union of states whose governments are subordinate to a central government.

federation: A union of states or other groups under the authority of a central government.

fetishism: The practice of worshipping a material object that is believed to have mysterious powers residing in it, or is the representation of a deity to which worship may be paid and from which supernatural aid is expected.

feudal estate: The property owned by a lord in medieval Europe under the feudal system.

feudal society: In medieval times, an economic and social structure in which persons could hold land given to them by a lord (nobleman) in return for service to that lord.

final jurisdiction: The final authority in the decision of a legal matter. In the United States, the Supreme Court would have final jurisdiction.

Finno-Ugric language group: A subfamily of languages spoken in northeastern Europe, including Finnish, Hungarian, Estonian, and Lapp.

fiscal year: The twelve months between the settling of financial accounts, not necessarily corresponding to a calendar year beginning on January 1.

fjord: A deep indentation of the land forming a comparatively narrow arm of the sea with more or less steep slopes or cliffs on each side.

fly: The part of a flag opposite and parallel to the one nearest the flagpole.

fodder: Food for cattle, horses, and sheep, such as hay, straw, and other kinds of vegetables.

folk religion: A religion with origins and traditions among the common people of a nation or region that is relevant to their particular life-style.

foreign exchange: Foreign currency that allows foreign countries to conduct financial transactions or settle debts with one another.

foreign policy: The course of action that one government chooses to adopt in relation to a foreign country.

Former Soviet Union: The FSU is a collective reference to republics comprising the former Soviet Union. The term, which has been used as both including and excluding the Baltic republics (Estonia, Latvia, and Lithuania), includes the other 12 republics: Russia, Ukraine, Belarus, Moldova, Armenia, Azerbaijan, Uzbekistan, Turkmenistan, Tajikistan, Kazakhstan, Kyrgizstan, and Georgia.

fossil fuels: Any mineral or mineral substance formed by the decomposition of organic matter buried beneath the earth's surface and used as a fuel.

free enterprise: The system of economics in which private business may be conducted with minimum interference by the government.

free-market economy: An economic system that relies on the market, as opposed to government planners, to set the prices for wages and products.

frigate. A medium-sized warship.

fundamentalist: A person who holds religious beliefs based on the complete acceptance of the words of the Bible or other holy scripture as the truth. For instance, a fundamentalist would believe the story of creation exactly as it is told in the Bible and would reject the idea of evolution.

game reserve: An area of land reserved for wild animals that are hunted for sport or for food.

GDP see gross domestic product.

Germanic language group: A large branch of the Indo-European family of languages including German itself, the Scandinavian languages, Dutch, Yiddish, Modern English, Modern Scottish, Afrikaans, and others. The group also includes extinct languages such as Gothic, Old High German, Old Saxon, Old English, Middle English, and the like.

glasnost: President Mikhail Gorbachev's frank revelations in the 1980s about the state of the economy and politics in the Soviet Union; his policy of openness.

global greenhouse gas emissions: Gases released into the atmosphere that contribute to the greenhouse effect, a condition in which the earth's excess heat cannot escape.

global warming: Also called the greenhouse effect. The theorized gradual warming of the earth's climate as a result of the burning of fossil fuels, the use of man-made chemicals, deforestation, etc.

GMT *see* Greenwich Mean Time.

GNP *see* gross national product.

grand duchy: A territory ruled by a nobleman, called a grand duke, who ranks just below a king.

Greek Catholic: A person who is a member of an Orthodox Eastern Church.

Greek Orthodox: The official church of Greece, a self-governing branch of the Orthodox Eastern Church.

Greenwich (Mean) Time: Mean solar time of the meridian at Greenwich, England, used as the basis for standard time throughout most of the world. The world is divided into 24 time zones, and all are related to the prime, or Greenwich mean, zone.

gross domestic product: A measure of the market value of all goods and services produced within the boundaries of a nation, regardless of asset ownership. Unlike gross national product, GDP excludes receipts from that nation's business operations in foreign countries.

gross national product: A measure of the market value of goods and services produced by the labor and property of a nation. Includes receipts from that nation's business operation in foreign countries

groundwater: Water located below the earth's surface, the source from which wells and springs draw their water.

guano: The excrement of seabirds and bats found in various areas around the world. Gathered commercially and sold as a fertilizer.

guerrilla: A member of a small radical military organization that uses unconventional tactics to take their enemies by surprise.

gymnasium: A secondary school, primarily in Europe, that prepares students for university.

hardwoods: The name given to deciduous trees, such as cherry, oak, maple, and mahogany.

harem: In a Muslim household, refers to the women (wives, concubines, and servants in ancient times) who live there and also to the area of the home they live in.

harmattan: An intensely dry, dusty wind felt along the coast of Africa between Cape Verde and Cape Lopez. It prevails at intervals during the months of December, January, and February.

heavy industry: Industries that use heavy or large machinery to produce goods, such as automobile manufacturing.

hoist: The part of a flag nearest the flagpole.

Holocaust: The mass slaughter of European civilians, the vast majority Jews, by the Nazis during World War II.

Holy Roman Empire: A kingdom consisting of a loose union of German and Italian territories that existed from around the ninth century until 1806.

home rule: The governing of a territory by the citizens who inhabit it.

homeland: A region or area set aside to be a state for a people of a particular national, cultural, or racial origin.

homogeneous: Of the same kind or nature, often used in reference to a whole.

Horn of Africa: The Horn of Africa comprises Djibouti, Eritrea, Ethiopia, Somalia, and Sudan.

housing starts: The initiation of new housing construction.

human rights activist: A person who vigorously pursues the attainment of basic rights for all people.

human rights issues: Any matters involving people's basic rights which are in question or thought to be abused.

humanist: A person who centers on human needs and values, and stresses dignity of the individual.

humanitarian aid: Money or supplies given to a persecuted group or people of a country at war, or those devastated by a natural disaster, to provide for basic human needs.

hydrocarbon: A compound of hydrogen and carbon, often occurring in organic substances or derivatives of organic substances such as coal, petroleum, natural gas, etc.

hydrocarbon emissions: Organic compounds containing only carbon and hydrogen, often occurring in petroleum, natural gas, coal, and bitumens, and which contribute to the greenhouse effect.

hydroelectric potential: The potential amount of electricity that can be produced hydroelectrically. Usually used in reference to a given area and how many hydroelectric power plants that area can sustain.

hydroelectric power plant: A factory that produces electrical power through the application of waterpower.

IBRD *see* World Bank.

illegal alien: Any foreign-born individual who has unlawfully entered another country.

immigration: The act or process of passing or entering into another country for the purpose of permanent residence.

imports: Goods purchased from foreign suppliers.

indigenous: Born or originating in a particular place or country; native to a particular region or area.

Indo-Aryan language group: The group that includes the languages of India; also called Indo-European language group.

Indo-European language family: The group that includes the languages of India and much of Europe and southwestern Asia.

industrialized nation: A nation whose economy is based on industry.

infanticide: The act of murdering a baby.

infidel: One who is without faith or belief; particularly, one who rejects the distinctive doctrines of a particular religion.

inflation: The general rise of prices, as measured by a consumer price index. Results in a fall in value of currency.

installed capacity: The maximum possible output of electric power at any given time.

insurgency: The state or condition in which one rises against lawful authority or established government; rebellion.

insurrectionist: One who participates in an unorganized revolt against an authority.

interim government: A temporary or provisional government.

interim president: One who is appointed to perform temporarily the duties of president during a transitional period in a government.

internal migration: Term used to describe the relocation of individuals from one region to another without leaving the confines of the country or of a specified area.

International Date Line: An arbitrary line at about the 180th meridian that designates where one day begins and another ends.

Islam: The religious system of Mohammed, practiced by Moslims and based on a belief in Allah as the supreme being and Mohammed as his prophet. The spelling variations, Muslim and Muhammed, are also used, primarily by Islamic people. Islam also refers to those nations in which it is the primary religion.

isthmus: A narrow strip of land bordered by water and connecting two larger bodies of land, such as two continents, a continent and a peninsula, or two parts of an island.

Judaism: The religious system of the Jews, based on the Old Testament as revealed to Moses and characterized by a belief in one God and adherence to the laws of scripture and rabbinic traditions.

Judeo-Christian: The dominant traditional religious makeup of the United States and other countries based on the worship of the Old and New Testaments of the Bible.

junta: A small military group in power of a country, especially after a coup.

khan: A sovereign, or ruler, in central Asia.

khanate: A kingdom ruled by a khan, or man of rank.

kwashiorkor: Severe malnutrition in infants and children caused by a diet high in carbohydrates and lacking in protein.

kwh: The abbreviation for kilowatt-hour.

labor force: The number of people in a population available for work, whether actually employed or not.

labor movement: A movement in the early to mid-1800s to organize workers in groups according to profession to give them certain rights as a group, including bargaining power for better wages, working conditions, and benefits.

land reforms: Steps taken to create a fair distribution of farmland, especially by governmental action.

landlocked country: A country that does not have direct access to the sea; it is completely surrounded by other countries.

least developed countries: A subgroup of the United Nations designation of "less developed countries;" these countries generally have no significant economic growth, low literacy rates, and per person gross national product of less than $500. Also known as undeveloped countries.

leeward: The direction identical to that of the wind. For example, a *leeward tide* is a tide that runs in the same direction that the wind blows.

leftist: A person with a liberal or radical political affiliation.

legislative branch: The branch of government which makes or enacts the laws.

leprosy: A disease that can effect the skin and/or the nerves and can cause ulcers of the skin, loss of feeling, or loss of fingers and toes.

less developed countries (LDC): Designated by the United Nations to include countries with low levels of output, living standards, and per person gross national product generally below $5,000.

literacy: The ability to read and write.

Maastricht Treaty: The Maastricht Treaty (named for the Dutch town in which the treaty was signed) is also known as the Treaty of European Union. The treaty creates a European Union by: (a) committing the member states of the European Economic Community to both European Monetary Union (EMU) and political union; (b) introducing a single currency (European Currency Unit, ECU); (c) establishing a European System of Central Banks (ESCB); (d) creating a European Central Bank (ECB); and (e) broadening EC integration by including both a common foreign and security policy (CFSP) and cooperation in justice and home affairs (CJHA). The treaty entered into force on November 1, 1993.

Maghreb states: The Maghreb states include the three nations of Algeria, Morocco, and Tunisia; sometimes includes Libya and Mauritania.

maize: Another name (Spanish or British) for corn or the color of ripe corn.

majority party: The party with the largest number of votes and the controlling political party in a government.

mangrove: A tree which abounds on tropical shores in both hemispheres. Characterized by its numerous roots which arch out from its trunk and descend from its branches, mangroves form thick, dense growths along the tidal muds, reaching lengths hundreds of miles long.

manioc: The cassava plant or its product. Manioc is a very important food-staple in tropical America.

maquis. Scrubby, thick underbrush found along the coast of the Mediterranean Sea.

marginal land: Land that could produce an economic profit, but is so poor that it is only used when better land is no longer available.

marine life: The life that exists in, or is formed by the sea.

maritime climate: The climate and weather conditions typical of areas bordering the sea.

maritime rights: The rights that protect navigation and shipping.

market access: Market access refers to the openness of a national market to foreign products. Market access reflects a government's willingness to permit imports to compete relatively unimpeded with similar domestically produced goods.

market economy: A form of society which runs by the law of supply and demand. Goods are produced by firms to be sold to consumers, who determine the demand for them. Price levels vary according to the demand for certain goods and how much of them is produced.

market price: The price a commodity will bring when sold on the open market. The price is determined by the amount of demand for the commodity by buyers.

Marshall Plan: Formally known as the European Recovery Program, a joint project between the United States and most Western European nations under which $12.5 billion in U.S. loans and grants was expended to aid European recovery after World War II.

Marxism *see* Marxist-Leninist principles.

Marxist-Leninist principles: The doctrines of Karl Marx, built upon by Nikolai Lenin, on which communism was founded. They predicted the fall of capitalism, due to its own internal faults and the resulting oppression of workers.

Marxist: A follower of Karl Marx, a German socialist and revolutionary leader of the late 1800s, who contributed to Marxist-Leninist principles.

massif: A central mountain-mass or the dominant part of a range of mountains.

matrilineal (descent): Descending from, or tracing descent through, the maternal, or mother's, family line.

Mayan language family: The languages of the Central American Indians, further divided into two subgroups: the Maya and the Huastek.

mean temperature: The air temperature unit measured by the National Weather Service by adding the maximum and minimum daily temperatures together and diving the sum by 2.

Mecca (Mekkah): A city in Saudi Arabia; a destination of pilgrims in the Islamic world.

Mediterranean climate: A wet-winter, dry-summer climate with a moderate annual temperature range.

mestizo: The offspring of a person of mixed blood; especially, a person of mixed Spanish and American Indian parentage.

migratory birds: Those birds whose instincts prompt them to move from one place to another at the regularly recurring changes of season.

migratory workers: Usually agricultural workers who move from place to place for employment depending on the growing and harvesting seasons of various crops.

military coup: A sudden, violent overthrow of a government by military forces.

military junta: The small military group in power in a country, especially after a coup.

military regime: Government conducted by a military force.

military takeover: The seizure of control of a government by the military forces.

militia: The group of citizens of a country who are either serving in the reserve military forces or are eligible to be called up in time of emergency.

millet: A cereal grass whose small grain is used for food in Europe and Asia.

minority party: The political group that comprises the smaller part of the large overall group it belongs to; the party that is not in control.

missionary: A person sent by authority of a church or religious organization to spread his religious faith in a community where his church has no self-supporting organization.

Mohammed (or Muhammedor Mahomet): An Arabian prophet, known as the "Prophet of Allah" who founded the religion of Islam in 622, and wrote *The Koran,* the scripture of Islam. Also commonly spelled Muhammed, especially by Islamic people.

monarchy: Government by a sovereign, such as a king or queen.

money economy: A system or stage of economic development in which money replaces barter in the exchange of goods and services.

Mongol: One of an Asiatic race chiefly resident in Mongolia, a region north of China proper and south of Siberia.

Mongoloid: Having physical characteristics like those of the typical Mongols (Chinese, Japanese, Turks, Eskimos, etc.).

Moors: One of the Arab tribes that conquered Spain in the eighth century.

Moslem (Muslim): A follower of Mohammed (spelled Muhammed by many Islamic people), in the religion of Islam.

mosque: An Islam place of worship and the organization with which it is connected.

mouflon: A type of wild sheep characterized by curling horns.

mujahideen (mujahedin or mujahedeen): Rebel fighters in Islamic countries, especially those supporting the cause of Islam.

mulatto: One who is the offspring of parents one of whom is white and the other is black.

municipality: A district such as a city or town having its own incorporated government.

Muslim: A frequently used variation of the spelling of Moslem, to describe a follower of the prophet Mohammed (also spelled Muhammed), the founder of the religion of Islam.

Muslim New Year: A Muslim holiday. Although in some countries 1 Muharram, which is the first month of the Islamic year, is observed as a holiday, in other places the new year is observed on Sha'ban, the eighth month of the year. This practice apparently stems from pagan Arab times. Shab-i-Bharat, a national holiday in Bangladesh on this day, is held by many to be the occasion when God ordains all actions in the coming year.

NAFTA (North American Free Trade Agreement): NAFTA, which entered into force in January 1994, is a free trade agreement between Canada, the United States, and Mexico. The agreement progressively eliminates almost all U.S.-Mexico tariffs over a 10–15 year period.

nationalism: National spirit or aspirations; desire for national unity, independence, or prosperity.

nationalization: To transfer the control or ownership of land or industries to the nation from private owners.

native tongue: One's natural language. The language that is indigenous to an area.

NATO *see* North Atlantic Treaty Organization

natural gas: A combustible gas formed naturally in the earth and generally obtained by boring a well. The chemical makeup of natural gas is principally methane, hydrogen, ethylene compounds, and nitrogen.

natural harbor: A protected portion of a sea or lake along the shore resulting from the natural formations of the land.

naturalize: To confer the rights and privileges of a native-born subject or citizen upon someone who lives in the country by choice.

nature preserve: An area where one or more species of plant and/or animal are protected from harm, injury, or destruction.

neutrality: The policy of not taking sides with any countries during a war or dispute among them.

Newly Independent States: The NIS is a collective reference to 12 republics of the former Soviet Union: Russia, Ukraine, Belarus (formerly Byelorussia), Moldova (formerly Moldavia), Armenia, Azerbaijan, Uzbekistan, Turkmenistan, Tajikistan, Kazakhstan, and Kirgizstan (formerly Kirghiziya), and Georgia. Following dissolution of the Soviet Union, the distinction between the NIS and the Commonwealth of Independent States (CIS) was that Georgia was not a member of the CIS. That distinction dissolved when Georgia joined the CIS in November 1993.

news censorship *see* censorship

Nonaligned Movement: The NAM is an alliance of third world states that aims to promote the political and economic interests of developing countries. NAM interests have included ending colonialism/neo-colonialism, supporting the integrity of independent countries, and seeking a new international economic order.

Nordic Council: The Nordic Council, established in 1952, is directed toward supporting cooperation among Nordic countries. Members include Denmark, Finland, Iceland, Norway, and Sweden. Headquarters are in Stockholm, Sweden.

North Atlantic Treaty Organization (NATO): A mutual defense organization. Members include Belgium, Canada, Denmark, France (which has only partial membership), Greece, Iceland, Italy, Luxembourg, Netherlands, Norway, Portugal, Spain, Turkey, United Kingdom, United States, and Germany.

nuclear power plant: A factory that produces electrical power through the application of the nuclear reaction known as nuclear fission.

nuclear reactor: A device used to control the rate of nuclear fission in uranium. Used in commercial applications, nuclear reactors can maintain temperatures high enough to generate sufficient quantities of steam which can then be used to produce electricity.

OAPEC (Organization of Arab Petroleum Exporting countries): OAPEC was created in 1968; members include: Algeria, Bahrain, Egypt, Iraq, Kuwait, Libya, Qatar, Saudi Arabia, Syria, and the United Arab Emirates. Headquarters are in Cairo, Egypt.

OAS (Organization of American States): The OAS (Spanish: Organizaciûn de los Estados Americanos, OEA), or the Pan American Union, is a regional organization which promotes Latin American economic and social development. Members include the United States, Mexico, and most Central American, South American, and Caribbean nations.

OAS *see* Organization of American States

oasis: Originally, a fertile spot in the Libyan desert where there is a natural spring or well and vegetation; now refers to any fertile tract in the midst of a wasteland.

occupied territory: A territory that has an enemy's military forces present.

official language: The language in which the business of a country and its government is conducted.

oligarchy: A form of government in which a few people possess the power to rule as opposed to a monarchy which is ruled by one.

OPEC *see* OAPEC

open economy: An economy that imports and exports goods.

open market: Open market operations are the actions of the central bank to influence or control the money supply by buying or selling government bonds.

opposition party: A minority political party that is opposed to the party in power.

Organization of Arab Petroleum Exporting Countries *see* OAPEC

organized labor: The body of workers who belong to labor unions.

Ottoman Empire: An Turkish empire founded by Osman I in about 1603, that variously controlled large areas of land around the Mediterranean, Black, and Caspian Seas until it was dissolved in 1918.

overfishing: To deplete the quantity of fish in an area by removing more fish than can be naturally replaced.

overgrazing: Allowing animals to graze in an area to the point that the ground vegetation is damaged or destroyed.

overseas dependencies: A distant and physically separate territory that belongs to another country and is subject to its laws and government.

Pacific Rim: The Pacific Rim, referring to countries and economies bordering the Pacific Ocean.

pact: An international agreement.

Paleolithic: The early period of the Stone Age, when rough, chipped stone implements were used.

panhandle: A long narrow strip of land projecting like the handle of a frying pan.

papyrus: The paper-reed or -rush which grows on marshy river banks in the southeastern area of the Mediterranean, but more notably in the Nile valley.

paramilitary group: A supplementary organization to the military.

parasitic diseases: A group of diseases caused by parasitic organisms which feed off the host organism.

parliamentary republic: A system of government in which a president and prime minister, plus other ministers of departments, constitute the executive branch of the government and the parliament constitutes the legislative branch.

parliamentary rule: Government by a legislative body similar to that of Great Britain, which is composed of two houses—one elected and one hereditary.

parochial: Refers to matters of a church parish or something within narrow limits.

patriarchal system: A social system in which the head of the family or tribe is the father or oldest male. Kinship is determined and traced through the male members of the tribe.

patrilineal (descent): Descending from, or tracing descent through, the paternal or father's line.

pellagra: A disease marked by skin, intestinal, and central nervous system disorders, caused by a diet deficient in niacin, one of the B vitamins.

per capita: Literally, per person; for each person counted.

perestroika: The reorganization of the political and economic structures of the Soviet Union by president Mikhail Gorbachev.

periodical: A publication whose issues appear at regular intervals, such as weekly, monthly, or yearly.

petrochemical: A chemical derived from petroleum or from natural gas.

pharmaceutical plants: Any plant that is used in the preparation of medicinal drugs.

plantain: The name of a common weed that has often been used for medicinal purposes, as a folk remedy and in modern medicine. *Plaintain* is also the name of a tropical plant producing a type of banana.

poaching: To intrude or encroach upon another's preserves for the purpose of stealing animals, especially wild game.

polar climate: Also called tundra climate. A humid, severely cold climate controlled by arctic air masses, with no warm or summer season.

political climate: The prevailing political attitude of a particular time or place.

political refugee: A person forced to flee his or her native country for political reasons.

potable water: Water that is safe for drinking.

pound sterling: The monetary unit of Great Britain, otherwise known as the pound.

prefect: An administrative official; in France, the head of a particular department.

prefecture: The territory over which a prefect has authority.

prime meridian: Zero degrees in longitude that runs through Greenwich, England, site of the Royal Observatory. All other longitudes are measured from this point.

prime minister: The premier or chief administrative official in certain countries.

private sector: The division of an economy in which production of goods and services is privately owned.

privatization: To change from public to private control or ownership.

protectorate: A state or territory controlled by a stronger state, or the relationship of the stronger country toward the lesser one it protects.

Protestant Reformation: In 1529, a Christian religious movement begun in Germany to deny the universal authority of the Pope, and to establish the Bible as the only source of truth. (*Also see* Protestant)

Protestant: A member or an adherent of one of those Christian bodies which descended from the Reformation of the sixteenth century. Originally applied to those who opposed or protested the Roman Catholic Church.

proved reserves: The quantity of a recoverable mineral resource (such as oil or natural gas) that is still in the ground.

province: An administrative territory of a country.

provisional government: A temporary government set up during time of unrest or transition in a country.

pulses: Beans, peas, or lentils.

purge: The act of ridding a society of "undesirable" or unloyal persons by banishment or murder.

Rastafarian: A member of a Jamaican cult begun in 1930 as a semi-religious, semi-political movement.

rate of literacy: The percentage of people in a society who can read and write.

recession. A period of reduced economic activity in a country or region.

referendum: The practice of submitting legislation directly to the people for a popular vote.

Reformation *see* Protestant Reformation.

refugee: One who flees to a refuge or shelter or place of safety. One who in times of persecution or political commotion flees to a foreign country for safety.

revolution: A complete change in a government or society, such as in an overthrow of the government by the people.

right-wing party: The more conservative political party.

Roman alphabet: The alphabet of the ancient Romans from which the alphabets of most modern western

European languages, including English, are derived.

Roman Catholic Church: The designation of the church of which the pope or Bishop of Rome is the head, and that holds him as the successor of St. Peter and heir of his spiritual authority, privileges, and gifts.

romance language: The group of languages derived from Latin: French, Spanish, Italian, Portuguese, and other related languages.

roundwood: Timber used as poles or in similar ways without being sawn or shaped.

runoff election: A deciding election put to the voters in case of a tie between candidates.

Russian Orthodox: The arm of the Orthodox Eastern Church that was the official church of Russia under the czars.

sack: To strip of valuables, especially after capture.

Sahelian zone: Eight countries make up this dry desert zone in Africa: Burkina Faso, Chad, Gambia, Mali, Mauritania, Niger, Senegal, and the Cape Verde Islands. *Also see* Club du Sahel.

salinization: An accumulation of soluble salts in soil. This condition is common in desert climates, where water evaporates quickly in poorly drained soil due to high temperatures.

Samaritans: A native or an inhabitant of Samaria; specifically, one of a race settled in the cities of Samaria by the king of Assyria after the removal of the Israelites from the country.

savanna: A treeless or near treeless plain of a tropical or subtropical region dominated by drought-resistant grasses.

schistosomiasis: A tropical disease that is chronic and characterized by disorders of the liver, urinary bladder, lungs, or central nervous system.

secession: The act of withdrawal, such as a state withdrawing from the Union in the Civil War in the United States.

sect: A religious denomination or group, often a dissenting one with extreme views.

segregation: The enforced separation of a racial or religious group from other groups, compelling them to live and go to school separately from the rest of society.

seismic activity: Relating to or connected with an earthquake or earthquakes in general.

self-sufficient: Able to function alone without help.

separation of power: The division of power in the government among the executive, legislative, and judicial branches and the checks and balances employed to keep them separate and independent of each other.

separatism: The policy of dissenters withdrawing from a larger political or religious group.

serfdom: In the feudal system of the Middle Ages, the condition of being attached to the land owned by a lord and being transferable to a new owner.

Seventh-day Adventist: One who believes in the second coming of Christ to establish a personal reign upon the earth.

shamanism: A religion of some Asians and Amerindians in which shamans, who are priests or medicine men, are believed to influence good and evil spirits.

shantytown: An urban settlement of people in flimsy, inadequate houses.

Shia Muslim: Members of one of two great sects of Islam. Shia Muslims believe that Ali and the Imams are the rightful successors of Mohammed (also commonly spelled Muhammed). They also believe that the last recognized Imam will return as a messiah. Also known as Shiites. (*Also see* Sunnis.)

Shiites *see* Shia Muslims.

Shintoism: The system of nature- and hero-worship which forms the indigenous religion of Japan.

shoal: A place where the water of a stream, lake, or sea is of little depth. Especially, a sand-bank which shows at low water.

sierra: A chain of hills or mountains.

Sikh: A member of a politico-religious community of India, founded as a sect around 1500 and based on the principles of monotheism (belief in one god) and human brotherhood.

Sino-Tibetan language family: The family of languages spoken in eastern Asia, including China, Thailand, Tibet, and Burma.

slash-and-burn agriculture: A hasty and sometimes temporary way of clearing land to make it available for agriculture by cutting down trees and burning them.

slave trade: The transportation of black Africans beginning in the 1700s to other countries to be sold as slaves—people owned as property and compelled to work for their owners at no pay.

Slavic languages: A major subgroup of the Indo-European language family. It is further subdivided into West Slavic (including Polish, Czech, Slovak and Serbian), South Slavic (including Bulgarian, Serbo-Croatian, Slovene, and Old Church Slavonic), and East Slavic (including Russian Ukrainian and Byelorussian).

social insurance: A government plan to protect low-income people, such as health and accident insurance, pension plans, etc.

social security: A form of social insurance, including life, disability, and old-age pension for workers. It is paid for by employers, employees, and the government.

socialism: An economic system in which ownership of land and other property is distributed among the community as a whole, and every member of the community shares in the work and products of the work.

socialist: A person who advocates socialism.

softwoods: The coniferous trees, whose wood density as a whole is relatively softer than the wood of those trees referred to as hardwoods.

sorghum (also known as Syrian Grass): Plant grown in various parts of the world for its valuable uses, such as for grain, syrup, or fodder.

Southeast Asia: The region in Asia that consists of the Malay Archipelago, the Malay Peninsula, and Indochina.

staple crop: A crop that is the chief commodity or product of a place, and which has widespread and constant use or value.

state: The politically organized body of people living under one government or one of the territorial units that make up a federal government, such as in the United States.

steppe: A level tract of land more or less devoid of trees, in certain parts of European and Asiatic Russia.

student demonstration: A public gathering of students to express strong feelings about a certain situation, usually taking place near the location of the people in power to change the situation.

subarctic climate: A high latitude climate of two types: *continental subarctic,* which has very cold winters, short, cool summers, light precipitation and moist air; and *marine subarctic,* a coastal and island climate with polar air masses causing large precipitation and extreme cold.

subcontinent: A land mass of great size, but smaller than any of the continents; a large subdivision of a continent.

subsistence economy: The part of a national economy in which money plays little or no role, trade is by barter, and living standards are minimal.

subsistence farming: Farming that provides the minimum food goods necessary for the continuation of the farm family.

subtropical climate: A middle latitude climate dominated by humid, warm temperatures and heavy rainfall in summer, with cool winters and frequent cyclonic storms.

subversion: The act of attempting to overthrow or ruin a government or organization by stealthy or deceitful means.

Sudanic language group: A related group of languages spoken in various areas of northern Africa, including Yoruba, Mandingo, and Tshi.

suffrage: The right to vote.

Sufi: A Muslim mystic who believes that God alone exists, there can be no real difference between good and evil, that the soul exists within the body as in a cage, so death should be the chief object of desire, and sufism is the only true philosophy.

sultan: A king of a Muslim state.

Sunni Muslim: Members of one of two major sects of the religion of Islam. Sunni Muslims adhere to strict orthodox traditions, and believe that the four caliphs are the rightful successors to Mohammed, founder of Islam. (Mohammed is commonly spelled Muhammed, especially by Islamic people.) (*Also see* Shia Muslim.)

Taoism: The doctrine of Lao-Tzu, an ancient Chinese philosopher (about 500 B.C.) as laid down by him in the *Tao-te-ching.*

tariff: A tax assessed by a government on goods as they enter (or leave) a country. May be imposed to protect domestic industries from imported goods and/or to generate revenue.

temperate zone: The parts of the earth lying between the tropics and the polar circles. The *northern temperate zone* is the area between the tropic of Cancer and the Arctic Circle. The *southern temperate zone* is the area between the tropic of Capricorn and the Antarctic Circle.

terracing: A form of agriculture that involves cultivating crops in raised banks of earth.

terrorism: Systematic acts of violence designed to frighten or intimidate.

thermal power plant: A facility that produces electric energy from heat energy released by combustion of fuel or nuclear reactions.

Third World: A term used to describe less developed countries; as of the mid-1990s, it is being replaced by the United Nations designation Less Developed Countries, or LDC.

topography: The physical or natural features of the land.

torrid zone: The part of the earth's surface that lies between the tropics, so named for the character of its climate.

totalitarian party: The single political party in complete authoritarian control of a government or state.

trachoma: A contagious bacterial disease that affects the eye.

treaty: A negotiated agreement between two governments.

tribal system: A social community in which people are organized into groups or clans descended from common ancestors and sharing customs and languages.

tropical monsoon climate: One of the tropical rainy climates; it is sufficiently warm and rainy to produce tropical rainforest vegetation, but also has a winter dry season.

tsetse fly: Any of the several African insects which can transmit a variety of parasitic organisms through its bite. Some of these organisms can prove fatal to both human and animal victims.

tundra: A nearly level treeless area whose climate and vegetation are characteristically arctic due to its northern position; the subsoil is permanently frozen.

undeveloped countries *see* least developed countries.

unemployment rate: The overall unemployment rate is the percentage of the work force (both employed and unemployed) who claim to be unemployed.

UNICEF: An international fund set-up for children's emergency relief: United Nations Children's Fund (formerly United Nations International Children's Emergency Fund).

universal adult suffrage: The policy of giving every adult in a nation the right to vote.

untouchables: In India, members of the lowest caste in the caste system, a hereditary social class system. They were considered unworthy to touch members of higher castes.

urban guerrilla: A rebel fighter operating in an urban area.

urbanization: The process of changing from country to city.

USSR: An abbreviation of Union of Soviet Socialist Republics.

veldt: In South Africa, an unforested or thinly forested tract of land or region, a grassland.

Warsaw Pact: Agreement made 14 May 1955 (and dissolved 1 July 1991) to promote mutual defense between Albania, Bulgaria, Czechoslovakia, East Germany, Hungary, Poland, Romania, and the USSR.

Western nations: Blanket term used to describe mostly democratic, capitalist countries, including the United States, Canada, and western European countries.

wildlife sanctuary: An area of land set aside for the protection and preservation of animals and plants.

workers' compensation: A series of regular payments by an employer to a person injured on the job.

World Bank: The World Bank is a group of international institutions which provides financial and technical assistance to developing countries.

world oil crisis: The severe shortage of oil in the 1970s precipitated by the Arab oil embargo.

wormwood: A woody perennial herb native to Europe and Asiatic Russia, valued for its medicinal uses.

yaws: A tropical disease caused by a bacteria which produces raspberry-like sores on the skin.

yellow fever: A tropical viral disease caused by the bite of an infected mosquito, characterized by jaundice.

Zoroastrianism: The system of religious doctrine taught by Zoroaster and his followers in the Avesta; the religion prevalent in Persia until its overthrow by the Muslims in the seventh century.

INDEX

This index contains terms from all nine volumes of this encyclopedia. The number of the volume in enclosed in brackets. The volume number is followed by the page number. For example, the reference [8]73 means that the indexed term can be found in volume 8 on page 73.